Rich Mulligan

Mulligan's Shenanigans

For Mum,

No one gave so much tea and toast to the young punks of Coventry

Contents.

Part 1
The Boy from County Coundon....................7
A couple of young punks set out to explore the other
side of the sea and find adventures, squats and the mishaps
of youth through Europe

Part 2
Jung Bloods..71
Education in Israel and Russia, and meeting an old friend
in the USA.

Part 3
A Foreign Posting....................................123
Working at the post office, knowing every letter was a mile
towards a lost backpack, a trusty toothbrush and a ticket
around the planet.

Part 4
The Lion, The Bitch and the Warzone............189
Misadventures across Africa, travelling with a truckful of
Fellow eejits.

PART 1
The Boy From County Coundon

I

Johnny Rotten crouched on a stage and sneered at us.

I guess when you're a kid, you're a natural born explorer. From those first moments that your eyes opened and you looked around at this new world, to that first morning when you learnt to slide about on your arse, or even managed to crawl, and then as you toddled around the house, picking everything up, risking death by Lego and realising that you don't eat muck, you explored everything, judged everybody, and learnt, learnt, learnt. The mere act of being alive itself is an adventure and it's taking place in a world that gets bigger every single day. Until it doesn't.

I'm sure that there isn't an exact moment that the adventure stops, and you begin to worry about what day it is, or think twice about how old you will be on your next birthday, or debate which one of the 30 or so different dishes you generally eat through your life that you are going to make for dinner later on. It does, I imagine, creep up on you unawares and you may never actually notice it. Well, maybe the odd midlife crisis, which could well be the inner soul asking, "What the hell happened to all those things I was going to do and when did I start wearing shirts like this?", or it could just be the fact that the kids are grown up and you can have a fun car now.

Alternatively, you may well find that the adventures never actually stop. Which raises the question of what do adventurers do in a mid-life crisis? Buy emulsion? Or maybe a pouffe, which they sent off to Morocco for and had to stuff the leather cover themselves and then realised that they may never use that sleeping bag again so it might as well go in there. Along with old towels, of course. There's always old towels. And some of those T-shirts with band logos on that haven't fitted since their tracks turned up on a Best Of album.

Even going to school was a bit of an adventure. It would have been 1969 or 70 or something when I took the mighty leap as an 8 year old to "Junior school" as it was called then, or year whatever it is that they call it now. And that meant, back then, probably walking to school all by yourself, or more likely with a group of other kids, not because you knew them, but because they were going that way. Some of them you liked. Some of them you certainly didn't. It meant 'shortcuts' that took longer than the streets, that involved entries and alleyways, and in our case walking past the River Sherbourne somehow, which was actually on the other side of the school. Oh, and daring each other to go into Webfoot's front garden.

There was this poor old feller known only as Webfoot, who I don't recall ever actually seeing, who lived in a bit of a dilapidated house right on the corner from the school. It had an overgrown pond, or former pond maybe - it was hard to tell - in the front garden behind a huge unkempt hedge that, legend had it, Webfoot had drowned his wife in. As kids are the moral upholders of the law when the police had clearly missed things like this, we felt obliged to shout WEBFOOT as we pushed one of us into the garden, and some of the kids threw stones at his house. Year after year, kids tortured that poor old man for the crime of having a pond and the fact that possibly his wife had left him for someone else years ago. That's assuming that he didn't actually drown his wife in it, of course, and the police let it go.

This was County Coundon. The UK didn't have ghetto districts in the same way that, say, the US would have, but certainly the towns and cities had areas that could be ethnically diverse from each other. And so it was with Coventry. Most of us growing up in County Coundon were of

8

parents that had come over from mainly Ireland, but also Scotland, or elsewhere in England even, and had come for the work. A booming Car Town, that saw Rover, Triumph, Jaguar, Rolls Royce, Peugeot and Daimler amongst others, with hundreds of feeder companies providing parts. My old feller told me that you could walk out of a job in the morning and walk into another one that afternoon. Though actually in my old feller's case, he'd walk out of a job in the afternoon and walk straight to the pub. Sometimes he didn't walk back for days, either. But he always worked. Everyone did, we just didn't always see the money, but that's another story.

Because everything is a story, really. You learn that as you go through life. All the adventures you have, all the stuff you see, all the people you meet. It's always about the story. Always.

But we played, we read Just William, we visited newsagents for comics and sweets. And we had bikes!! Oh yes, we had bikes. And we went everywhere on them. If ever there was a device built to let kids explore, it has to have been the bike. We explored our district, moved through the city, then explored the small towns nearby. Of course, we were hitting the ripe old age of 11 by then, and starting "Big School." Or year whatever the hell that is called now. And leaving our huge Catholic Comprehensive school when the home time bell rang, we'd be on the bikes, taking at least an hour or more to make the 20 minute cycle home, sitting down to dinner, listening to Mum cursing my Dad as he was no doubt in the pub again, then getting on the bikes and heading off for a few adventures before bedtime. Or TV time. If Dad still hadn't got back from the pub....Which was most likely....Mum would let me stay up a bit later to watch the 9pm shows. The World At War. Play for today. Whatever. She said it was because I was the oldest, which I was quite proud about, as It seemed to imply that I'd won some kind of race, which I also liked as I wasn't really the sporty type, and generally lost any race I might be in at school sports. I couldn't really kick a soccer ball straight either and would be the last kid picked for games. So winning the sibling race was quite the achievement, probably deserved a trophy, and got me to stay up till News at 10. There was a downside to that....I'd hear just the headlines while Big Ben chimed, and would go to bed wondering what the news story was about. So I only really knew a snippet about what was going on, without knowing the full facts. It was four decades

9

later that this turned out to be how people spoke to each other on social media, and so was quite the skill to hone at the time.......

Oddly, I don't recall that anyone knew, or would have cared anyway, that the bike as we know it was a Coventry invention, so to speak. This was down to a certain Mr James Starley who moved here to set up the Coventry Sewing Machine company in 1861 with his friend, whose expensive and rare Sewing Machine he had once fixed. He was quite the inventor, whose devices included...And I love this...a kind of mechanism that would allow a duck to get through a hole in a fence, upon which a door would close, stopping any pursuing rats.

At some point in his sewing machine days, his nephew brought along a new-fangled French boneshaker, a kind of proto-bicycle, and Mr Starley set about inventing gears and metal spokes and things, till eventually, via the basic bike, came up with a contraption that could only steer if the two people needed to sit on it were about equal in strength whilst they peddled. They usually weren't, so James carried on till one Saturday, over a cup of tea, he had a bit of a Eureka moment. He had invented the differential gear, and had the prototype built by Monday. It is still incorporated in the back axle of every car today and job done, he went on to found Rover cars, and set Coventry on its road to being the huge car town that attracted the future Mr & Mrs Mulligan to County Coundon as teenagers with parents who came for the work.

So as we kids explored the world around us on our bikes, we never knew that our freedom, and indeed our very existence as Coventry kids, was down to a bloke who knew how to fix his mates sewing machine. I'm sure that had we known, we'd have been kind of grateful, though to be fair, he hadn't invented the Raleigh Chopper, which would have actually made him pretty cool. Especially if he'd invented the yellow ones.

Even with that hindsight of his ingenuity though, and discovering the inventive and industrial genius of himself, his friends and his family and all they did for this town, I'd probably say that of all his achievements, the fact he invented a device that helped ducks escape from rats is the one I'd probably talk about down the pub. Well you would, wouldn't you?

So the boys from County Coundon explored, and we got into schoolboy fights, and we learned that if we stole beer bottles from behind the social club, we could get the deposit for them in a nearby pub with an off-sales. Or even in the same club, if we were brave. And we brewed a disgusting home brew in one of our sheds that we thought was great, but made us sick. We also sold cigars in school, as one of the lads had a brother in the Merchant Navy who brought boxes of them home. Along with the homebrew and cigars, we sold saucy mags in school as well. By now we were 15, and we gave the young kids 5p each for the mags, which we told them they would find under their dads beds, and we sold them on for 10p each or 15p, if none of the pages were stuck together. We'd also find these in hedges. Weirdly, hedges and spinneys were a great source of saucy mags. Or, at a pinch, one of the boys, Colm, was a pretty good shoplifter and managed to get them from the top shelf in newsagents. We were at a bit of a strange crossover age where we were kind of like junior contraband dealers, but who spent the money on sweets and Marvel comics.

I was arrested once as a kid. The police brought me home after we were caught in an old pavilion on the local recreation ground that had been vandalised. In actual fact, we hadn't done it. We stashed our saucy mags and cigars and home brew there, and it was in our interest that it had a good roof. But we couldn't really tell the police that, so we all got a caution. That made us feel pretty damned grown up and the apologetic humility we showed our parents changed into brag rights at school.

And through all this, our little gang listened to 50's Rock & Roll and swore we were going to be Teddy Boys, like our dads had been. Or Greasers with leathers, like in cool movies we never really watched, but would see posters in poster shops for. We'd become aware of girls of course, but had no real idea how to approach them. The girls in class we'd made fun of were now strangely bumpier and were meeting lads who had left school, and became Teddy Boys like their dads had been, or were wearing flares with 20 buttons on their waistbands. 20 buttons!!! Selling all the cigars in the world, we couldn't compete with that.

But generally, life was good. We had all begun to get career advice in school. In Coventry, this meant that you wrote down three jobs you thought you'd like to do. I hadn't got a clue, a condition that stayed with me till this day, and wrote down Journalist, (I thought you'd meet the topless page 3 girls from the papers), cinematography, (I had heard of it the day before and thought it sounded good) and a Lawyer. (My mate in class had watched a show about some young lawyers, and said they were always getting off with girls because they had good suits). Dutifully, we

11

all handed our choices to the careers teacher, who took them home and the next week brought us a list of all the car factories in Coventry with their recruitment phone numbers, and then for the rest of the term told us the history of the car factories in the city, though probably missing out Mr James Starley. Everybody did. That was apart from the day they brought the army recruitment people in , who performed a little play involving stupid looking teenagers who were bored and ready to become criminals, but instead joined the army and became smart, upright and happy citizens. All of our fathers had either been forced to do national service, or were singing IRA songs in pubs at the weekend, hence a mainly Irish Catholic school in the 70's wasn't going to be their best recruiting ground. So we went back to learning car factory history and the topic of journalism was never mentioned again. We were about to become adults and we were exploring our options of jobs in the same car factories in which our parents were working, and we sat down on a Thursday night to watch Top of the Pops on BBC1, listening to the same music our parents listened to.

Then Johnny Rotten sneered at us, and a new chapter in many of our stories began.

II

I was sitting on a bridge in Amsterdam and felt it was one of the most content moments of my life.

The cool thing to say would be that Punk Rock changed my life. You know, like a huge WOW moment, where I came into the house one day covered in chains and safety pins, and my parents spat their tea out, threw me out on the streets, and suddenly I was the working class rebel, up against the world.

That would be the cool thing to say. However, that's not what actually happened. I was still at school when punk hit the UK, and me and the boys were still thinking we would be Teds. Or rather, that's what we were telling each other. There was a lad in school who somehow had access to the very early punk singles and used to play them in the school music room. I'd go along with a couple of classmates on the pretence of sneering, but actually found it exciting. But the papers had told us that Teds and Punks hated each other, because they saw the opportunity for a new Mods and Rockers Fight on Brighton Beach style headline, and hell, everything the papers say is true, right, so we duly decided we hated the punk kids in school. It was in later years that I was to find out that in fact all of us had been doing the same thing, and we'd managed to keep up the pretence till we left school, once we had become grand old wise men of 16. Most of the boys from County Coundon had phoned the car factories, and gotten apprenticeships, but I somehow missed it. We didn't have a phone in the house, and had to use the old public phone boxes. By this time, my old feller had taken to going out for a drink and not coming back for weeks or months at a time, and things like phones were a no-no. My Dad's mum used to bring us bags of clothes from the second hand shops, full of really bad clothes. And I mean bad. Or my Mum knit. Let's hold that thought. So I'd gone to the phone box up the road, armed with a good few 2p coins, and found as I'd begun to speak, the time would run out, and a huge beeping sound interrupted the call till another 2p would slowly go in. So I gave up.

I mentioned sports weren't my thing, and I couldn't kick a ball straight. But I found in the 4th year, I wasn't bad at Rugger. It involved picking a ball up and running into people, which I could handle quite well. In fact, I was picked for a try out for the school Rugger team, which was quite the big deal for me. It meant, of course, that I needed a full kit, a fact I impressed upon my Mum, probably much to her dismay. I'd got most of it from the school 'spare' box, meaning crappy old kit that had been left behind at some point, but no socks. I just needed socks. So my Mum knit me a pair. And there amongst all the lads in their gleaming new kits they would get at the start of the year, as we kept, you know, growing, was me in a clearly not brand new, ill-fitting kit with big chunky hand knitted socks. Let's just say, kids can be cruel, eh? Especially to kids in little position to defend themselves. The others on the team made it quite clear that if I turned up at another school with those socks on, if the other kids didn't get me, they certainly would. I didn't try out. I didn't tell my Mum why either, even though she was angry at me for not getting on the team, as my lack of sporting prowess had been an on-going thing for my parents. Not that either of them was sporty. Not at all.

In fact, I remember the odd occasion my Dad took me to see Coventry City play at their Highfield Road Ground. Now my Dad had always moaned at me about my disinterest in Soccer. And in fact, I really didn't have an interest in it, and never ever did in later life either. Though I'm sure he didn't really think it through, he equated my lack of interest in soccer, or any sport, with a potential for homosexuality. Though that wasn't exactly the words he used to make this point. I should say that for all his faults, which were mainly based around the drink, he was actually a pretty good bloke. He was a cracking singer, and was in a number of bands over the years, an occupation he enjoyed as it involved pubs and social clubs. When he was sober and at home, he was a typical Dad,

14

though you could always tell he got twitchy around opening time. Anyway, there was the odd occasion he took me to see Coventry City play. You still stood up at matches then, and to be honest, I could never really see anything over the taller adults. But the thing that occurred to me much later in life, and kinda made me chuckle, was that about 15 minutes before the end, we would leave the match, and go to the bar below the stand, so that my Dad didn't have to wait in a queue when everyone else poured in on the final whistle. He explained this by saying that nothing really happened in the last 15 minutes, which I believed for years. Or didn't care about. Probably the latter.

I loved books though. I couldn't read enough books. From the moment I learned to read, I read everything I could, from novels to science journals. As a younger kid, I especially loved the Narnia books. Younger than that, Enid Blyton. It's a shame about Enid Blyton really. Frig, she could write a great kids book. In later years, we (and I mean the society I am in, not myself) became intent on destroying everything that was nice, in the name of the truth, apparently. So whenever I think back to those happy , carefree kids stories, that cheered me up when things were a bit bleak at home, someone will inevitably and merrily point out that she was a fascist, and wrote about golliwogs in the Noddy books. I suppose she did, really. But naïve as it may sound, I had no idea as a kid that toy golliwogs were a caricature of black people. I thought they were just a thing. I have no idea if Enid knew this or not either, I never met the woman any more that her destroyers did. So she's up there with Adolf Hitler , and on the banned books lists. Noddy has been edited. He now has trouble with goblins. Which is odd, as he lives in Toytown. To the best of my recollection I never had a toy goblin. I don't think any kid ever has. I think that there were eventually toy goblins, but they were for the kind of adults that played dungeons and dragons, and would never dream of getting into a taxi with a little boy with a nodding head. Hopefully.

This love of books, and my constant trips to the Coundon Library were also a source of my Dad speculating on my sexuality. A lot of things seemed to worry him about that, including the time he caught me helping with the washing up. It's a shame that he couldn't have seen our collection of magazines that we had stashed in the old pavilion. That would have put his mind at rest, but we had taken the rap for the vandalism we didn't do instead, so he never knew. On saying that, I don't recall him calling us out on the vandalism thing. I guess he considered that to be a pretty manly activity. Especially if you went about it in socks that hadn't been hand knitted.

There was a woman called Mrs Bolter who lived on our corner, who would always seem to be standing by her gate when I went past. She'd often give us old comics that belonged to her son. And at some point she gave me a great big book that is still in my house to this day. It was The Readers Digest Atlas of the world, 1966 edition. Or somewhere round that. What a book. It was full, naturally, of maps. But not just countries, but contour maps. And the solar system. And where the dinosaurs lived. And old empires. This book had everything. I don't know how many times I would sit reading it, tracing all the different countries, and letting my imagination run riot. I remember thinking how brilliant it would be to visit these places, and see the exotic looking people in the photos. Even Just William didn't have adventures like that, and he was my childhood hero!! As yet, no one has called Richmal Crompton, his creator, out on being a fascist yet to my knowledge, but I'm sure it's only a matter of time. For frigs sake, don't tell them his gang of 11 year olds dressed up as Red Indians once, or they'll be organising book burning parties.

And then there was punk. So on leaving school, I pretty much immediately lost touch with the rest of the lads I'd spent 5 years with, for no real reason that I can remember. This also allowed for a bit of a change of style. It was quite common at that time for people to start using pubs at 16. Effectively, the barmaid asked you how old you were, you said 18, and that was pretty much it. On the odd occasion that the police did question a pub, they said they had asked and you'd said 18, and it was left there. So at 16 the bike got put in the shed where it pretty much stayed, and off I trotted to the pub with newly cut spiky hair, straight jeans, and a pyjama jacket to consolidate my originality. I had seen some older punk wearing one once, and it struck me as really original, so I decided to be that original too.

The crowd of men I drank with in the pub.....Because at 16, we had left school, so knew we were men now....didn't particularly dress punk, though New Wave and Punk music were pretty much our background songs. It was mainly just me. The lads were a mix of people from the 2 local schools that hadn't got on of course, but no one cared any more, now we had left and were in the same car factories. The lads from my school were mainly people who never mixed at school, but we all lived near the pub, and that was more important now. Oh, and I also pierced my nose. You couldn't get it done in a shop then, well, not in Coventry, so I did it myself. With a sharp keyring. Made of tin. It wasn't long till it went septic, and various coloured pus would come out of it, but I persevered till it hurt too much, and gave up. Then I would write in marker on myself, like a line with "CUT HERE" written across my chest. Or something.

Oddly, I was never barred from that pub, which was a large pub in Coundon called the Holyhead. It was an old Irish guy that ran it at the time. Mind you, to say a pub in Coundon had an Irish landlord was a bit like saying it had beer. However, he did bar me from room to room. Later in the 80's, lots of pubs knocked their bars and lounges into one, and renamed themselves with awful names. The Silver Sword became Silvers, Golden fleece would be Goldies, and the Holyhead became Hollies. Luckily I had gone off a separate way by then , but was there in the 70's when it had a good old bar and lounge. I was, as I say, constantly barred from one room to the other. So I came down with a ring in my nose, and was told I would have to drink in the bar so as not to offend the nice people in the lounge. Then I'd have band names written on my face one night, and would be barred back to the lounge, as the good people in the bar didn't want to see that kind of thing. This went on a lot, and my drinking buds begrudgingly moved from room to room with me, over and over again. Yet the bloke never barred me completely. I'd like to think he had a kind of respect for me, but my guess is that it gave his mates something to laugh about.

In any case, a little behind the others from school, I got myself a plastering apprenticeship secured, but not till the next year. So in the meantime I found myself on a Youth Opportunities Programme course on Brickwork till the starting date came round, where I absolutely never really learned how to lay bricks, but instead found that a lot of punks were doing such courses in the same building as getting proper jobs was nigh on impossible if you looked a bit different back then. And so I eventually fell in with the punk crowds, drank in punk pubs, and ditched the pyjama jacket for a leather one. Along the way, I took up my apprenticeship, and got the sack from it after 3 months, partly due to trapping some other builders overnight in a temple that we were working on by taking their ladder away, (Ah, no mobile phones then, eh?) but

17

mainly due to the fact that I absolutely never really learned how to put plaster on walls.

I left my parents' house at some point, and a bunch of us on the dole got a flat together, on a public housing estate. We had trashed it by the time we left, not on purpose, but by it being a kind of punk party flat. But hell, there were some great people passed through those doors, and though we had no money as such, we always seemed to be drinking, mainly cheap but potent scrumpy cider, and a kind of homebrew we made in the bath, which we could as no one actually used it as a bath.

We looked after each other, and I could share many a tale. Many a tale indeed. Suffice to say, we bludgeoned through life, getting by, having fun, being drunk, and coming up with plans. Some we did, others got forgotten. But in any case, we were all of a nature, I guess, and found that adventures just seemed to come to us, whether we wanted them or not. And firm friendships were made, which is a key in enjoying life. Which we most certainly did.

And one adventure led to another, until, sometime later, I found myself one day sitting on a bench on a bridge in Amsterdam with one of my best friends at the time, eating a sandwich and not really talking. It was raining, and we had just made a decision. And I looked at the canal, and sat reflecting on how I'd come to get there, and I still remember thinking it was one of the most content and happiest moments of my life so far.

III

We were shot at once.

I'd taken up with a Swiss punk girl, Eva, who was staying in Coventry, in a hostel of some kind. I can't honestly remember where we first met her, but she was soon seeing a mate of mine, briefly. And at some point I began to see her instead, but I'm sorry to say I cannot remember how that came about either. I say sorry, because I really should know. I'll explain later. But in any case, at some point she left the hostel she was staying in and began living at the flat we all kind of existed in. That wasn't so unusual, as at any given moment you wouldn't know exactly how many people were staying there. I'd noticed, for example, a kind of rockabilly lad who'd been there about a week once, and I hadn't really spoken to yet. When I mentioned that he'd been there a lot lately, he told me he lived there. So naturally I pointed out that it was my flat. He thought about this for a moment, and then said that he'd thought I'd been there a lot too. Nothing really to say about that. I'm sure he was there about a month after that, then like so many, vanished.

But Eva stayed there with me till it was time for her to head back home for a while. That's when we decided that it would be a great idea to go part of the way with her, as she'd been intending to hitch Hike back to Zurich. I say we, as one of the other original occupants of the flat, Brody, decided that he should come along as well. Oddly, he was the only one out of us to have a full time job, so I guess he took time off.

So, with whatever funds we could muster, we set off one night, intending to hitch to London, catch a train to Folkestone, then arrive in Boulogne. Seemed a straight forward enough plan.

When it comes to travelling, there is never really a straight forward plan. There seems to be a couple of golden rules that never fail to kick in. One is that if it can go wrong, it probably will. The other is that it is these wrong happenings that tend to make the adventure. If you're going to set off on adventures, you should always be prepared for just that. Adventures. And for some reason I have yet to fathom, the moment you set off on a journey, right from the moment you lock your front door - after checking the cooker, the lights, the iron, and everything else about 6 times - then returning to check the front door at least twice, anything can happen. You just go with it. Now, we were excited about setting off. We couldn't wait until we reached France, and have ourselves a great time, ready to explore the world. You know, get away from the routine of punk ,anarchy, chaos and all that. Because, as I was to find out, it's always about the story and even then we knew we were setting out to have one.

We actually reached the spot on the road where we were going to hitch from when the story began. We were actually a bit naïve about hitching, and the fact that 3 multi coloured haired Punk Rockers in leathers with backpacks hitching at 11pm at night didn't strike us as an obstacle. To be honest, we'd actually intended to head off in the afternoon, but one of us needed to go to the toilet on the way, so we popped into a pub, and it would have been rude not to have a drink. Let no one say we were rude. But , after proving our lack of rudeness for a good few hours, we eventually wandered along the A-road that led to the motorway, assuming we'd be picked up in no time. We'd even made a sign that said LONDON. Well, we'd made one, but Brody had left it in the pub. So we stuck our thumbs out.

No-one stopped. We ended up all the way to where we could walk no further, and found that spot occupied by another Hitcher, this time a guy on his own with a sign that actually said London.

"Been waiting long, mate?"

"Yes", he said, in a Welsh accent. " About an hour."

Well that was worrying. It began to dawn on us that maybe this wasn't the best plan we'd ever made.

"Ah. We're going to London too. We'll stand back a bit, so they don't think there's four of us. As you can see, we might have a few problems getting a lift, now we think about it."

"Why?"

"Just the way we look."

"How do you look?"

"Eh? Like this...you know, coloured hair, leathers, studded belts. We might not have thought this through."

"Are you punks then? "

Brody interceded. "Are you blind, mate?"

"Yes."

"What?"

"I'm blind."

He was. He explained that he'd missed a coach to his destination in Wales, and was stuck in Coventry. He'd got a relative in London who could put him up, but not collect him, so he'd decided to hitch. He'd got a taxi out to this spot, and used the last of his money to do it.

"To be honest," he said, " I think the fare must have been more than I had. I thought Coventry was smaller. I think the taxi driver felt sorry for me, and got me here anyway."

So there we were. Three Punks and a blind guy, hoping to get to London at night. Naturally, it started to rain. Not teeming down, but that annoying drizzle that gets you really wet with very little effort.

"By the way, would you know what to do if I started having a fit?"

"Are you likely to start having a fit?"

"Well, I'm epileptic, you see. So you never know"

Apparently, Eva did know what to do. Even so, I was a little worried. I could see that if a blind guy was lying on the floor with a bunch of leather clad youths loosening his clothes, that the odds were a police car would be coming past. I could see in my mind the officers jumping out, shouting, Hey, is that guy alright? Thanks for your help, folk, we'll take it from here....

Actually, I couldn't see them doing that. Generally they stopped us for the sinister crime of walking around, or shopping. Shopping was always a problem back then. As soon as you wandered into a shop to, say, get some milk, or maybe beans, all eyes trained on you. The shopkeeper, or security if it was a bigger shop, would fix his gaze on you till you reached the counter and paid, and even then they'd look at you like you'd just pulled a fast one, and there was actually enough food to feed the 5,000 hidden behind your loaf of bread and a copy of The Coventry Evening Telegraph. Shoplifters loved us. I suspect they'd wait outside supermarkets till one of us would walk in, then have a field day walking behind the security people that were following us. We should have charged them. Not money, but maybe a block of cheese, or something. I like cheese. I guess if there'd been Punks when my old schoolmate was pinching saucy magazines we'd have been set up in Soho by now.....

So anyway, it's raining, and there's four of us in one place, hoping to get to London. Then a couple of student types, also with a sign for

London wandered up the road, and said Hi, and asked us if we'd been waiting long.

"Fuck off, mate." Brody piped up. And they simply did.

Which was a good job, as a bloody car pulled up! Luckily for us, the blind guy hadn't had a fit, and was also still holding a sign saying London. It occurred to me that the driver may actually have pulled up to see if our new friend was OK, but Eva started talking to him first, and it was fair to say she was a good looking girl. Tall, blonde, classic Germanic looks, and an incredibly ample chest. We were to find over the course of time that when it came to getting lifts off guys, this would be a huge asset, even with me and Brody being there. It's like her bosom was some kind of cloak of invisibility shrouding the rest of us. But anyhow, she told him our plight, and how the guy was blind, and he managed to fit all four of us in a not particularly big car. He suggested it would be best if Eva sat in the front for room purpose, even though I was bigger than her. We were learning.

So we got to London at stupid o' clock, via a stop at services, where the driver then told us he was short of cash for fuel, and could we put in, which is when I realised that he wasn't so much a concerned citizen who was worried about a disabled feller, but in fact just broke and saw an opportunity to get petrol. Fair play to him.

But we got there, he even dropped us at St Pancras, or whatever the station was – I never did know London much – and went on to take the other guy to his mates house. Well, we assume that he did. However, the station was shut, so we had a nice wait in a bus shelter till it opened in the morning. It opened at the same time as a small newsagent next door, where Brody headed in to get a couple of bags of crisps and Mars Bars for breakfast. I'm not sure, but probably some scruffy guy with huge pockets went in after him.

I'm guessing that the train ride was fairly uneventful. I'm guessing that, because I can't remember a single thing about it, but perhaps we were asleep. But at some point we arrived at the harbour, and got tickets for the ferry, which it turned out wouldn't be leaving till much later. It's easy to forget how things were before the internet. Finding ferry times and such from another town involved phoning up and stuff, and, living sort of hand to mouth as we did, we didn't have a phone in the flat. It's also easy to forget what life was like before mobile phones. And when it came to getting information, quite frankly we hadn't got a clue. So we just had headed off, with no real plan. Probably Eva was a bit wiser on that score, having gotten to Coventry from Zurich, but at this point she spoke limited English, and we spoke zero German, so it was a moot point, plus we never actually asked her anyway.

This gave us time to kill. However, we were very aware of our limited funds, so we were aware that we shouldn't really go and spend any of it in a pub, and maybe go and sightsee instead. Around the time we decided to do that, it began to rain again, plus Eva needed the toilet, so we thought we'd best pop in a pub after all, and maybe have just the one, so as not to be rude. Again.

Hence, come the time to get the ferry, we were pretty rat arse drunk. Now, the funny thing about people travelling, whether they be soul seeking hippies, day-trippers, seasoned travellers or tourists, is that their normal social conventions on who they will or won't mix with seem to fall by the wayside the further they get from home. So as punks, sitting in a pub at home we could be absolute pariahs, if we were let in the pub in the first place. We would usually only be approached by other people if they were the sort of pub loudmouth who wanted to ask us about why we looked the way we did, (kinda went with punk), what our philosophies about it all were (Beer. Music.) why we hated society, (I didn't know we did) and what we were rebelling against. (Sod all. We liked beer and music.) We were to find that this applied right across Europe. But, find yourself amongst anyone on the road and that changes.

And so it was at the docks. We found ourselves drinking in the company of a group of mods, a bunch of squaddies, and some Scottish feller. In fact, we all drank so well together that we continued on the ferry, and were all very merrily drunk by the time we disembarked in Boulogne. The Scottish bloke had been particularly drunk, in fact paralytic, and also pretty generous, beer wise to us, so as we all hugged, laughed and wished each other well, I looked out for him to say cheers, but couldn't see him anywhere. I guessed he'd staggered off. It was a couple of days later I mentioned this in passing, and Brody told me that the last he'd seen of him, he'd climbed into a lifeboat to have a bit of a kip, and asked him to give him a shout in half an hour.

"Did you?"

"What?"

"Give him a shout?"
"No."

So I guess that explained that then.

We had arrived! The only time in my life I had been out of England before was a school skiing trip to Scotland, which somehow my Mother had managed to pay for. It probably meant she'd sacrificed a lot somehow, but I only realised that in retrospect. Now, there's always a bit of debate on the road whether or not England and Scotland should count as two countries. As far as the UN listings go, the United Kingdom is all one country. My answer to that has always been well, pop into a bar in Glasgow on a Saturday night and loudly announce that Scotland isn't a country, then come back and let me know how you got on with that! But that aside, I hadn't been on what we would call Foreign soil before. So the mere act of landing somewhere else was incredibly exciting for me. I wasn't to realise it then, but this sense of excitement, this feel for adventure, this amazement that I was actually somewhere else, was never to go away. Almost like a young child in awe of almost every new experience, This was an excitement that would live with me, as it does with most travellers, forever and it started in France.

It was near the end of the summer and we had each only brought a sleeping bag and some clothes. We intended to just sleep wherever we could. Which in fairness is what we ended up doing. But after exploring Boulogne, and discovering that punks were just as unwelcome in French shops as they were at home, we decided to do an evening hitch, especially as no bar would serve us.

We were on the edge of town, when a car pulled up almost immediately. It was a couple of guys who asked us if we wanted to go to a punk club. We were a little sceptical, as these were clearly not punk guys, but they seemed friendly. And they were true to their word, and we ended up in a small club in the middle of nowhere where we had a great time, everyone talked to us, and our faith was restored. Hell, we liked Boulogne now. The guys drove us back to town after, and we stopped by the sea to get chips as we hadn't eaten all day.

That was the first time I had tried Mayonnaise. Seriously. Never heard of the stuff before. And they had it on chips there instead of vinegar. Even Eva was surprised that this was new and exotic to me . But as we sat in the car eating, another group of guys went past and gave us some quite evil looks. Not just us, but our new friends as well. Brody, who was shockingly short sighted, but refused to wear glasses, apparently missed this, and called after them.

"You got a light, mate?"

They came back. We never established if they had a light or not, as one of them threw a punch through the window at Brody, and caught him by surprise. He was a tough cookie for a little guy, and went to get out, but our driver started the car and sped off. These guys seemed to somehow quickly be in another car and speeding after us. That's when something hit the car, and we realised they had shot at us with something. A second shot caught the driver in his shoulder, and he yelled out in pain and then drove the car with one arm as blood appeared on his shirt. I have no idea to this day what they were firing. It couldn't have been anything too serious, but enough to make the driver throw up when we stopped. Which was luckily only a couple of minutes later, as they pulled into the drive of a huge mansion-like house. The pursuing car drove straight on. The driver's friend, who was the one that had invited us to the club, ran straight into the house, apparently to make some calls. It seemed that we had stumbled into some local dispute. These people knew each other. While he was making the call, the driver, and some other guys who had come out, all gave us some kind of signal to scat. This struck us as a good idea, so we hit the lane and ended up sleeping under a bridge.

So day one of our trip abroad, eh? We were obviously a little shaken up, and tried to speculate exactly what had just happened as we bedded down. It was the summer, so having just a sleeping bag was no problem. Brody went to sleep first, after grumbling that he still hadn't actually got a light for his cigarette. I snuggled up with Eva, and she came up with the theory that our guys owned the club we had been in, and the other guys were French Teddy boys. They did have that kind of hair, thinking about it. She speculated that this was an ongoing turf war, and noted the other car hadn't followed us into the mansion-like grounds, even though they were seemingly armed. I reflected on this for a while.

"I'll tell you what, "I eventually said...

"What?"

"I've honestly never tried that Mayonnaise stuff before...."

It seems that at this time the French were not too keen on picking up hitchhikers either. We'd picked up a map of north Europe back in the town, and figured that the next place to aim for should be Lille. We had not, of course, planned any kind of route to take. We knew we would arrive in France, and Eva needed to be in Switzerland, but everything in between these two facts was somewhat of a mystery. I wanted to take in as many countries on the way as we could, Eva wanted to take the shortest route we could find, and Brody said he didn't really care, so long as he could get that bloody cigarette lit at some point. We came to a sort of compromise that we could cross a few borders, but not go deep into the countries, and that we would stop at the first place we could find to get some matches to shut Brody up. This worked for all of us.

So we got to the main road and came up with a sign saying Lily. Brody had written it, and we only had one piece of cardboard. He scribbled the Y out, but could only get the E on the end. To be honest, I don't think it would have made much difference, we mainly just got abuse shouted at us in French. Or at least, we assume it was abuse. It would be funny to think they were in fact shouting "Does anyone need a light?" and wondering why we were ignoring them.

We ended up walking all day and nobody stopped. We were hot, thirsty, and pretty pissed off. Luckily, we passed a small village at some point, which meant a walk off the route during which I imagine would have been the time groups of punks in vans would have been driving by on their way to a gig, wondering if anyone needed a lift. But we got some bread, ham and water to keep us going. Water in bottles, I thought. Plastic bottles!! I really am through the looking glass here!

Back to the road, and we carried on walking. And walking. And walking. Night came, and we figured we'd eat the last of the bread and cheese – Brody had eaten the ham along the way – and bed down in a field behind a lay-by. We found a suitable place, off sight from the road, and somewhat dejectedly bedded down. There wasn't really much to talk about.

"Mulligan?" Brody eventually did say.

"What?"

"This is the last time I'm coming with you when you walk your girlfriend home. "

We all were laughing. You know, it wasn't such a bad day after all.

Waking up the next morning we were all slightly damp, and were pretty pissed off that we had eaten all the food. We still had a long way to go, and had resigned ourselves to probably walking. We hoped we'd come across somewhere to get food soon. And water. Or tea. I could murder a cup of tea.

We hit the road more or less at first light, so it was pretty damned early. We had literally just set off when a car pulled up about 20 yards ahead of us, and out got possibly the ugliest three people, a man and two women, I'd ever seen. They seemed to be pulling cases out, and rearranging them back in. It was a small Citroen, and was pretty full, so we guessed that they hadn't stopped for us. Nevertheless, Eva walked over to the man who'd been driving, breasts first, and asked him if they were going to Lille. The man laughed.
"Sure!! Can drop you there." The women laughed too.
I'm not sure how we all got in, but Eva was on my lap, Brody on one of the women's laps, and cases were taking up every other inch. And the three ugly people laughed all the way. Eva spoke a bit of French, but said later she thought they were Flemish speakers from Belgium. In any case, you couldn't fault three people who missed out when looks were granted, had a clapped out tiny car, a vast amount of luggage, and still found giving a bunch of Eejits a lift to be a joyous occasion. And in no time at all, we were in Lille.

One of the interesting things about Eva was that she seemed to know a lot about art. Not that me and her talked about it much, as I knew nothing about it whatsoever. That was never to really change. But Eva most certainly did, and whenever she had the chance, would chatter away for ages to people who knew about such things. This, in the early punk days, was a surprising amount of people. According to the TV or media view of punks, we were kind of semi-literate junkies, working class, comically dressed morons in need of saving, or should be in jail for something. However, the reality was far from that. Yes, indeed there were a lot of working class kids who got into it quite seriously, though usually far from thick. And there were the currently fashionable types, who looked positively pristine, with perfectly dyed hair, and brand new leathers, before moving to the next scene. (And why not...Life is about having fun.) But somewhere in the middle were the "art school" Punks and New Wavers. A mix of classes, this smaller group tended to look a bit more individual. Many were in bands, and developing music, others were studying fashion, and though usually called poseurs, a lot of innovation came from these people. And it was amongst these that Eva seemed to be in her element. I didn't really know much about her family, nor could I tell a "posh" Swiss accent..(If there was such a thing...) but I kinda guessed she fell more into that group than working class street punk.

So she was quite excited to find that a couple of exhibitions were on that she would love to see. She asked if I wanted to go, and to be honest, maybe I should have, but did not. This annoyed her, so she decided to see one that day, and the other the next. Luckily, over a coffee and breakfast in a cafe, a couple of hippy types at the next table asked us where we were staying, and when hearing we were on the road, gave us their address to come round later and crash.

Our first port of call was the train station, not to get tickets anywhere, of course, but back in the pre-terrorist bomb days, they generally had lockers. These lockers proved of great service to us as we travelled around, to stash our sleeping bags and other pitiful amounts of clothes we brought. After that, Eva headed off to one of the exhibitions she was interested in, leaving me and Brody to wander around. As in all situations like that, it involved a half hour or so walk around the centre looking at nothing in particular, but being disproportionately excited when we found a chain store with the same name as back home. Brody became especially excited as he found a chocolate bar called Raider, that was what we knew back home as Twix. I noticed that till the day we headed home, he made a point of looking out for these, and staring at the whole box in the shop, possibly wondering if there were actually Twix's in there, and the Raider thing was some kind of mistake. I pointed this out to him a few weeks later, observing that he never actually bought one.

"Nah." he said. "I don't really like Twix."

During our wandering, a rather well-to-do woman came up to us, speaking in French at first, but switched to perfect English when she presumably saw the blank looks on our face. She had kindly decided to give us the advice that this wasn't the town for us, and warned us to be very careful.

"There are very angry people about. " she told us. "They would not like this.", pointing at our clothes. " Just be very, very careful. " But if you have to stay, there is a cafe you could go to, you'll be safe there." And off she went. She actually didn't tell us where the cafe was.

We wandered around a bit more, looking for signs of anger in people, but didn't really spot anything. We eventually sat outside a little cafe to get a coffee. A waiter came out and told us to go.

"What, we can't even buy a coffee?"

He paused. "One moment." then went back inside and spoke to someone.

He came back out. "Non."

"Fuck, I suppose a Tea is out of the question as well then, " Brody said, sarcastically.

"One Moment", and he went back inside.

"Oui. Two teas?"

He brought them out. With the bill. "You must pay the bill first today."

We did.

And we were enjoying our tea – though if truth were told, we actually would have liked coffee – When two skinhead looking lads and a punky looking girl walked past, took a double take, then walked back and sat at the next table, and lit up some cigarettes. The waiter came out, and they had a bit of a long conversation, ending with him going back inside and bringing out some cola.

"Where are you guys from?" , one of the skinheads asked, but as he spoke in English I'm guessing he knew."

"A place called Coventry. " Blank looks.

"Near Birmingham".

"Ah, Birmingham."

It is worth noting that this was to be an ongoing conversation for the rest of my life on the road. The latter half of my life, I found it easier to just say Birmingham. Though in fact, I'm not completely convinced that anyone outside the UK, or even southerners in the UK, knew where Birmingham was exactly, but it tends to move the conversation on a bit.

So after a bit of chat with the skinhead – The others didn't speak, but seemed to nod their heads at appropriate places, so I guess they understood – He told us about a bar, or cafe, we could go to later where the music was quite good, and there might be a band on. We wrote the address on a bit of beermat, and bid farewell. He did point out we should be careful, as there were a lot of angry people about.

"What do you think?" Brody asked.
" Don't know. We haven't had a lot of luck with the French teddy boys, nothing to say the skinheads will be much better. Could be a set up?"
"She's more punk though."
"True. Maybe meet up with Eva later, see what she knows about European skinheads. Shall we find a bar?"

We were turned away from the first bar we went into, and got waved away from the second, which caught the attention of a young barman outside another place opposite. He waved too, but this time to come in.
"Hey, what are you guys having? Couple of beers?"
"Oh yes." He put a couple of bottles on the table. This was something else a bit new to us, as beer came in pint glasses, and even though we knew we weren't, we always felt a bit cheated. Or I did. Brody didn't seem to really care.
"And where are you guys from?"
"Coventry." Blank look.
" It's near Birmingham."
"Ah.....Birmingham."

He was a cheerful kind of fellow, and showed us to a table with a huge grin on his face. There was only one other customer, an old boy sat on a stool by the bar. He would mutter something to the barman every so often, and the barman would laugh loudly. At any point in our conversation if we laughed, he would look round at us, like he'd forgotten other people were there, and wondered where the noise was coming from.
"Music?" The happy barman called out.
"Yeah," we laughed, "why not." Don't suppose you have the Clash? Nah, we are just kidding, anything's great."
He grinned, and went through a pile of tapes on the back of the bar. 2 minutes later, we were listening to White Man in Hammersmith Palais. Brody thought it hilarious to shout out Hammersmith Calais a couple of times, which seemed to make the barman's smile even bigger.

New York Dolls, Television, Patti Smith, The Fall, Ramones and the Slits all followed. And some stuff we didn't recognise, including some French punk. We were quite enjoying this. We stayed for a few beers, then left to meet Eva at the train station, something we had arranged earlier. By this time, only one other customer had come in, a kind of fat "heavy rock" guy. He was wearing a Led Zeppelin T-shirt, and had that scraggly long rock guy hair, but seemed to enjoy the tunes that were on too. We nodded at him in a friendly way, and he nodded back, but seemed content in his own company, occasionally agreeing with the old boy when he muttered stuff that made the barman laugh.

We left a tip this time, as Eva had pointed out how rude we had been in other places so far by not tipping. We weren't rude really, we just didn't really know much about tipping. It was another strange European thing that we hadn't been aware of. We would find plenty of such things, which is the great thing about travel. Till this day, I have never been able to put my head into the mindset of people who save up to go on holiday "abroad" and then complain that things are different. This turns out to be a surprisingly huge amount of people. They will spend a huge amount of time seeking out a place that serves food they recognise, or complain that local taxi drivers don't speak English, or if they are ticked off by a local policeman for jaywalking, point out patronisingly that it's not against the law in England, as if that is a perfectly reasonable defence against breaking the local law.

But we headed off and met Eva, who had been given a lift to the station by a rather smartly dressed German chap from the exhibition who greeted us with a warm handshake, and took us for a drink in a cafe next door. Though we got disapproving looks, it seemed being with a suit opened doors. Either he or Eva would bring up something they had seen at the exhibition, then chat and laugh in German, something that began to bug me a bit.

"Anyway," Eva explained, "There is a large art festival in a nearby town tomorrow, and Dieter is willing to take us all over there."

"I'm not sure," I answered, "Art's not really my thing"

"You'll love it" said the German guy, "It is more contemporary than classic." Eva and him laughed at this. So did Brody, but I'm sure he didn't find that comment any more funny than I had.

"But you haven't really seen Lille yet. Maybe explore tomorrow?"

"You smell like you've been exploring already" she said, smiling, before saying something in German to Dieter, who laughed back.

Now I was really bugged, but trying to not show it.

The conclusion was that Dieter would pick Eva up from the train station the next day, and they would go and look at art. Probably. He bought us another drink, then headed off, shaking hands in an admittedly friendly way. We sat with the drinks, and I have to admit to being a bit sulky. Eva could see this, but seemed happy to chat to Brody about the exhibition, even though he was looking blankly at her.

"Oh, by the way," She finally said to me, with a knowing smile. "Did you see how Dieter looked at Brody"

"Condescendingly? " I remarked, giving in to sarcasm.

"No, he was quite taken. Very disappointed he's not going to the festival."

"Eh?" Brody said, cocking his head. "Why? Because I was changing my mind about that and was thinking of going now..."

I glared at him. Seriously?

"You couldn't tell?" carried on Eva, with a winning grin. "Why, Dieters homosexual. And he was very taken with Brody. He said he'd like to help you explore all sorts of new things......I'm sure he didn't mean anything about art, ha ha."

Brody seemed to take a moment for this to sink in.

"What? Don't be stupid. That bloke can't be queer...."

"Homosexual"

"Whatever. But he can't be anyway."

"Why not?

"He was wearing a suit for fuck's sake. And a nice one at that."

So, after much taking the piss out of Brody and his belief that it was unlikely for a homosexual man to be wearing a smartly pressed suit, and be at an art show, and then eating a kind of sandwich and chips for food, we decided to look for the music place the skinhead had recommended. Eva's guess was that skinheads here were like at home, and could blow a bit hot and cold on who they mixed with. We took the chance. As we passed the bar we'd been in earlier, we decided to pop in, get a beer, and ask the way to the other one, as we had no idea how to get there. We had stopped and asked a couple of people, but they angrily told us they had no idea, and stomped off. We sat down, to a warm greeting by the same barman, and he brought us some drinks. We asked him if he knew the music place, which we had written on the beermat..

"You are going there tonight?"

"Yep....Was told about it earlier."

"You will like it. You turn left outside of here. Then walk straight. Second left at the top of the hill......In fact, I'll write it down."

He wrote instructions on a bit of paper, and then put a tape of the Clash on. Great guy.

Off we headed later. Followed the instructions with the badly drawn map.

"I don't know why we left there," Brody pointed out, " it's pretty good, and the beer was quite cheap. "

"We are here to explore. Meet new people. Broaden our horizons. And all that shit."

We turned at the top of the hill, followed a little road, went down an alley, and walked along a main road. Found the small cobbled street, went up another hill that looked like the first one. Went up a street, walked round a traffic island, and down the other side of the street. We walked for about half an hour, thinking this didn't seem right. Then, on the last road, we had to look for a shop called, amusingly enough TittZ, and the place would be opposite. We spotted TittZ, and looked at the music place.

We looked at it for a while.

"So," I finally said. "None of us thought to check the name of the last bar we were in, or what street it was on."

And so it was that we walked back into the same bar, where the grinning barman put three beers on the counter, laughed, and said, "Welcome to The Music Place..."

Well, the place filled up later, and all in all a good night was had by all. We were to learn that another difference between Europe and the UK was the times that people went out at. We would arrive at a bar about 7pm, with no one in it, and start to see people arrive at midnight. This was due to the bizarre British drinking laws of the time. When I started going to the pub after I left school , the pubs closed at 10.30pm. And also closed in the afternoons from 2.30 to 6pm. The exception was the Market and Docks clause, allowing for anti-social times. Hence, one pub by the Coventry Market could open at 5pm on an evening, and there would be a queue for half an hour before that. This law went back to WW1 – yes, world war one! - to stop people drinking instead of getting on with their war work, and wasn't reversed till most of a century later. Hence, a kind of unique British binge drinking culture , where people necked as much as possible in a short time emerged. Even by the time I hit Europe, the extension was the grand old later time of 11pm. There was back then though, I recall, a remarkable amount of parties after the pubs closed, which you don't see as much of now. Or, the Indian curry house, another way of a later drink. There were nightclubs (which shut at 1am then), but outside of London this meant nothing to punks, or anyone not wearing a suit, white shirt, and definitely never trainers. It was, quite frankly, shit.

So a night not starting to get going till midnight left us in the same boat of generations of Brits. We would be already drunk when everyone else arrived. And we were this night too. Eva met a couple of Swiss-French girls, and spent the night dancing. We were at a table with the skinhead guy, who promised to beat up anyone who hassled us (There was, he reminded us, a lot of angry people) and the girl from earlier and her friend. Now, these were two very cute punk girls, that Brody tried his hardest to "get to know" better, but to no avail. But they were friendly. Come time to leave, another guy that was a friend of theirs, gave us a lift to the hippy house, who were surprised to see us, and in truth, I'm not sure they remembered meeting us at all. But we got to crash out, and went our separate ways the next day. Brody decided for whatever reasons that he was not an art fan after all!

We ended up in the same place the next night, as it seemed a great choice. Eva was to meet us, but didn't show up. Meanwhile, the two punk girls were there again, and one of them sat with us, with Brody buying her beers in the hope of, ahem, getting to know her better. The other one came to and from the table, and we met a couple of pretty laid back New Wavers from Belgium, who gave me a few bits of paper with addresses and phone numbers written down to contact once we reached Belgium. I enjoyed these guys' company whilst Brody unsuccessfully engaged with the girl.

Near the end of the night, Eva had still not shown up. This gave me a bit of a sinking heart.

"I don't think she's coming then." I said to Brody.

"No shit. You let her go off with a bloke in an expensive suit."

"FFS, it's not that," I muttered, trying to convince myself. "He's homosexual, maybe his car broke down or something."

"Bollocks," Brody reasoned, "queer my arse. That was just a ruse so you'd not object to them going off together. I told you, didn't I ? I said, of course he's not queer."

"And why are you so sure?"

"I told you.....He was wearing a suit. Now who's laughing at who?"

Not that I held with the suit theory, but it sure was beginning to look like Brody was right. I was putting my jacket on, when the more elusive punk girl came up.

"You going now?"

"Yep. Nice meeting you all. We are probably going on to Belgium tomorrow."

"Do you want to come back to my apartment?"

"Me and my friend?"

"No. Just you. It's a very small apartment."

I considered this. After all, it seemed that Eva had bailed on me. However, our stuff was at the hippy place, and so was Eva's, so I told her this, and she said that my girlfriend had clearly left me, so she would come back to the squat too, just to show us the way. She did, and came straight in and asked me where we were sleeping. In fairness, I was a bit beer-angry with Eva, the girl was hot, so we went to my sleeping bag on the floor, and Brody lay on the other side of the scruffy little room in his own sleeping bag.

"I won't listen," he said. "I'm gonna pass out anyway."

"Cheers bud"

"We could share?"

"Fuck off."

We were just about to get down to some naughty shenanigan's, when we heard the door of the squat knock and the sound of one of the hippies letting Eva in.

"Shittttttttt"

"Is that your girlfriend?"

"Yes....Fuck!"

"No problem. " My new friend got up, walked over the room and lay next to Brody, who was noisily snoring.

Eva came in.

"Hi. I am so sorry. The car broke down on the way back, so we decided to get dinner as it was late in the town we were in. Dieter actually made an arrangement to meet the waiter after his shift finished, so we hung on, and the waiter guy drove us back here. They have gone back to his. Did you have a good night? And is that one of the girls from last night with Brody?"

"Shit, I was worried about you....And yes it is. I think they are asleep now."

The night before, Me and Eva had zipped our sleeping bags together, so had a double one, and she got in, gave me a quick peck on the cheek and promptly fell asleep straight away.

Then for the next hour I listened to Brody having very noisy sex with the hot punk girl. So this is why everyone here is so fucking angry, I thought.

IV

So there was this fat lady that couldn't get out of bed, and everyone fed her.

We slept quite late, and headed off in the afternoon. Me and Brody were obviously a bit worse for wear, so were not too chatty.

"Funny thing is," He began eventually, in reference to waking up next to the girl, who had promptly got up, said Au Voir, and headed off, "Is that I don't even remember getting back to the house last night. I barely remember leaving the club. Surprised the hell out of me when I woke up next to that girl. It was her mate I was chatting up all night. I just sort of remember waking up to a blow job, then getting laid. Result, eh?"

"Good for you," Eva said. "I was feeling a bit bad about me and Mulligan being together, and you on your own. But you and her, Dieter and the waiter....Looks like everybody was happy last night.

Yes. I was frigging ecstatic.

But we got a lift quite quickly off a woman, who said there were two main routes to Brussels, our destination, and she was going via Ghent, where she could drop us or we could wait and see if we got a straight ride through. Eva suggested Ghent, so we could get to a Bureau de change. So we did that, and, as tended to happen, bumped into some punk guy who gave us an address, and the name of a bar, so we dumped our stuff in the train station locker, and explored a bit. We had a good night in the bar, but somehow lost the address to stay at, and ended up getting our bags and sleeping in a park near the station. We went for a coffee and some bun type thing, and I looked at the money.

"I like this money," I remarked.

"Oh yes," Eva said, " I've been meaning to ask you. Why did you change all your money? You did the same in France. You changed all your money to French Francs, and now you changed all that into Belgium Francs."

"What's wrong with that?"

"Well, it's more commission paid. If you do that everywhere, you'll lose lots of money. Why don't you just change the amount that you might need?"

"What? I didn't know that. I thought they just changed it. There's commission?

"Didn't you know?"

"Well, of course I didn't! Or I wouldn't have done that. Why didn't you say?"

"I thought you knew. I thought it was a bit strange though."

Well, thank you Eva. Twice now I'd paid a percentage to the money changers on money I didn't need to change, and she thought it was 'a bit strange'. So I decided to keep the Belgium money and just change what I needed from now on.

We had a bit of another look around, then headed out. We got a lift pretty quickly, and were in Brussels in about an hour. Done the usual with the train lockers, and were barely out of the station when a small, runt-ish looking punk kid.....and I mean kid, he looked about 12... told us about a house we could maybe stay at. "Tell them Runt sent you." It figured.

We got our stuff straight back out of the lockers and headed there first, as we planned a few days in Brussels, and knocked on the door of a fairly big, but dilapidated house just outside of the town centre. A spaced out looking girl opened the door, and said Hi, come in.

"Don't you want to know who we are?"

"Oh. Oui. Who are you?"

"We need a place to stay. Runt sent us."

"OK. Come in. Who is Runt?"

So we went in, and found ourselves in a large living room which had a couple of equally spaced out punk guys sitting in it. They spoke in French, then German, and Eva told us they said that if we wanted to stay, we had to ask Mama. Mama was in the bedroom, they said.

"Ok...We'll wait here till she comes out."

"She won't come out. Go and see her."

So we went to head upstairs, when one of the guys shouted out, in German, not upstairs....Go in the other room. So down the hall was another door which we knocked.

"Come in."

We did, and there facing us was a huge, old fashioned iron bed, in which sat possibly the fattest woman I had ever seen. She was eating a big bag of what we call crisps, but are called potato chips there, and she smiled a toothless smile at us. Surrounding her, sitting either on the bed, or the floor, or on stools, were a whole bunch of maybe about 12 or so punks and odd looking kids all watching a black and white TV with a really bad picture. We were, it must be said a little taken aback.

"Hi.....Runt sent us...."

An older punk guy who looked like he'd been through the mill a few times answered in English.

"Who is Runt?"

"We met him by the station. Said we might get a place to crash? We are here for a couple of days.

The woman just smiled at us, then carried on eating crisps and watching TV.

"Sure," the older punk guy said, after looking at Mama smiling." There's a space in one of the rooms just upstairs. Just a couple of days though. You won't need a key. We don't lock the door.

And so that was our base camp. We asked if anyone knew any good bars or anywhere, and as with any other time that we asked anything, they all kind of looked at Mama, who smiled and said nothing. Occasionally someone would actually tell us something. Every time we came back to the house over the next few days, no matter what time of day or night, Mama was in bed, and the others would bring her tea or food, and she would smile. I never once saw her get up, and wondered how she went to the toilet, but really didn't like to ask.

"We are just having tea," a skinny hippy type girl had said on that first occasion. "Do you want some?

I have never seen such a huge kettle in my life. I'd followed her into the kitchen, which was huge but didn't seem to have much in it, not even a fridge that I could see. She told me it was OK, she'd bring the tea in, so we found a space round the bed. After half an hour she came back with an equally large teapot, which seemed too heavy for her, and another girl brought a lot of cups and mugs in. All chipped, none matched, but clean. They poured the tea, there was no milk, and we politely tried to follow whatever the hell was on the TV. We eventually secured a space in a room upstairs, which had signs of people staying, a couple of mattresses on the floor sort of thing, and boxes of, well, stuff, and then we headed out.

Brussels was a pretty great city. We found a few interesting bars and cafes, and caught a local band somewhere that was pretty impressive, even if we had no idea what they were singing about. And we knew we could always get a decent cup of tea back at the house, as the kettle was always on. We'd go back, say hallo, and Mama would smile at us and then eat, always surrounded by the punks in the house. None of whom we ever saw outside of there.

The morning we left, we popped in the bedroom to say goodbye, and a girl who looked remarkably like a younger Patti Smith was in there, who we hadn't seen before.

"We just thought we'd say goodbye. Thanks for the stay."

Mama smiled at us, and ate a banana.

"Who are you?" the new girl asked, quizzically.

"We got this address a few days ago. Mama let us stay. Or some bloke did. I'm not sure who let us.

She looked thoughtful.

"How did you know about here? " she asked.

"A young punk kid called Runt gave us the address....said to say he sent us."

"Who? Ah, never mind. Hope you enjoyed Brussels."

We had and said so. We figured we knew the best place to hitchhike, and would catch a bus out there. We were at the bus station when, of all people, Runt walked past, and called us..

"Hey, guys, " He shouted across the road. "Did you go to the house?"

"We did....Thanks."

" Did you tell them I sent you?"

"Er, we did.....Thanks again..."

"No problem. If you're ever back here, ask for Runt....Everyone knows me, and I'll make sure you are Ok...."

With that, he cheerfully swaggered off down the road.

That Runt, eh. What a guy.

V

I was mistaken for an old car chassis once.

Well, not exactly. But close. Leaving Brussels, we headed off to a town called Namur for the night, which was a rather attractive, if somewhat unremarkable City, other than it proved exceedingly difficult to leave. The weather had taken a turn for the worst, and no matter what way we went to head out, we seemed to get lost, and end up back in the centre. So, we decided on a bus, and found one going to Liege, which Eva told us was supposed to be rather pretty. Though this struck Brody and myself as a rather funny reason to go somewhere, we hadn't got a better plan and so laughingly agreed.

Actually, Liege was indeed rather pretty. Though wet. Not that we could help that, mind you. So a particularly uneventful day was had mainly , not helped by the fact we had not brought anything in the line of waterproof clothing. So we tended to wander from cafe to cafe, drinking tea or coffee, till we were so wet that it was getting depressing. We headed outwards from the town to catch a lift, deciding that we might as well carry on. During a particularly heavy shower, we popped into a nice relaxed bar to shelter, ordered a couple of coffees, and sat by a heater to try to dry out.

A large, bearded chap in his 50's who had been sat at the bar sent a couple of shots of a spirit I didn't recognise over, (though I never was a spirit drinker) and loudly announced to the bar in general that these poor wet people needed a good warming drink on such a day.

"Liege is sorry for the weather on your vacation!!"

"Thanks....Though we are not taking it personally."

At this he guffawed loudly, and sent us over more shots. I liked this guy.

So he came over and joined us, and we spent the evening in his company, with him buying us drinks, all of which seemed to come with various snacks, which was quite handy as we hadn't eaten since our now-habitual ham and cheese rolls in the morning. He had been, he explained, a traveller in his day, and said he admired our spirit, setting off on adventures without much money and not caring about the weather. A nice thing to say, but in fact, I'd have liked to have had more money, plus we hadn't actually said we didn't have much, so I guess we just looked poor. We also would have liked the weather to be better, and I kinda did care about that as I sat dripping.

He had travelled across America when he was younger and found work in California. He seemed to make that point by saying "Right on" a lot, and in a Californian accent too. Just that phrase, mind you. I found myself quite fascinated by some of the stories he told, and was a little embarrassed that my complete travellers' tales were about France last week, and a ski trip to Scotland as a kid.

"Ah, Scotland," He mused. " A very beautiful country. With beautiful women. I fell in love with a girl in Scotland once. She was exceptionally beautiful."

"A Scottish girl?"

"No, Norwegian. There are very beautiful women in Norway"

Over the course of the evening, we were to find that there were very beautiful women in Denmark, Ireland, Thailand, California, Russia, Korea, Yugoslavia, Czechoslovakia, and pretty much everywhere else that he had been.

"But do you know where the most beautiful women are?" he asked.

"No...But you haven't said England yet..."

"Here. Right here. In Liege. Here, all the women are beautiful."

Brody thought about this.

"It was hardly worth you going away, then......"

Well, it was a most pleasant evening to be sure. He also explained to us about Wallonia.

It would seem that Belgium, for such a small country, is quite the mix of cultures. Its history took it between France, The Netherlands, and Germany, and at the moment, he told us, there is much tension between the Flemish speakers of the Flanders region, a language close to Dutch, and the French speaking Belgium community. To make matters more complicated, the area we were in, it seems, is the Walloon region, which is separate from the rest of the French speaking community based around Brussels.

The name Walloon has its origins in the German word, Walha, which translates as the Strangers. Interestingly, this is also where the names Wales and Cornwall, amongst others, derived their names. The strangers in question referred to the Celtic or Gallic people of the regions. Though whether it meant that they were strange, or, you know, just didn't visit very much I really don't know.

("Hey, Caesar, the Walloon's are at the door"

"Really? Send them in.......Well, Hi, strangers, how's the low countries?")

So it seems that Namur is the capital of the region, but Liege has the bigger population of Walloons. And the best comparison seems to be the Cornish people of South England who retain their own cultural identity. Unfortunately, during much of his conversation, possibly down to the drinks, I thought he was saying that they were Balloons, and tried not to laugh whenever he said it. The evening drew to an end, however, and he bought us one last drink "for the route."

"Cheers...We say one for the road back home."

"Yes," he said, "But the Californians speak English better."

42

To this day, I have never heard an American say one for the route.

Off out into the night we went, realising that it was much too late to get a lift, and so should find some shelter. Especially as we were dry now. We weren't far from the main road out, it seemed, and came to a part where a flyover went overhead. I'm sure it wasn't legal, but we scrambled up the elevation to a kind of ledge just under the flyover, and bedded down. Just in time. The heavens opened again, and it poured down all night. In fact, when we woke up, we found that the rain had been soaking the concrete, and we were lying on the only dry patch left. Never mind, the road was busy, and we got a lift straight away from a guy who told us it was illegal to be on that road, so he'd drop us at the Dutch Border. Which he did and soon we entered Holland.

It is worth mentioning our passports, now that we had crossed a couple of borders. Eva had a full Swiss passport, which was no problem. I had, what they called at the time, a visitors passport that was only valid for one year, but cheap to get, and you could get them from the post office. They were a flimsy bit of card, which were stamped like a normal passport as you went over the border. Brody, on the other hand, had an Irish passport, for reasons I'm not sure about. In fact, I'm sure he told me he'd been born on a British Army base in Germany. This, for reasons unknown, was becoming a bit of a problem.

Coming from County Coundon, with its high Irish population back home, we were always brought up to believe that the Irish were the toast of the world. Be careful, my Mother and neighbours warned me when I said I was going abroad. Don't let them know your English. They're not liked.

The strange thing about my parents, and in fact most of my friends' parents, was they always seemed to be oblivious to the fact that their children were English. They spoke to us about 'The English ones' and their faults, totally missing the point that they were actually putting their own offspring down.

"Just tell them you're Irish", they would say, "Everyone loves the Irish."

Well, customs officials didn't seem to! Every border we came to.....(And this was before the Treaty of Maastricht, and the right to roam across what would later become the EU, and so meant that you had to get a stamp at each border.)....we would be alright till they saw the Irish passport, then things would slow down. They would take the passport, examine it, talk amongst themselves, or leave us in a room for a while. No one ever explained why, though it was possibly linked to IRA activity at the time, though in all honesty, the chances that three punk rockers were heading onto the European Mainland to cause Fenian bombing activities with one Irish passport between us struck me as highly unlikely. But never-the-less, this occurred at nearly every crossing. Nothing ever happened about it, we just got stern looks (Do border guards have any other look?) and after a long delay they stamped his passport and sent us through. I mentioned this to my Mother when I got back.

"Well, that's odd." she decided. "They must have heard your English accents."

And so we arrived in Maastricht, where we went to the Bureau De change, wisely converted only some of my money into Gilder, and headed to the train station. Where we had quite the result. When Brody opened one of the lockers, he found there was an envelope with a small bundle of Dutch Guilders in it. Not a fortune, but enough for a decent meal and night out! I suppose that the right thing to do would have been to hand it in to someone, but we weren't really sure to who, it wasn't a huge amount, and we were, to be honest, a bit over what we'd planned on spending, if you could call what we had done planning.

So we headed off to explore a bit and in no time at all we had got talking to some punk couple who told us there was a good place to go called, I think, The White Balloon Cafe. We spent the day wandering about and then headed there in the evening. Not being able to find it, we figured we would go into another bar, get a drink and ask directions. And maybe something to eat. Hey, we were rich now. And there was only so much living on bread and cheese we could do.

Eventually we found a place, and walked in. I guess the point to remember was that I was wearing a cut off leather jacket with studs and badges on, a studded belt, and D-rings on a pair of black bondage trousers. In fact, we all had something similar on, which is what prompted the owner, an English guy, to loudly announce,

"Fuck me, what's this? I'm a barman, not a scrap metal dealer!!!"

Well, that drew a laugh from the other people in the bar, but at least it was in fun, as he served us and went on to have a bit of a laugh at seemingly everybody who walked into the place. And flushed with our new found wealth, we ordered the best meals we had had so far, and all feelings of guilt about the found money disappeared in a satiated happiness.

After a few more drinks, we bid farewell, took another insult about watching out for magnets, and headed off to the white balloon.

Which turned out to be a pretty good find. It was a bit of a dump, truth be told, with no furniture that actually matched, nor had four equally sized legs, the toilets were just about usable, but the clientele was definitely of a punkish kind. Apart from one older fat rock type guy, who was balding but had long hair, and was wearing a Genesis T-shirt. He stood on his own at the corner of the bar, nursing a beer. As my adventures and shenanigans continued over the years, I was to learn that with regards to rock bars or punk bars, or anything similar, in any country in the world, there is a God given constant that is that all such places were basically dives, and every one of them must have a fat rock type guy wearing a musty looking prog or classic rock band t-shirt who was based alone at the bar.

In fact, over the years I came to the conclusion that somewhere in the centre of each continent, there must be a giant warehouse called "Rock bar Furniture." Here you would find countless tables, benches, stools, etc, with the important factor being that NOT ONE PIECE of this furniture would match another. That was the guarantee. Also, a small piece of one leg of each piece, maybe about half a centimetre, would be planed off so they wouldn't sit quite straight. This would complement the odd angle of the table-tops, that meant once your pint spilled, which it would, the beer would go straight into your lap, no matter what side you were sitting at. You would also be able to pick up well-worn triple-extra-large t-shirts by rock bands that no longer released albums for your fat rock guy, and, unique to rock bars, you could buy a kind of piss coloured paint for the toilets, along with an air freshener that smells of shite. Just add the type of beer generally regarded as the worst in the country at an overpriced and slightly out of date taste served in a dirty glass, and you, my friend, have yourself a rock bar!!

We were sitting at a wobbly table having a drink when a couple of lads who had been playing bar football came over and asked if we wanted a game. Me and Brody rose to the challenge, and were totally wiped out by these guys. However, they had asked just to be friendly, and so we all got chatting. Amongst their group was a girl with a completely shaven head, something I hadn't seen before. I'd seen plenty of girls, especially amongst the skinheads back home with close cropped hair, but never shaven. She got chatting to Eva, and they nattered away in German. I was quite taken by the fact she had introduced herself to us by the name of Tits, which in fairness, was very apt, as her ripped red and black stripy t-shirt did very little to keep them in. With the best will in the world, it was hard not to keep looking. Mind you, I was a young, hormone filled bloke on the road and would be lying if I said that seeing her and Eva getting on so well didn't stir up a few imaginings that served me well for a few months!!

"She's quite a looker, that Tits girl, " I remarked to one of the lads we were by this time playing pinball with.

"Yes. That's why she's my girlfriend," he grinned.

Oddly, I really don't remember what he looked like, or what his name was.

Our new friends told us of a squat we could stay at, that had recently been vacated. It was still used as a party house though. But for tonight, after the bar closed, we headed off to one of the guys' apartments, where we took a few take out bottles, and sat drinking with him and a couple of his friends. One by one, people started to fall asleep, pretty much where they sat. It seemed to be basically a large room, with a small shared kitchen down the hall. First Brody dropped, then one of his friends, then Eva, and then the other friend.

"Right...Everyone's asleep....I have something," the guy whose apartment it was said to me when we were the last two awake. We went to the kitchen, where he went to the fridge and took out some cartons of Chinese food.

"Thing is," he explained, "I really only had enough for just about 2 people. So I thought I'd see who was the last person awake."

Getting out a large wok, he fried up the various contents of the cartons in one delicious, mixed up meal, and we had half each.

"Just don't tell the others tomorrow!"

Two good meals in one day!! Hell, I was living like a king at the moment.

Next day, they showed us the empty house, and we got our stuff from the train lockers and left it there. We hung around the cafe, and got to know a good few people while we were there, and got to quite like the place. The house was bare, but there was running water, and it was dry.

"Just be careful of the police," we were warned. "They come down really heavy on squatters."

Wandering around the town a couple of days later with Eva, (Brody took to wandering off on his own, for whatever reason), I found myself looking in a touristy shop window, and spotted something interesting.

"Hey look, are those little iron-on patches of countries' flags?"

It was. I went in to have a look. They were indeed some of those patches you can iron, or sew onto a backpack, or whatever, hanging on a bit of card. For some reason they caught my imagination. I bought a France, Belgium and Holland one, and also one with the European flag which had EUROPA and 12 stars on it. I also picked up a Brussels and Maastricht one. I didn't know it at the time, but I had just unwittingly begun what was probably to become the most expensive hobby I would ever have. As I carried on my travels, I would always try to pick up a patch if possible. It even had a pattern. First, the patch of the country. It didn't have to be the flag, but I do like flags. Then, if I passed through the country again, I picked up a patch of the city I was in instead. If the place was, say an island or a territory but had their own flag, even if they were part of another country, I bought their patch first if I didn't have the country flag....For example, the Canary Isles, though part of Spain, warranted their own patch because they have a flag and autonomous government, as would, say, the Faroe Islands even though they are part of The Kingdom of Denmark. These patches, even more so than the journals that every good traveller keeps, became my diary. They live in a box. And I'm convinced that if my house caught fire, I would probably be stupid enough to run back in to rescue them. I say an expensive hobby jokingly, for any money spent travelling is money well spent, but though these little embroidered 'souvenirs' – A word I really hate by the way – cost very little each, the money, the time, and the joy I have had gathering them up is priceless. And that day in town began all that. It was many years later that the gaps in the patches from places where I couldn't get them, and a little thing called the internet, kicked my ass back onto the road again. But that's a story for later. And it is, as I say, always about the story.

Happy with my new possessions, we had headed back to the squat, where we found Brody looking quite pleased with himself.

"Look what I found."

It was a bike. Quite an old rusty looking thing, one of those typical Dutch sit up and beg types that remind Brits of vicars cycling through little villages.

"You've stolen a bike?"

"Not stolen....found. It was out by some big waste containers I passed. Just dumped there. So I rode it back here. I feel proper Dutch now."

It was true, the Dutch did seem to like their bikes. We kept being nearly hit by them, and got swore at a lot, mainly due to the fact we tended to look the wrong way when crossing roads. It takes a long time to accept that the rest of the world stubbornly drives on the wrong side of the road.

Naturally, I felt obliged to have a go, noting that I should remember which side of the road to cycle on. And off I went. I'd never rode one of these types of bikes before, and quite enjoyed it, it made me feel very local. That was until I was cycling up a fairly busy street, feeling a bit unsure of the traffic flow where I needed to turn, so mounted the kerb, intending to push it across the fairly busy junction. Well, I pulled the bike up, and indeed most of the bike followed. However, the front wheel didn't and just carried on rolling along ahead of me. I landed hard on the floor, man and machine all kind of mixed up in one big, painful and embarrassing heap.

No one seemed to care, except one large, fat gay guy in a red flowery shirt who drew a sympathetic sharp intake of breath, and said something in Dutch.

"Sorry?" I muttered, disentangling myself, and noting a lack of skin on one knee.

"Loose nuts?" He translated, looking concerned.

"Yep. Yep, I guess I had loose nuts."

I recovered the wheel, and decided to push the stupid thing back to the squat. Or I did till I saw some big waste containers, and dumped it there. I noted the next day that it was gone again. Circle of life, I guess.

Eventually, much as we were enjoying Maastricht, we decided it was really time to move on. We had a last night with many of our new friends in the White Balloon, and, picking up a few beers, headed back to the squat for one last party. We had all just got there when that was the night the police decided to storm it. One of the Dutch guys spotted them coming, and called out for everyone to hide. This was due to the quite large amount of illegal substances they, and Brody, had amongst themselves. I should really point out that though most drugs, especially speed, were pretty common amongst a lot of the punk crowds, I was, and still am, just a drinking bloke. Not for any particular moral reasons, I just was never interested in trying anything like that. I was very much in the minority, mind you. However, I knew darned well that the police were not going to believe that, and we would be arrested and treated collectively. I also knew hiding in a basically empty house was not really going to work, though the others had already scattered.

So on a whim, I sat on the stairs and watched as four armed policemen burst through the door. They stopped and shone a bright torch right at me, and I continued to sit there.

"Hi." I said.

This clearly surprised them, and one of them said something angrily, and I asked them if they spoke English.

"What are you doing here? This is not your house."

"Yeah, I know. Sorry. "

I then, (and I have no idea where this came from) told them that I had arrived in town that morning, was leaving tomorrow, and had stashed my luggage in there while I explored town. Luckily, we had packed our bags earlier, and these were by the front door, which I pointed out..

"Just you?"

"No. My girlfriend too. But we had a bit of a row earlier, and I got back here first. I'm waiting here for her. We want to be on the road tomorrow. Well, later this morning at this time, I guess."

They looked through the bags , which couldn't be pleasant as they contained nothing except a few clothes, which were by now getting a bit rancid, as we had intended to find a launderette, but had drank instead. They beckoned me down, quite politely, really, and did a quick search in my pockets.

"Why not stay in a hotel?"

"Can't afford it. We are just hitching around Europe, and sleeping where we can. We were given this address, but no one was here, so we stashed our stuff."

Surprisingly, they simply told me I would have to leave there, and head probably to the train station. They quickly shone the torch about a bit, and we left, with me holding all three bags. I thanked them and headed off in the direction of the station. They left.

About 5 minutes later, all the others came running after me, laughing and whooping.

"Fuck, man, that was unbelievable. The police would usually just arrest you, and probably hit you a bit." C'mon, let's go to another place we know. So we did, had a few beers, (Or I did....The others still had their stash) then crashed out till the afternoon, where we bid farewell to those that were awake enough to hear us, and headed off to the road to Germany.

VI

There was that time we conquered Germany.

We had gotten a lift through to Aachen pretty quickly, with just the usual hold up at the border whilst they examined Brody's passport. As usual, we stuck the stuff in a locker, changed money, and went off to get something to eat. This turned out to be a little more difficult than we imagined.

To say the place was quite unwelcoming was an understatement. We spotted a shop selling what looked like nice pastries and pies, and went to walk in, but were told in no uncertain terms to leave. This happened in the next couple of places we went to, until we found a small convenience store run by an Indian guy, who regarded us with a bit of suspicion, but let us buy biscuits and crisps and stuff anyway, and we retired to a little park to eat these.

There was some punk graffiti on a bench we sat on, and a little symbol that Eva said she thought was some kind of drug related thing, though I hadn't got a clue what she meant by that. But I'm guessing it was part of the reason why our local counterparts were not too popular around here.

We tried a couple of bars, but we were equally unwelcome. We decided that enough was enough, went and got our stuff, and decided to try a night hitch on towards Bonn. We got out to a road OK, but no luck on lifts, which we suspected would be the case, so found a cosy looking bush to chuck the sleeping bags down behind, then crashed till the morning. We had literally just packed the bags, and walked back to the road when a van pulled up, and offered us a lift. On hearing we were going to Bonn, he said he could get us to a town just 10K up the road from it called Bornheim, so we took it. He only spoke German, so full marks to Eva.....

Bornheim seemed a bit friendlier than the last town. We went into a small cafe sort of place and managed to purchase a breakfast without being thrown out. We also spotted a launderette across the road, so wearing the minimum amount of reasonably clean clothes managed to wash and dry the rest of our underwear and t-shirts and spare trousers we had actually brought. Feeling like quite the dandy's, we headed off to the local train station toilets for a wash and change. We'd found train or bus stations to be best for this, as the little old ladies were too busy to notice us.

I say little old ladies. It had taken me completely by surprise at first that seemingly most public toilets on the continent seemed to be manned by a little old lady by the door, who never smiled, but had a stack of coins on the little table she sat by. The function of this virtual army of little old ladies was to take a coin off us, and presumably to keep the toilets clean. The first time I used a public toilet, not long after we arrived, I had walked straight past her, not knowing her role. I was quite harshly rebuked, and informed by Eva that this was the norm. So I made sure that I always had a couple of coins on me, as even at a younger age, I was a frequent user of toilets. I also learned not to bother reading a paper, or anything whilst in the cubicles there, as they would bang on the door when they considered that you had been in there too long. They also were not keen on you trying to have a full strip down wash.

So, washed and changed, we felt a bit human again, and had a look around. It was a sunny day, so we found a nice little cafe to sit outside and have a couple of beers. The waitress seemed very pleasant, and Brody kept trying to engage her in chat every time she walked past. I guess he felt his new cleanliness made him more attractive or something. As she spoke no more than a few words of English, he kept directing his conversation to Eva to translate, which I could see was beginning to irritate her. I'd noticed before about Eva that this tendency of ours to use her to translate usually annoyed her. She felt that we really didn't try hard

51

enough to speak other languages, which in all fairness was true. Speaking English naturally can make you quite lazy in that respect, and her ability to speak a bit of French and Italian on top of English and German really brought that point across. It didn't push me to learn another language, mind you, I never even got the hang of German all the time we were together. Just before we left, the waitress said something to Eva, and looked like she was giving directions, and mentioned what sounded like the name of a bar or something, and smiled at Brody.

"What did she say?" He asked.

"That she thinks you are very funny, and she will be in a certain bar tonight if you want to join her there."

"Really? What time?"

"She said late, about 11pm-ish. And don't worry, you'll have no problem getting in with your leather jacket. This is a friendlier town than the last one."

We had picked up some snacks and drinks for later, and went and sat in a nice little park we'd spotted. We sat on the grass, quite content, reflecting on some of our adventures so far. The funny thing is, the worse time we had had, the funnier the story seemed.

"Look what I've made," Brody said at some point, after being quiet for a while.

"It looks like a little flag."

"Yes, look, I peeled the labels off those beer bottles, and used the coloured bits to make a little flag."

He had actually done that. The bottles had a blue, red and white label, and he'd taken the trouble to carefully rip the labels up, and stuck together a bit of a union jack on a beer mat, then attached a bit of twig as a pole.

"Present for your date? That should impress her."

"No, it's just the labels sort of reminded me of the flag, so I thought I'd make one."

"Brody, the bottles looked nothing like our flag. I think you're getting homesick, you thought that the froth on top of a beer we had the other day looked like a map of the UK."

"It did."

"It did not. It looked like froth on a beer. But a nice flag though."

"Let's plant it."

Actually, that seemed like a good idea. There was a little hill just by us, so we marched the whole 20 paces up it, and planted the flag. Not only that, Brody wrote on the other side of the beer mat that this territory was now under British rule.

"We now declare that Germany officially belongs to us!" I announced, and we saluted the little flag, now stuck in the ground.

"From this day forth, you will all hail Good King's Mulligan and Brody. Long live the kings"

That was it, then, that was the day we conquered Germany. And even as we proudly walked back to Eva to tell her the great news, we saw two ladies walking their dogs stop and pick up the flag, and talk about it. They even laughed and stuck it back into the ground. This was good to know, as we wanted to win over the hearts and minds. We were ahead of our time.

It was getting dark around 9, so Brody decided to head off to the bar. He was quite confident we wouldn't see him later, so we arranged to meet at the bus station the next day, and we'd get a bus through to Bonn. It wasn't far, so it should be cheap.

Eva and myself walked down a main road, and debated where we should sleep. Let's get a drink, we decided, and sat and mulled it over.

A guy at the next table must have spoken a bit of English, and asked Eva if we needed a place to stay. He told her we could crash overnight at his place, but would need to leave early. This seemed like not a bad call, so we asked him to join us.

"No. Just let me know when you want to leave.", he said, and continued to sit with his rather large, but well behaved dog.

We had another beer, then a coffee, and Eva said we were ready to go. He paid his bill, and we walked not more than 20 yards down the street, went through what looked like a side door into an old apartment block, and up an awful lot of stairs.

His apartment was not exactly the place of dreams. It was a long, thin room, and he showed us a place on the floor where we could put our sleeping bags down. Though obviously friendly, he didn't really chat with us much. We couldn't help but notice – and smell – a fair amount of dog shit on the floor, so we were extra careful as we bedded down. We had just nodded off when we heard him shouting loudly. We looked over to the far side of the room where he was, and saw he was sitting with a big CB radio set, and wearing headphones. And that was it for the night.

He sat up the whole night talking loudly down his radio set, and laughing, and then shouting. I had no idea what about. Morning came, and we got up, and he walked us out of the block, waved goodbye, and went off with his dog.

"Sleep well?" I asked Eva, laughing.

"No, not at all. He was talking about some weird shit to people there. Really weird shit. I decided it's better to stay awake."

Well, that was a bit worrying then.

"Well, Let's see if Brody fared better," I said.

She laughed.

"Not with the waitress, he won't have."

And I laughed too. "You sent him to a gay bar, didn't you? I wondered why you said his leather jacket would be fine."

She had done just that. Every time he asked her to translate something, she had been telling the waitress he was a bit simple, or that he needed a chemist to get piles ointment, and finally that he was gay, and was wondering if she knew anywhere in town he could find some company. Preferably with wealthy older men. The waitress had known just such a place, and off Brody had set.

He was already at the bus station when we got there, looking remarkably dishevelled, like a guy who had sat outside a closed bus station all night.

"Bloody waitress didn't show up." He said when we walked up to him. We laughed.

"And to be honest," He carried on, " I couldn't even try to pull anyone else. Place was full of blokes."

"That's because it was a bloody gay bar, you twat"

"What? Bollocks. It was quite a nice place. I got chatting to a few blokes in there......"

"I bet you did"

"........and they told me that Bonn might be a bit of a problem. Apparently, the punks and skinheads there have quite the reputation as junkies and scroungers, and we may be judged on that, a bit like Aachen. But they say that we might like Trier. Plus, it's near Luxembourg, and we were thinking of going there."

"And where did you stay? Didn't your new friends offer you a room?"

"Actually, one of them did, but when I said we could try to go to another bar to meet some girls, he remembered that his mother was staying, so he couldn't really bring visitors."

"So he blew you out," Eva laughed. "Because you wouldn't blow him off?"

"For fucks sake, he wasn't queer!" Brody said loudly, giving us all a sense of Deja vu.

"He was wearing a fucking suit."

Taking that into account, we caught a bus to Trier instead. And it really wasn't what we expected. We walked out of the station and onto the main street, and it appeared that we had accidentally left Germany and got off the bus in the Good Ol' U.S. Of A!

The thing is, we weren't in Germany as we know it today in any case. In actual fact we were in The Federal Republic of Germany. Or, as we called it then, West Germany. The USA and Russia were still engaged in the cold war, with posturing on each side, and Germany was right on the cutting edge of all that, after being divided between The US and allies on one side, and Russia on the other, after world War 2. Bonn, not Berlin, was the current capital. Berlin was itself divided between the two, with the now infamous Berlin wall being the most famous evidence of the split.

Hence, across West Germany, was a number of US military bases, including Trier. And boy, how the locals had adapted. All along the main street were the sort of outlets that would be seen as more American at the time than German. McDonald's, for example. I knew of them, but hadn't seen one. And Burger King. Believe it or not, I had never heard of Burger king till that moment in time. And all along the street were American military personnel, some in uniform, but others being loud enough to identify pretty easily.

And we caught their eye! Not in a bad way, either, we had plenty of young lads stopping us and chatting in a really friendly way about how we looked, and how England was, and if we'd met the queen or not.

"So, where are you guys from?"

"A place called Coventry. Actually, it's near Birmingham"

"Hey, we have one of those too. Is yours near Trafalgar Square ?"

"Yeah. Just North"

"Cool....."

I had the first McDonald's of my life. The closest thing I'd had back home was from a fast food place called Wimpy, which served a rather tasteless thing in a rather tasteless bun, and I didn't really bother with them. Actually, this McDonald's thing wasn't half bad. I never went on to be a lover of the burger in a bun kind of places, but as the years went by, I discovered that you could not go wrong with their coffees! No matter what country you arrived in, a McDonald's, or Burger King, or whatever, coffee would be exactly the same. And it came in a large cup, which also pleased me, as I could never get on with those one gulp Espresso things that the continental folk seemed so keen on.

"I don't like this place." announced Eva.

"Why? It's pretty laid back?"

"I don't know. I just don't. Listen, I want to get home."

"Switzerland?"

"Yes. I feel dirty all the time, even though we have had a great time, but I'm done now. We never know where we will sleep, and, well, I just want to go home."

"So you think we should get on the road to Zurich?"

"Actually, no. I have another plan."

"Go on..."

"Well, we are just over the border from Luxembourg. It is supposed to be lovely. And it's literally a few miles away. Let's get over the border, enjoy Luxembourg for a day or two, then I will catch the train down to Zurich. You two could get the train to London from there, it would include the ferry. Or carry on thumbing. But our money is running low now, and I am sick of sleeping in parks, so what do you think?

She was right.

"OK, tell you what. It's early, there will be a bus there, let's have just one drink, so we can say we had a drink in America on the way, and head over."

So we went back to the bus station, and sat in a little cafe next door and had a bottle of Coors. I also managed to pick up a Deutschland patch that matched my others. As a result, we just missed a bus, but were assured another one was coming soon. We had time to have a bottle of bud each, then boarded the bus.

VII

We slept under the tower of Radio Luxembourg one night.

Well, Brody's passport worked its magic again, and we found ourselves stuck at the border for longer than we expected. We then had to get a lift into Luxembourg City, where we found we had missed the Bureau De Change. So we were stuck with a few German Marks and our Belgium Francs meaning that we were, effectively, broke. We really should have caught the earlier bus.....As Brody kept reminding us.

So we just wandered around a bit, admiring the scenery, but with a nagging feeling of hunger setting in. I had kind of argued with Eva about her going back, but she pointed out it was only for a couple of months or so whilst she worked, and get more money to stay in the UK – she was self-supporting, not being able to access any kind of British benefits, or legally work – and, well, this was proving her argument correct.

It started to rain. Not a downpour, but that miserable drizzly rain, that just gets you wet enough to feel uncomfortable on the outside, whilst sweating in your jacket because it was still actually quite warm. We wandered around a bit more, and walked past cafes and bars, looking in at very happy people sitting relaxed, eating, or sipping coffee, or enjoying wine or beer. We knew we were buggered till the morning, so decided to head out a bit and see if we could find shelter for the night. Luckily, in Maastricht, we had liberated some large sheets of plastic from the squat we had been in, just in case. Looked like this would be that case.

We were walking uphill, seemingly heading out to the countryside, and it had got dark.

"You know what," I said, "We're not going to find any shelter to crash out in. We might as well just bed down, and wait till the morning."

So we walked a bit into what seemed like woods beside the road. It was pitch black, and we couldn't see anything. We were also pretty hungry by now, and getting a bit snappy with each other. The rain had stopped, but the ground was wet, so when after a few yards into the trees we found what seemed, in the dark, to be a clear space, we just chucked the sheets on the floor, and put our sleeping bags on top. We just had to hope it didn't rain again.

It didn't. However, we were woken up in the morning to the sound of Brody shouting,

"Fuck....Fuck....Fucking hell!!"

"What's up?"

"Don't stand up quickly..."

"What??"

"Just don't get up quickly....roll this way towards me..."

Me and Eva sat up slowly, and then saw what he meant. It appeared that we hadn't actually wandered into the woods and found a clearing at all. What we had stumbled into was a thin bit of spinney, separating the road from the edge of a whopping large drop, of which we were sleeping right on the edge. Brody only discovered this as he got up to have a leak, luckily after it became light.

An interesting thing about Luxembourg is that it isa country of beautiful valleys, and we had found ourselves nearly falling over a main one.

"And this," reiterated Eva, "Is why I am catching a train to Zurich today."

It was, of course, shockingly early. Probably around six, meaning we had about 3 hours before we could get some money. We walked back along the road, this time going downhill, till we were back in Luxembourg city. We sat down on a bench near the train station, our stuff all wet, and our stomachs taking it in turn to see who could rumble the loudest. And boy, could I murder a hot cup of coffee!! We watched local people merrily walking into little cafes for breakfast, and no doubt delicious cups of coffee. We amused ourselves by joking about various puns concerning our rather precariously balanced sleep..

"Hey, we just dropped into Luxembourg for the day."

"We are really falling for this place."

"Edgy kind of town"

Then finally, we figured a Bureau De change would be open, so we wandered along to one, waited in a queue, and presented the man at the desk with our Belgium money.

"What do you want to change it to?" He asked.

"Luxembourg money, please."

"That is Luxembourg money."

"What? It's Belgium"

"It's the same currency here."

Well, there's times you do stupid, and times you do stupid. I had taken the money in, whilst the others were outside, and walked out and presented them with the little bundles of notes they had given me.
"What's going on?"
"We are twats. Now let's get breakfast."

We had watched people eating and drinking forlornly, we had a hungry night's sleep, an equally hungry morning walk, and all the time we had money in our pockets, as Luxembourg used the Belgium Franc, and had done since 1944. We had also nearly fallen down a valley. So far so good.

We went and got a decent breakfast in a cafe, and wandered up to the train station where Eva bought herself a ticket to Zurich, leaving in a few hours' time. Me and Brody figured on hitching back to the coast, though we did price up the cost of a ticket, rejected the idea and so would stay another night here. And probably drink.

We had a look around, and the sun was shining wonderfully now, and it must be said this was a pretty nice place. It seemed very relaxed and quite friendly. Well, till some biker types walked past and shouted abuse at us. We just waved back cheerfully and laughed. And the time came to see Eva off, so Brody waited in a cafe, whilst I walked her to the train. Though we were laughing about the shenanigans so far, I could see she was relieved to be going back. I said I'd phone her once we got back to England, hugged, kissed, and I waved her goodbye, like in the old movies.

Right. Time to go on the piss then.

Which is what we did. Though I did notice Brody looking a bit thoughtful during odd moments. We met a group of two couples in a bar, who insisted that they would show us all the best beers and drinks the country had to offer, and had quite the evening of it, and they told us about another good place near a municipal park. We headed off that way, didn't have any luck finding it, but did come across a place called Villa Louvigny, which we ended up sleeping in the shadow of, so to speak.

What was interesting about this place was that it was, I believe, the headquarters of Radio Luxembourg. I myself was too young to remember the days of pirate radio, when illegal radio stations such as Radio

Caroline broadcast from boats, due to the monopoly by the BBC in the UK, and its reluctance to play "modern" music. But the other alternative to that was Radio Luxembourg, which was still broadcasting in the 80's. I used to listen to it, as it played a pretty good variety of music, including New Wave. The BBC didn't especially, except for the outstanding John Peel Show, and one or two other DJ's who played a token nod to it.

John Peel was, of course, a living legend at the time. As a teen first getting into punk and New Wave, this was the "go to" show. So whilst I worked at not being able to lay bricks straight until not being able to plaster walls properly, I would listen in the evening to John Peel, and write down the best songs and then go and purchase these from the local Virgin Record shop, the purveyor of all things punk then. I was usually served by a particularly grumpy looking bloke who would take my little list off me, tick what they had in and give me it back. I would then say, all of them you have please. He would look like this was quite the annoyance, then go and get them for me, like he was doing me a great favour, rather than serving in a record shop, which was odd, as that was his job. This was every pay day, until one day I gave him my list, and he actually smiled, got the records straight away, thanked me greatly, and said Bye, see you next week. This actually caught me on the hop, and I wondered what was wrong.

Till about a week later, when a picture of a new Coventry group appeared in the Local paper, the Coventry Evening Telegraph, and there was the record shop man, right in the middle of them. The band were The Specials, (then the AKA Specials), and had released their debut single, the brilliant 'Gangsters'. They went on to big things, but at this point were just part time musicians spearheading what became Two-Tone Ska, a blend of Punk and Ska that developed quite naturally in a city like Coventry, a working class city with a high unemployment problem at the time, and a highly creative young Caribbean population. So I had bought Brad, the drummers, own band's record off him, and actually made him smile. Which oddly, he seemed to refrain from doing in any publicity photo I ever saw of them since.

And of course, there was the mighty Radio Luxembourg. I actually remember the night it was announced that Elvis died, Tuesday, August 16th, 1977. The year punk really broke in the UK. I tuned into Radio Luxembourg and it had turned its entire night into a dedication to Elvis. Elvis, growing up, was my all-time favourite, and I'd still probably put him up there today. I started recording it with my little cassette player.

The technology of the day meant that it was a cassette player with a plug in microphone which I propped up in front of the house wireless, which was an old sixties thing, which I'd liberated to my bedroom ages before, to my parents annoyance. Though we did have a black and white TV which was more important to them. This meant that on top of the Elvis tributes, it picked up the sound of me walking around the room, my brother going to bed, (as we shared a room), a couple of rows with my parents about why I was playing music loud all night, and every time the toilet flushed. It also meant I taped over all the music I had on tape, which was early punk tracks I'd accumulated secretly, during the time that me and my friends were still kidding ourselves that we would be Teddy boys.

All this meant that I felt quite honoured sleeping beside the legendary station. I've often wondered what they were playing whilst we were out there.

Waking up the next morning, and counting my remaining money, I suggested to Brody that hey, we'd had a great time, but why not do what Eva had suggested, and catch the train back. We walked back to the station, to enquire about the times and prices. It was while we were in the queue that I found out what had been on Brody's mind.

"I don't want to go back yet. I want to go to Amsterdam. Let's go to Amsterdam first."

"Yeah, great plan, except we just about have enough cash to get home. We'd be fucked if we hitched up there now, and still had to get back."

"No. We are OK. We can do it."

"Why," I laughed, "you got some secret money?"

"Yes."

"What?"

"Yes. I've got some secret money. We can get a train to Amsterdam and be OK."

"What are you talking about? How have you got secret money? And why is it secret?"

"Remember that money I found in Maastricht? Well, there was more of it than I said."

So that was it. It seems when Brody found that money, he only told us about a quarter of it. This caused a bit of a row, as I felt a bit cheated, which was totally wrong, as it wasn't any of ours, and we really should have handed it in anyway. Yet cheated I felt. Brody said that he thought he'd hang on to it in case we were really buggered, and if not, well, finders keepers. I was really pissed off about this. Here was a dilemma, that my friend had lied about some money that wasn't ours, but now was offering to pay for us to go on towards Amsterdam, even though I'd told Eva we were going back home as we were skint too. So it meant either telling him to stuff it, which seemed right, or carry on travelling.

A minute later we were at the front of the queue, and had two singles to Amsterdam.

VIII

So this rat bit my penis.

We finally pulled into Amsterdam Centraal Station. And no longer just the two of us either. We had gone via Brussels, and whilst at the station a couple of guys we knew from nearby Birmingham got on, and we carried on together. They were doing something similar to us, but mainly by train. Sitting comparing notes, they had had quite a few adventures themselves. Ah, travellers' tales. Sitting swapping stories is something that I don't think you ever get tired of. And sitting swapping them with alcohol available, as in the cans in our hand at the moment, only ever enhances the experience.

So we got to Amsterdam fairly late, but that was never going to be a problem in such a city. Jed and Marco, the two Brum lads, already had an address of a place to stay, and were convinced we could probably crash the night there too. We caught a tram to some area that the address was in, and it was a pretty run down affair, not too far from where we arrived. After a bit of wandering around, we found the address, which had a huge heavy door, and was clearly a squat, and banged for ages till finally a girl came out and asked what we wanted.

It seemed that the guys which our Birmingham friends knew had moved on, and had never really lived there, but crashed for a while. It seems they hadn't left on the best of terms, either. However, the girl took a bit of pity on us, and said we could crash there that night, but only for one night. We took it.

She was a nice, if odd looking girl, who called herself Snail, and she was German. She'd been living in Amsterdam for a couple of months, and had moved into that squat with her boyfriend, who went out one night after about a week there, and never came back. The primary residents of the squat were a couple of punks from Eindhoven, who made a bit of money drug dealing, but seemed fairly amicable. Others came and went. They recommended a couple of bars where we might get talking to people who might have an address where we could get digs.

Amsterdam had a huge squatting scene. It was not long since there had actually been riots, which we were to learn left a bitter taste, as many of the squatters in the surrounding places had been caught up. It was, as these things are, complicated, but the essence was the fact that landlords left so many buildings empty vs the fact so many people needed a place to live. Many had been hurt, and a tank was even deployed at some point. So many of the squatters were incredibly defensive over their homes, and who came and went in them. For a while, it became popular for people to "go to the squats", as they had heard of the riots and fancied being cool. Not us. We'd never heard of the riots, and were just sick of sleeping in parks and lay-bys.

The next day, Snail offered to show us about, but Brody and Jed had decided it was time to go and get stoned, and worry about digs later. So Marco , Snail and myself went for a wander round the red light district. Now this I liked. The area I was living in at home, Hillfields, was in fact the local red light district. Certainly the place for kerb crawlers, though the local girls were a bit rough, to say the least. This place , however, though indeed seeming ten times as sleazy, did have what seemed to be remarkably good looking women sitting in little shop windows.

"Wait till we come here at night" Snail remarked.

Yep. That was one of my plans.

In a moment of good sense, but much to his annoyance, I had agreed to go to Amsterdam on the basis that Brody split the money in half, so one of us wouldn't get stuck. From what I could see and smell of the coffee shops, that was probably the wisest decision I had made. Hell, it sure smelt different to the "Happy Shopper" home brand coffee we had back home! Snail said she wasn't much of a smoker herself, but If anyone was, Amsterdam was the place to be. After a while, Marco decided he too would retire to a coffee shop, and Snail went off to meet a friend, so I found myself having a bag of pretty English style chips, and finding a Hard Rock Cafe.

I'd heard of the Hard Rock Cafe in London, and today we know them as a chain of rather expensive burger bars with musical stuff stuck on the walls, and the need to book ahead to eat the said expensive burgers and maybe buy a t-shirt to let people know that you are prepared to spend a stupid amount of money on a block of mince in a bun. However, this was not one of them. It was well after getting home I was surprised to hear that there was no Hard Rock Cafe in Amsterdam, (in fact, there wasn't one till the late 90's, I believe.) So I'm guessing this place was just some kind of rip off. Anyhow, it was small, and quite a bit of a dump, and had clearly invested in furniture from the Central Warehouse that specialises in unmatching furniture, and piss coloured paint for the toilets. However, I did get chatting to a punk girl – or rather, a punk woman – that sat and chain smoked by the bar. She told me about a bar called, I think the Appel, or Karl Appel, or something like that. Her and some friends would be there later, so why not come down and join them?

Having no idea where anyone else was, I just wandered about, before bumping into Snail again. She told me she might have an address for us to stay for a bit. We got something to eat, and eventually were given a flyer for a local band playing in a bar called the Octopus, and decided to go our separate ways and met up later there.

Snail didn't show up, but Brody and Jed, still stoned, had been given a flyer too, and we managed to catch up. The gig was not bad, and we headed to the Appel after, where the woman from earlier was indeed there, with two friends.

I found myself thinking of her as a woman, as opposed to a girl, because most of the girls I had ever met or still knew on the punk scene were either in their teens or early to mid-20's. Punk was, after all, a relatively new culture. However Chicci, as I soon found out she was called, was in fact the grand old age of 33. This seemed at the time remarkably old to me, and I found her quite intriguing. One of her two friends was a much younger, though amazingly tall punk girl that smiled a lot, even when, as Brody told me later, she took her teeth out, and the

64

other was a very normal looking girl, with almost model looks, or rather would be if not for a kind of hard knock life look about her face.

We all sat and got on pretty well. As the night went on, we found ourselves kind of pairing off, Jed with the straight looking girl, Mona, Brody with the tall girl, Snax, who literally loomed over him, and myself with Chicci. It seemed they were all German. A lot of people here seemed to be. They were working here, Chicci told me, and had a small squat to themselves. We were invited back.

It went pretty much the way you might expect. The squat wasn't one of the large ex-warehouse or old business buildings, but what seemed to be an apartment in an already occupied building. They had a key, so I guess it was official in some kind of way. After the squatters' riots, various arrangements had been made with squatters , apparently. So the girls had a room each, and after the others all had a smoke, we went to the rooms and did what young lads do when on the road, given half a chance.

Chicci's room was a couple of bits of furniture, an old t-chest which she kept her clothes in, and a mattress on the floor. Oh, and a rat cage, where her pet rat lived. In fact, they all had a pet rat, all of which ran around the flat mostly at night. I'm not sure how they knew whose rat was who, but they had names which the rats totally ignored, but they insisted on using anyway.

And so, this became our home for the rest of our stay. We had heard that an English band we liked, The Anti-Nowhere League were playing in a huge squat the next night, and went along. It was well organised. It had a public bar, a venue, and I even found a room that had chickens. In fact, a lot of the squats got caught up in the anti-squat movement, or laws, as time went by, and there are still businesses to this day that have their origins in this period. We found Marco at the gig, who was also welcomed back to the squat. He had been so out of his head, he had no idea where or who he had been with since we left him last. I think he was grateful for the couch.

It turned out that the girl's work was doing a bit of hooking. They clearly were not the sort of prostitute's who sat in the windows in the Red Light Districts, but more so street girls. It seemed they had a couple of scams and ripped drunken punters off more than they actually fucked them, but they worked most nights, and we would meet up with them in a bar somewhere afterwards. There was a guy in Snail's squat, a Dane who had been crashing there and who had been working in a nearby market, doing general sweeping up and humping stuff about kind of work for cash and he was leaving to go to Berlin. Snail had a word with him, and he got me his job there. This was well before the Maastricht treaty, and so any work you got had to be cash, and off the books, so naturally meant you didn't get paid much. But it was enough to keep going for the time being. Brody very quickly found himself helping the girls do a bit of dealing on the streets, and took a couple of hidings off the local bikers, but he seemed to find this quite funny.

As for Jed and Marco, they left before us. A few weeks after moving in with the girls, they took a yen to head to Sweden, so we all went out for a big night out in a bar called Fizz, where we got shockingly drunk, and Marco started getting loud about the fact he hadn't had sex for so long.

"Pay someone. You're in fucking Amsterdam"

"I ain't paying for it. You all think you're dead cool, bagging off with the girls, eh? Well fuck you. Fuck you all."

He stomped out, and headed back to the squat. Minding the journey they had ahead, we left just after him, laughing about his hissy fit, and yet arrived back before him somehow. We fell into bed, a bunch of ruins, but pretty happy. A bit later we heard Marco arrive, slam about, and then there was a knock on my bedroom door.

"Mulligan...."

"What?"

"It's my last night....."

"So? Get some sleep...."

"Can I fuck Chicci"

Chicci was passed out cold, so didn't hear it at first.

"What? No. Fuck off."

"Go on....I'm dying for a fuck....."

"Marco, piss off..."

Chicci started coming round and asked what was going on. I told her.

"He fucking asked you? Not me?"

She shouted at Marco in German something that I believe was definitely NOT an invite into bed.

"I'll pay you...."

She came round even quicker, grabbed a bat she kept by the bed, and went to get up. Apparently, even with what she did, this pissed her off that it was from a friend. I get that. I also held her down and said forget it, he's just a twat. We told him to fuck off again and he left. Next thing was, we heard a knock on Brody's door, and some muttering.

"Fuck off, Marco," we heard, and Brody laughing.
"Come on....It's my last night." We then heard Snax say something to him, and the sound of him being pushed over and hitting the ground hard. She was a big girl, Snax.
"Jed next" Chicci said.

"Jed..." we heard, after a knocking on Jed's bedroom door.
"WHAT? " he shouted. We found out the next day that Jed and Mona had had a bit of a row on arriving back, and he took some kind of pill with his smoke, and was not in the best frame of mind.
"Can I fuck Mona? It's my last night."
"Fuck off."
"Come on, mate...."
"Do what you want. Sure, fuck her. I don't give a fuck"

And, unbelievably, that's what happened. Jed came out of the room, Marco went in, and then we heard about two minutes of fucking and some heavy snoring.

It seemed though, that Jed did give a fuck. When we all got up the next day, he'd gone. Marco was looking sheepish, but madly hung over, and Mona took the trouble to make a cup of coffee and throw it over him. Marco decided to head on to Sweden, and hoped to catch Jed up. I bumped into Marco years later, in Birmingham, and asked about it. He'd got so far and gave up and went home. When Jed arrived back, they made it up, and laughed about it, but Jed developed a serious drug problem, and topped himself a few years later. Marco did the same about 10 years after that. Shame. Good guys.

Brody took a particularly bad kick in off a Hells Angel one night about a month and was in bed for 3 days. We were chatting, as I mocked his swollen eyes, and he decided it was time to head back. I said I'd think about it, as I'd got quite comfortable, though the thing with me and Chicci was completely a non-decider. We never interacted outside the squat, in fact, I drank more with Snail. We basically slept in the same bed and fucked sometimes, and that was about it. And that night after Brody said about going back, we had fucked, and I was on top of the bed as it was warm, when I woke up with a scream to find one of the rats biting my dick.

"What are you screaming about?" Chicci asked, barely looking round.

"The bloody rats just ate my dick," I yelled. It did feel like that.

"My rat?"

"What? I don't know...does it matter?"

"Yes. If it's my rat, it likes cheese. Probably thought your dick was strong cheese. Maybe you could wash it better tomorrow?"

So that was that really. Me and Brody went out the next day, I collected some money from the market, and we bought some fresh bread and pate, sat on a bench on one of the bridges and made some sandwiches, even though it was raining.

"You know what?"

"What?"

"You're right. It's been brilliant. But It's time to go home."

And that's when I sat by the canal, only just aware of the people going about their business, and enjoyed the rain. Amsterdam has a strangely wonderful glow about it when it rains. For all the sleaze – well, where we were anyway – it is a beautiful City. So I quietly gazed into the canal, with my dick in pain and Brody with his black eyes next to me, reflecting on the journey that had got us there, and I still remember thinking that it was one of the most content and happiest moments of my life so far.

IX

Though we headed back just after that, it wasn't quite the end of the adventure out there. I'd let Eva know about our shenanigans in Amsterdam and she decided that she'd like to go there too. So we decided to pick up where we left off and I caught the train out to Luxembourg, where we would meet up on her return to the UK now she had saved up enough to stay for a while again. Another friend of mine,

Col, decided to come too, so we headed out a few days earlier than we were due to meet Eva.

As is the way of these things, we had been in Luxembourg all of an hour when we met two gorgeous punk girls who offered to show us around. I honestly meant to say we were out there to meet my girlfriend, but the time never seemed quite right and the fact got overlooked even as we stayed at one of their places. In fact, I kept meaning to say it right up to the moment Eva got off the train, causing quite the moment of silence for all of us standing there at the station, as the local girls came with us to meet our friend, but were clearly taken aback as a rather hot looking tall blonde Germanic girl stepped off the train, rather than some Swiss punk guy which I guess they had expected to see. To be fair, the look on Eva's face when she saw we'd brought dates was a bit of a picture as well.

Still, I generally always seemed to be in trouble over this kind of thing at home, so tried to take it my stride and somehow things worked out, though Eva decided she was not interested in seeing this lovely little country after all, so we headed off the next day, going a different route to Amsterdam than before, and naturally having a few more adventures along the way.

We found the squat that Snail had lived in, but I was disappointed to find that she had gone. The others in there let us stay, however. I felt it wise to go nowhere near the squat where Chiccy and the other hookers lived. Col didn't stay long, he'd been very smitten by the girl in Luxembourg and headed back down 2 days later. Even as he left, Eva began to feel sick, and we decided to cut short the trip and get a train and ferry back.

It turned out she was pregnant. After one more trip out that way, the hitching around Europe stopped, and due to the fact we could only live in one country or another unless we were married, Eva and I wed. And so it was that bang slap in the middle of the punk heydays, the first chapter of this traveller's life had drawn to an end, and my patches were put safely in a drawer.

The odd thing is, the memories of the different trips out there, which ended up including Switzerland, (where I finally discovered that Eva came from some pretty serious money), became one combined memory. It seems to me that once out on the road, you forget about what you do at home quite quickly, and like a folder on a computer, you draw on the memories of your previous journeys instead. I wonder if this is some ancient survival tactic, when early humans had to migrate, or just move about to follow food, and they needed to focus on the lessons of travelling? Because back then it would be do or die.

The other thing I noticed on getting back that first time was that we felt we had conquered the world (And not just Germany with a small beer mat!) yet when we looked on a map, we really hadn't gone that far. Well, maybe we hadn't if we measured it in miles by world standards, but we had gone far from our safety zone, and began exploring. A bit like when we were those kids on bikes, so wonderfully invented for us by the amazing Mr Starley in Coventry. And how we had cycled off to the next district, thinking that we were exploring the world, which is in fact what we were learning to do. How a new spinney, or an unusual building, or tormenting the monster that was Webfoot were the most exciting things ever, and learning which entries and alleyways got us from street A to B made us pioneers of exploration. And just like the kids that we had been then, we were about to find that the world was to keep getting bigger and bigger.

PART 2

Jung Bloods

I accidentally got a Diploma

You have a trust in people like teachers, coaches, and adults in authority when you are growing up, so it can be a bit of a shock when you find out they lied to you a lot. Well, let's say fibbed. Not the good kind of fibs, like Father Christmas, or the tooth fairy. You know that they are fibs for more of the time than you don't and go along with it because not only does it mean you get stuff, but it seems to keep the grown-ups happy. So you lie from your end that you believe their lie, and everyone is happy. It's a great system.

But that's the lovely lies you tell kids and they are very charming. But as you get older, early teenage years, say, they get a bit more complicated, Especially one in particular.

"You can be anything you want to be."

That was the real mother of all lies that was being pushed to us in school, and even when we left and couldn't find the jobs we wanted, (that's if you even knew what job you wanted in the first place), they carried on telling you that fib. When I was on my 'youth opportunities' bricklaying course, they had life skills tutors that were still spinning you this yarn, even though you were stuck on a £25 a week useless course because you couldn't get anything else, let alone what you wanted..

71

You can't be anything you want. Or we'd all just be rich enough not to work, or a kid with two left feet and bottle bottom glasses would be playing for Manchester United, along with the rest of the squad of 15,000 players. Colour blind airline pilots & tone deaf singers are a no go either.

But what we can do, and what we really should be taught, is that we can make the most of anything that comes along. So, in a factory full of people assembling car wheels to go on luxury models, you probably won't find anyone that left school with the burning ambition to stand on a production line and knock weights onto wheels. However, amongst them you will find people that are raising families, getting married, buying a house, going on holidays and enjoying their leisure activities, from anglers to kinksters, and generally getting on with life, mostly happy.

And sometimes you will get a break come along, and you take it or you don't, and so on and so on. Don't get me wrong, some people will get to be whoever they want. And some of them will be happy, and others will be not so happy, because they thought they wanted something they didn't. Life is a complicated old game, best treated as if it was simple, and just enjoy the flow sometimes.

On returning from my adventures in Europe, Eva and I got married primarily to raise our little lad rather than for romantic reasons. It didn't work out. The more we learnt to communicate, the more we knew we had very little in common outside of punk, and she eventually moved back to Switzerland where I am sure she did very well. I never saw the little lad again.

I had taken up Djing in punk bars, and putting a few bands on. The multi coloured hair became just bleached, or sometimes black, the leathers no longer had studs, and the accessories like wristbands, bum-flaps, bondage straps, etc became redundant. I was, it had to be said, a bit older.

Don't get me wrong, I don't believe there is a particular age to tone down and you probably don't even realise that you are. In fact, some don't at all, and fair play to them. But to get the opportunities that you will need to come along, you don't have to exactly give up non-conformity – Even though most of us hadn't actually become punk purely for non-conformity, but rather that we actually loved the music and style – but you find you will start to compromise. Learning to compromise is another factor of growing up. The trick is to seem to be compromising more than you really are, so both parties walk away happy. It's a bit like the Father Christmas thing.

And the chain of events meant that by Djing, (something me and a friend took up as there really were no places to go for this music at this time, so we done it ourselves), we were approached by small bands asking to play in the pub we were based in, so we found a bigger venue to accommodate that as it seemed like a great idea. We then asked bigger bands to play and started to get a name for being on the UK circuit, so to speak. A girlfriend who was doing a bit of acting in a youth group that needed funding at the time told me about a meeting where the local council were talking about grants to youth projects, so I went along to see if I could get any money for our "Total Noise" gigs and shows.

We couldn't. It wasn't that kind of thing at all. It was about youth ,and funding for youth, whatever that meant, in the city, as apparently it was the International Year of the Youth. But, being a bit of a big mouth at the time, I stood up and talked about some topic they were going on about, and caught some Education Department Executives attention, and they asked me if I would join a new "Youth council" thing they were forming. This was to give the appearance of youth having a voice in the city, and we would all look diverse and youthy, then pretty much follow the lead of the adults in authority that told us what it was we apparently wanted in the city, which was surprisingly awfully like their own ideas.

I swiftly got voted as the first chairperson, and for a little while was a voice of youth as far as the council were concerned, and all their boxes were ticked. Around the same time, the head of the council at the time had had a meeting with his Israeli counterpart, an American-Israeli called Yehudah Paz, both staunch Labour men, and over drinks they discovered they had both been in the army, but on opposite sides during one of the many middle Eastern conflicts, perhaps even shooting at each other. This made them firm friends, and they decided on an experiment - My guess is they were drunk, as this is when so many seemingly great ideas come about – to send a group of urban first world students to Paz's College, the Afro-Asian Institute in Tel-Aviv. Here, groups were taught how to set up worker's cooperatives in their usually third world countries, as Israel at the time was a great place for the co-operative movement, the Kibbutz's being the most obvious, and a great place for young travellers. They just needed a nice, box-ticking ethnically and sexually diverse group to go. Two Whites, Two Asians, Two Blacks, and one male & female of each.

73

There were plenty of minority activist groups to draw reps from, but not so many groups that represented young white males, as this would be a serious no-no in council fundings. The closest thing to organised groups of young white males at the time were the soccer hooligan mobs, which didn't count, so I guess someone remembered that punk guy who gets quotes in the paper about youth opinion on such and such, and I found myself the white male of our group.

Well, not quite, of course. This was, remember, a public funded educational trip, so to make sure that everything was OK with our racially and sexually balanced group, two well paid older white male members of the Education department also came along, but didn't count in the balance.

When they summoned me to the Education Department headquarters to tell me about the idea, and ask if I was willing to go -it was all expenses paid – I didn't even think about it. I said yes straight away. This was not anything to do with a particular affinity to the co-operative movement, or a desire to further my education. To be honest, I didn't really understand what it was actually about. I just heard the name of a country and was asked if I wanted to go, and that was in fact the sole reason why I agreed and said yes. I was jumping at the chance to get back out there again. I'd never thought of going to Israel, nor did I really know much about it, but that desire to travel superseded any other thought I may have had.

I was going to Israel.

II

I had to get a full passport. I'd never had one before. Travelling around Europe meant I could buy the cheaper, one-year visitors passports that were available at the time, but limited where you could go on them. My work on the Coventry Youth Council was time consuming, but all voluntary. I barely got by on the DJ and Promotion income, and was supplemented by benefits. So I had to lend money to get a passport, and borrow bits and bobs, like a camera, to take out there.

And off we flew. We had all met up once before going. I knew one of the guys, Melko, from around my district, and also from when he'd rented a floor once in my Dad's second Hand shop to sell records. Vinyl reggae records. He had a hell of a selection, but for whatever reason, it never took off. He was the black male balance. I knew the white girl balance as well, she was also on local youth councils and stuff. I'd never met the others, but we all seemed to get on.

The night we arrived, we went straight to the Afro-Asian Institute, and were shown to our dorms. Apparently, there was only one other group studying there at the time, a large group of Black South African Trade Unionists. We were to get close to this group, as once a week, the institute organised an excursion out to somewhere intriguing, and we all went together. We were familiar with the South African situation at the time. Apartheid was still going on, there were trade embargo's, and protests galore in the UK and other western nations. In fact, local Coventry band The Specials – who you may remember that I once bought their single from their grumpy drummer once – penned and released Free Nelson Mandela, which became an international anthem for the cause. There probably wasn't a university or polytechnic in the country at the time without a Mandela or Steve Biko bar. (I always thought the latter had a better ring to it, though I guess that wasn't really the point.)

Interesting thing. The whole point of the place was about co-operative and Labour values, the empowerment of workers, freedom, equality and education. On the second morning there, I was looking at the notice board in the lobby, with a list of rooms we were to take classes in. I was with Rose, the white girl, when a loud lecturer who was working with the

African group saw me, came over and shouted loudly to me about what I was doing in there.

"Studying."

" I don't think so. I'm going to ask you to leave this building."

"No, honestly, I'm studying here."

"I'll give you to the count of zero to GET OUT!"

The janitor, who we had met on arrival, happened to be there and said, "Yes. He studies here. Part of the English group."

The rude guy considered this, muttered sorry, and walked off. I guess he hadn't quite seen me, but instead saw the rather ripped jeans, leather cut off with The Ramones painted in red on the back, and black spiky hair with a blaze of bright red running through it. He didn't even seem to register Rose. I would probably have totally forgotten all about this, had it not been for a party we all had on the last night we were there. Since then I'd seen the guy lots of times, and in fairness, he seemed not a bad bloke. But he tapped me on the shoulder at the party and told me he wanted to say something.

"Hey, I'm sorry about that incident in the lobby when you first got here. I hadn't realised that a second course was running yet, and thought you'd just wandered in."

"That's OK," I told him, laughing, "I've been accused of worse. No harm done."

"Yes, thanks. It's just we'd had a bit of a problem with people wandering in and stealing stuff, so, as I say, Apologies."

Hmm.

"Well as I said, no harm done. But one thing I would say.....Try not to judge a man by the colour of his hair." I smiled, and winked at him. I think I'd made my point.

Studying was quite interesting. We were to pick a project of our choice, and develop it, with the guidance from our tutors and lecturers. I teamed up with Rose, and we worked on a project to do with a self-sufficient venue for arts, music and a base for general youth projects within the city. The excellent skills shared with us showed us how to run this as a co-operative venture, hence not being a financial liability to the city council, who would normally fund – or usually under-fund – such things.

At the end we received a lot of praise from the college staff, and we duly presented our project work and proposal to the Education Department when we got back, who thanked us, filed it, and it was never mentioned ever again. They went on instead to carry on under-funding a number of short lived projects that ticked a few boxes, and meant raising local taxes to do so.

I couldn't help but notice that the two guys from the education department were especially keen to meet the founder of the Institute, Yehudah Paz. I must admit to never having heard of him, but he was quite the character amongst international labour groups.

Though born in New York, he had emigrated to Israel in about 1950, where he swiftly became one of the founders of the Kibbutz movement, a solution to regional needs in labour and farming that was of a major concern at the time. Via hard work and entrepreneurialism, he made his way to being appointed Director General of the Jewish Agency's Youth and Youth Movement Division. He refused to join Israel's Diplomatic world as an ambassador, despite many offers, instead moving into politics, indeed the Knesset itself , heading various educational bodies, and pushing for solutions to conflicts facing Israel.

I went to dinner with him and his wife once. Not just me, of course, but a few of us from the group. He still lived on a Kibbutz. That's when he told us about the Six Day War in 1967, which is where I guess the conversation between him and the head of the Coventry council sprang from, and why two men with such similar views, ideals, philosophies and opinions could find themselves on two different sides of another armed conflict that followed, even if not on the front.

Food for thought. Though I admire completely, and respect the young men who went to the front lines in the world wars, if it were to happen today, with what I know of all the people I have met on my travels and shenanigans, could I shoot a young German man, or Arab, or anyone on the other side of a trench? A guy that I know that if I'd met in a backpackers hostel, I'd probably be drinking with him and talking about music and girls. I honestly do not think I could. The Politicians on both sides, mind you – That's a different story. I could possibly shoot them.

What really brought Paz to the world's attention, I learned, was what he did next. Seemingly outnumbered by the Egyptian, Jordanian and Syrian forces, as many as 150,000 volunteers came to Israel to support in mainly non-combative roles, but no doubt some came to fight. Many were there to replace workers that were called up in the military. Of these, around 80 per cent did not wish to leave afterwards, causing a huge unemployment problem. These were generally young, highly motivated people that could only, in the long run, be good for the country.

So Paz and the Kibbutz movement stepped in, and the new people were offered the chance to volunteer for the mainly agricultural, but also industrial Kibbutz's. This was revolutionary, as volunteering to be housed and fed for 6 hours a day of work had not been the way they had run before. It was to shape Kibbutz's to this day, and solved the problem.

In addition to food and board, they were given organised trips and tours, as Paz believed strongly in education, of course. This philosophy he carried on, even when he set up the Institute I found myself in. And that is how I was able to see so much of Israel when I was there. Talking to him, you could see the intelligence and sincerity of the man and I found that though I never went on to form a workers collective in a third world, or any other world for that matter, diploma or no diploma, I was to find I took many of Paz's values on board and applied them and the skills I learned there subconsciously for the rest of my life.

So thanks to the visionary Mr Paz, off we went on adventures around the country. Tel- Aviv itself was a thoroughly modern city, complete with plenty of little bars that Raj, the Indian Male balance, and myself took to exploring. There was also a reggae club that Melko managed to source out that we all took to going to at the weekend. A few of the younger South African guys joined us down there.

It became a challenge between me and Raj over who would meet a local girl first. The others found this amusing, especially the girls. Me with my cut off punk leather, and coloured hair, and Raj, the clean cut, immaculately dressed good looking Indian guy. There was a good natured banter between us, which was interesting as back home we would probably not have crossed paths socially. Not for any kind of prejudice on either of parts, but our respective groups had our own places to go, our own music's, our own fashions, neither having a particular reason to cross over.

This is another joy of travelling. After a while, the little bubbles, and self-imposed social villages we cocoon ourselves in begin to break down quite quickly. We find ourselves, usually by chance, with people we would walk past on the street at home and have nothing in common with.

We form groups, as humans do, based more on an instinct that manifests itself as simply as 'I like this person'.

So in this context we were no longer the white punk and the suave Indian, but two young males, far from home and competing to meet women. Possibly one of the most basic scenarios known to humankind.

The result was that neither of us met anyone at all while we were there, but enjoyed sitting in the couple of bars we found discussing what we would do if we did. This caused even more merriment amongst the girls, who liked to rub our failures in our noses, albeit in a good natured way. As for Melko, who was a good 15 years older than me and Raj, didn't have a particular image, and wasn't aiming at meeting women.......Well, he shagged someone in the group. Bastard.

III

We went out to Jerusalem. This is of course where someone who attended Sunday School regularly, except the days we cycled off in the wrong direction instead of going there, had heard about, but knew very little of. After Europe and Tel Aviv, this was the first time I explored somewhere 'different'. Capital cities, in fact any big cities, are great fun, and full of interesting stuff, but they are generally of a muchness. You don't notice this till you do a whistle stop tour of lots of them, and you find later that it is hard to remember exactly where you did what, and that they could all nearly be the same place. Especially western Capitals. But here in Jerusalem, I felt history. The buildings, the people, the smells, the air, this was absolutely amazing. Here, Judaism, Christianity and Islam met, in a shared, but tense common place. Cultures collided, and huge, dangerous looking soldiers could be seen at what we would think of as nice tourist places.

I visited the wailing, or western wall, where a tradition of writing prayers or thoughts on a piece of paper and shoving it in a crack caught my imagination. Though a Jewish tradition, I wrote something and put it in the wall. I have no idea what I wrote, but I wish I did. I've had a fortuitous life, so I would like to think that maybe my prayers were answered, but possibly my intact foreskin may have put paid to that, along with causing leakage problems in much later life.

It was also in Jerusalem that I first discovered hole -in-the-floor toilets, of which I had no previous knowledge. Finding myself in need of a number two, whilst wandering around with Melko, we located a large public toilet area. I went in, and opened a cubicle, and my first thought was, oh, this one's broken, the toilet's missing. But then so was the next one, and the next one, until the penny dropped. No paper either, but a little tap on the wall. Though a basket of used toilet paper showed that you could bring your own. I went native and washed. It was odd, enjoying the ancient sights with a wet ass for the next 20 minutes.

Another time, we went out to the Dead Sea, which is actually an extremely salty lake. Now, I think everyone knows that you are not supposed to be able to sink in this, so it had to be put to the test. And indeed, it was true. You couldn't swim either, which is good, as if you got the salt in your eyes, it rather stung! I found that by kind of sitting upright and paddling backwards, I could get a bit of speed up. It was odd to be sitting up on the water, but quite fun too. One other thing was when the African guys went in, and came out with salt all over them.

"So," one of them laughed, "This is how it feels to be white..."

We stayed in a hotel by the Dead sea that night, and a large group of white South African tourists were there too. Now, the information that we were given at home about the South African situation gave the impression that it was as simple as the nasty white Afrikaners lived like kings at the expense and humiliation of the larger black population, of whom we only saw pictures of living in slum townships. Now whilst there was some fact in this, nothing is ever that black and white, (albeit probably not the best expression to use). So our group commented amongst ourselves that this wasn't good, the two groups being there. So we were actually quite surprised when they began mingling and chatting, which went against what the militants back home told us should have happened.

There was a younger lad with the African group called Joey who I'd been getting on well with. He found my red and black hair interesting, though not from the point of view I'd expect.

"So, what is it with the red and black? Is it some kind of group you belong to?"

80

"What, my hair? Kind of, it's a punk thing."

"I know, but apart from that....The Red and Black. I have noticed you use it a lot"

"Eh?"

"Look at your jacket..... Red written on black. I've seen it on a few other things too."

It seemed he'd got it into his head it was some kind of code that others from my 'group' would recognise each other with. I laughed it off the first couple of times he mentioned it, but then began to just give him a knowing nod, or wisely tapping my nose with my finger. This got him all the more curious.

Anyhow, I mentioned to him in the hotel that we were surprised they got on with the white group, and he filled me in a bit about how many whites were against apartheid, whilst many Blacks, often Zulu, supported the government to a point, as they did not care for the ANC (African National Congress) opposition that they considered made up of people from outside South Africa. It had been a surprise to me that the black population had got trade unions, as our impression was that life there was about one step up from slavery. Another good reason why travelling is a way to see things for yourself, and to be very careful of biased people's political lecturing, no matter the rights and wrongs.

"So, sure we talk...they are our countrymen. Now let me show you something."

And so Joey took me over to a couple of the Afrikaners he'd been talking to, and introduced me. They politely said hello, then wandered off.

"See. They will talk to us. But you being British, and especially looking as you do, they want nothing to do with you. It's not as simple as black and white."

Nope. It never is.

We were in the hotel bar all night, and got rather drunk, to say the least. Which was a bit of a bugger, as I had the hangover from hell when I was woken up and told we only had half an hour before the coach left. I had a quick wash, missed coffee, and was on the bus. We were heading to Masada, an old fortress where allegedly a couple of hundred Jewish rebels committed mass suicide rather than be conquered by the Roman Legions laying siege to it.

It took about 3 minutes to get up there by cable car as the fortress was on top of a small mountain, or big hill maybe. And at the top I found myself not just in an amazing place, full of history, with incredible views of the desert, but I found myself up there in the hottest place I had ever been in my life nursing a hangover. This was my first lesson in the effects of searing heat and the effects of alcohol. However, it apparently taught me nothing, and I was to be reminded of that lesson over and over again through my life. But hangover aside, the view was well worth it, and I even decided to take a few photos on the cheap little camera I had borrowed to take out there.

"Look at that," Joey hissed quietly to me."

"The view? Yes, stunning, isn't it."

"No", he said. "Your camera. Even your camera is red and black." And he nodded his head, knowingly.

A week later we went out to Bethlehem. Now here was a town everyone who has sung a carol has heard of, though I was to find out that our Christmas cards had been lying to us. There were not, and possibly never had been, rustic looking wooden buildings everywhere, and the ancient village would have been a mix of stone buildings and places carved into the soft rock. Certainly the famous stable with its manger -that may have been a trough-, was a cave, over which the Church of the nativity had been built. This building too was surrounded by dangerous looking soldiers.

I was quite in awe of this place, truth be told, and had the feeling of the hairs standing up on my neck when I kneeled over the spot deemed to be the birthplace of Jesus Christ. Though at this time I wasn't a particularly practising Catholic, and indeed the lyrics of my music mocked the idea of religion, I wasn't exactly a non-believer either. So I found this place mighty inspiring. Faith aside, I was to learn that these old and ancient places do seem to give out some kind of enigmatic vibe. Is it our imagination, combined with the atmosphere of these mysterious locations? Possibly, but my own thoughts, as I visited more such places over time, is that you can seem to 'tune in' to the history and combine that with what your consciousness does with knowledge of the places, and that overwhelming feeling will raise those hairs. But whatever the reason, it is an amazing feeling, and you never forget it.

Similarly, I was struck by the fact that a mass was going on. I'm not sure if it was Catholic or Orthodox, but a mass never-the-less. And in this remarkable, ancient pace, I was struck by what mass meant. All my life it was a place the parents took us, till they couldn't be bothered, and sent us ourselves, until we couldn't be bothered and stopped, aside from Christmas, weddings, Baptisms and funerals. It was, quite frankly, a chore. But this mass I walked into seemed to make more sense. Of course the surroundings, the air of the place and a bit of active imagination helped, but there it was. And I suddenly realised what communion was. Not just the act of putting a bit of dry bread being put in our mouth and told it was the body of Christ, but the actual word communion. And not just being in touch with a higher power, and the millions of other believers for a moment....But also being in communion with the millions of believers who had come before us, and maybe even those to come. This was just one of many ways, I came to believe, of how people touch the collective mind of humanity, and maybe the real reason we can 'feel' these ancient meeting grounds. Quite the revelations for a day-trip....I'd never had that with Blackpool.

IV

The Scottish will never let a pair of Cossack boots ruin a good floor.

Eventually the course was done. Our projects completed, and studies complete, we received our Diploma's and headed back to England. As I say, the projects were ignored and the Diploma didn't really open any doors immediately , but though I didn't know it then, a number of different seeds had been sown in me that were to become bigger and bigger influences in my life, slowly but surely.

I was back about a week, when I was called into the youth services office where the Coventry Youth Council were run from. Well, it seemed that international relations were all the rage at the moment, and some of my group had been selected to do an exchange visit with Russians from one of the city's twin towns, Volgograd. Did I want to go?

I couldn't believe my luck. And of course I wanted to go. But first the Russians would come here. The powers that be laid on a number of activities to entertain and educate our young guests, mainly involving trips to places that were not in the city at all, and we were to accompany them and no doubt befriend them, all in the name of great international relations. I like to think that if the bombs were about to be launched, someone in Moscow would probably run in and stop the button being pressed by shouting,

"We can't do it, we can't launch the missiles, Mulligans' over there, remember? He presented us with that book about some bloke in the city who invented bicycles."

"The same comrade who enabled ducks to escape from the canine oppressors?"

"That is he."

"I read that book. Mulligan had written "Good luck" to us all inside the cover. Quick, comrade: STOP....THE......WAR!"

Along with conquering Germany, it would be the greatest act of peace that I never initiated.

So the Russians eventually arrived for the youth exchange and we were struck immediately by the fact that they didn't seem to really be youths at all. I'd have put over half of them in their 30's and 40's. Suddenly, it looked like the trips that were organised for them were less likely to be appealing. When asked what they wanted to do, their first suggestion was a nightclub, something no one had put on the agenda, as Education department people, especially the youth organisers, tend to think that young people not much younger than themselves in some cases want to play ping pong and take part in workshops, and this will stop them becoming drug addicts or racists. It's an odd theory, but was quite prevalent in the 80's.

Then one of the Russian organisers spoke to our people about venues and the penny dropped. Someone had not done their homework, and this wasn't a youth group at all, but in fact a company of traditional Cossack dancers, under the impression they would be performing to youth groups in the city as part of an educational swap. Our people had them down for things like a trip to Warwick castle with a visit to McDonald's after, to show them western culture. This, I thought, was brilliant, and was bound to be hilarious, and nothing over the next two weeks let me down.

After a few hurried phone calls to anyone who would answer a phone, a couple of venues were hastily put together, mainly infant schools due to one of the Education department people having been a teacher at one, and knew some headmistress's. As the Cossack dancing tells a story, lord only knows what the infants got out of this. However, it was fun to see the various city dignitaries that had been invited squashed onto those little chairs designed for 6 year olds that are in school halls everywhere. The trips also went ahead, and we discovered that contrary to what we had been led to believe in the press (Yes, think South Africa again), that all Russians were not trying to escape (which we had been briefed might happen and told the procedure for reporting it), were not prepared to pay a fortune for brand name jeans, and, disappointingly, did not all wear big furry hats. They also were not that impressed by the huge range of products in the shops.

"Why you have so many things the same?" one guy asked.

"To give people choice."

"Why?"

So they can choose which brand they like the best, and buy that."

"Why? The same thing, yes?"

You know, none of us could really answer that.

The grand finale, the highlight if you will, of the Cossack dancers tour was to be in a more adult environment. After as much publicity as they could do in two weeks, remembering that this was pre-internet days, hence an advert in the local paper, and a couple of plugs on the local radio station, the wise people from youth services managed to book a Saturday night in the Tam-o'-shanter Social club. Now, if this sounds like it could be a Working man's club for the local and aged Scots community in the city, complete with bingo and a free-and-easy (A kind of fore runner to Karaoke, where depressed people got up and sang the same songs every week with the backing of the house drummer and organist. They were hell on earth, and my Dad was a regular singer at them), then that's because it was exactly that. And to fit in the show, they had persuaded the committee to cancel either the bingo or the free-and-easy. The free-and-easy lost out.

At a guess, not one person from the city who had read the advert and thought, oh, Cossack dancing, that's Saturday sorted actually turned up, though few local councillors and Education department employees who weren't given a choice did come. Everyone else was the regular Saturday night crowd of mainly pension aged Scots, who hated change more than they hated the English. And the compère, no doubt a member of the committee, got the ball rolling quite early on. This was mainly to explain why the regulars hobbling in were finding their usual tables being taken by colourfully clad Russians, and patronising council people with false smiles. There was quite a bit of swearing, and the Russians politely moved about as each new group turned up, shocked at someone under 60 being at 'their' table, and with no concept of maybe sitting somewhere else.

"So, Ladies and Gentleman" he began, speaking slowly in a polite Scots accent, "We have a little surprise for you tonight. It's certainly a surprise for me. So, apologies, but we won't be having the free-and-easy later...."

Yes, he apologised for the Russians being there. The room erupted as much as a group of grumpy pensioners could erupt.

"What"

"Shame"

"Why?"

"What's going on, man?"

He carried on. "Aye, I'm sorry and all that. But tonight we have a group of young people (gasps from the room) all the way from the Soviet Union who are going to dance for us."

There was silence as this sunk in, then the questions.

"From Russia?"

"Dancing?"

Then the big question came....

"And what about the bingo?"

At this, people were out of their chairs and banging fists on the tables. The Compère tried to regain order.

"Ladies and Gentlemen, I can assure you that the Bingo WILL still be going ahead. I can tell you that Stalin himself will not stop the bingo."

This seemed to appease the crowd, who grumbled amongst themselves , but consoled themselves with a Scotch and purchasing their bingo tickets.

The Russians could not work the bingo out at all. They knew something was happening, and that during it, various miserable men would come over and ask them to be quiet if they spoke amongst themselves. This was the Committee in action. Anyone who remembers the old working men's and social clubs will know that the committee were the group of self-appointed 'guvnors' whose job it was to keep children in their seats and women out of the snooker room. Laughter outside of a paid comedian was forbidden, and getting past the member on the door if you were a new face was harder than Brody getting through customs with his Irish Passport. Volgograd had been utterly destroyed by the Nazi's during the war, and went on to live under the eye of communism and the KGB. But probably none of this prepared them for a group of Scottish Committee men on a bingo night in the Tam-o'-shanter.

Eventually the dancers came on, and danced magnificently. The costumes were amazing, the performers professional, the musicians astounding. The sound of heavy leather on the parquet was both dramatic and inspiring to hear as they danced as only Cossacks can. They even worked around the pillars without missing a beat. I had only seen the condensed version in the infant schools, so seeing the full shenanigan's was breath-taking, right up to the finish, where they gathered around, stood in front of the rows of tables and bowed, with beaming faces and beads of sweat dripping from their brows.

I clapped, others in our group clapped, then we were joined by some half-hearted clapping from the audience. This quickly waned, and rather than shouts of 'More' or 'Encore', a single Scottish voice called out.

"Well. I hope they hae nae damaged the floor with those big boots."

V

I dabbled on the Black Market in Russia for a while.

The Russians returned home with whatever impression of Coventry they had made, and in no time at all our motley group of Coventry representatives were heading out past the Iron Curtain . We had to contribute £100 to the trip each, but as I had in the meantime picked up a job working for a charity, this wasn't a problem. The job had been a temporary contract, for 6 months, with a chance for it to be renewed. This renewal was in fact offered to me, but it would have meant having to cancel the Russian trip, which I had no intention of doing. The beauty of being at an age when you have a whole life ahead is that you can – and should – take gambles. Sometimes they won't pay off, but you will have no problem clicking the reset button.

We arrived at Moscow airport and had no problem with customs. I was a little worried as my passport had a photo of me with red and black hair, which was now bleached blond. I also had to check that the Israel stamp in my passport wouldn't be a problem. There were a lot of countries that would not let you in with that stamp, and with hindsight I should have requested it on a separate piece of paper, which was possible, but I hadn't really considered it at the time.

Arriving at the hotel, our first concern was about getting money. Being a closed currency, we hadn't been able to get any Rubles before leaving, but had been advised by people in the know to take hard currency in US Dollars, Pounds or Marks, which of course we had and so we weren't too badly off. We found that in the hotel bar where we first stayed that they only took hard currency anyway, so it wasn't a problem.

There was a group of Irishmen staying there, who told us how to go about using the black market guys who hung around the hotels. This caused a matter of concern to the Education department supervisors who were there with us. There were two of these, one who I knew from the youth service, and another woman who I had never met. There was also a large Russian woman who they had brought as a translator. These wise educators were quite adamant that we should use a bank legitimately, but as the Irishmen pointed out, it was a one-to-one exchange. So 1 dollar = 1 Ruble, 1 pound = 1 Ruble, 1 Franc = 1 Ruble, etc. We knew enough to know that this was throwing money down the pan, with the Ruble being not especially a valuable currency. Most of the group, however, being quite young, agreed with the supervisors.

"How do we find these guys?" I asked, clearly not agreeing with the supervisors at all.

"They already know you're here," they laughed.

And so it was. I was probably the oldest 'youth' in the group, and headed off with one of my friends from the Coventry Youth Council, Rob, and wandered into the lobby. We were approached straight away by a young guy who hissed and whispered as if the hotel staff had no idea what he was doing, though quite clearly they did. He took us outside the back of the hotel, which I'm pretty convinced was for dramatic affect only, and we exchanged money. There. 6 hours in Russia, and I was breaking the law.

We came back, and the others asked us how much we had got. We had exchanged for 10 Ruble a pound, meaning 10 times as much as the bank rate. Suddenly, everyone's minds were changing, and they were asking us to go and change money for them. Honesty and money, eh? As it was, that wasn't a good rate, and as I learned to barter with the dealers, and they knew I could exchange for a sizable crowd, I eventually got that up to 15 per pound.

We were in for a bit of a shock about another subject close to our heart though. Apparently we had arrived during a period of partial prohibition in Russia. Apart from hotel bars for tourists only, there were no pubs or public bars. This came as a bit of a shock.

It seems that in 1985, Mikhail Gorbachev, the last president of the Soviet Union, had decided on a ban on alcohol in a bid to kick start the economy, as the workers were unmotivated, and often rolled into work drunk, or so it was reported. The general feeling was that with very few goods in the shops, and the Soviet guarantee of employment of some kind but with very little chance of bettering yourself, there was no real incentive for people to push themselves, but drinking was becoming a major problem. So an experiment in an alcohol ban took place that was in hindsight a complete failure. The Russian citizens, an inventive people used to coping when there was very little, took to brewing and distilling their own, with far more potency and dangers than before. Varnish, boot polish, vehicle fuel....There was no end to what people used. This lasted till 1989, when it was agreed it had caused more problems than it had solved.

We had been given a guide on arrival, Katya. She was quite a stunning looking young Russian girl, a Student. She was to be with us for the whole trip. I'm not sure exactly who allocated her to us, but as best I could tell, there was no way that we were ever going to be given a free hand in where we went. Everything was organised for us, from start to finish. Katya had the inventory.

The next night, before heading to Volgograd, we were taken to a place called the Sputnik Centre, to a disco. And of course, there was no alcohol so I was drinking cups of orange juice, much to my annoyance. By this time back home, I had moved on from Djing in pubs, and was working in the bigger Alternative clubs in the city, so I was interested in the DJ set up here. Basically, it was two guys and a tape recorder. They didn't have any records. But they were friendly, and gave me their addresses and virtually pleaded with me to send them tapes. They didn't mix tunes, which was no problem, but instead would play a song, talk while changing the tape and then play the next one. And in the meantime, everyone stopped dancing and stood patiently till the next track, and then resumed dancing. It was like some nightclub game of statues. I wondered if they had considered getting a second tape recorder.

I'm guessing that this was the Russian Education Department's idea of entertaining young people, as I did notice an unused ping pong table in the corner, which was great, and no doubt keeping the Russian youth from becoming Drug addicts or Capitalists.

Back to the hotel to discover that the bar shut early, so a good kip was had by all and we woke up, hangover free to head off to Volgograd.

It has to be said, The Moscow underground stations are something else. We travelled by metro to the main station, and I got to see a few on the way back, but they are beautifully decorated, with mosaics,, and art, and sculpture. In fact, you could spend a day just visiting the metro stations, if you wanted to do something different. This was a nice build up to the train we caught, which reminded us of one of those old Agatha Christie films, with ornate carriages, and a dining car, with staggered dining.

Well, it was a lovely train till you needed to go to the toilet, which was at the back of the train. Now, I'd experienced a hole-in-the-floor toilet before, in Israel, but finding one on a train that dropped straight to the tracks caught us by surprise indeed. And there in a box was a pile of newspaper, cut into fairly neat squares.

Most of the girls declined from using the toilet for the whole journey. This is something that to this day amazes me about girls, that they can refrain from going to the toilet if they don't like the look of it. This to me, who can get caught short anytime, and when you gotta go, you gotta go, strikes me as almost a superpower.

In fact, I always took my need to go quite seriously. To the point that before a DJ set, I would make sure that I went for a good crap before, as back in the days of 7" singles, getting to the toilet, hoping it wasn't being used for lord knows what, doing the business and getting back to the decks in a nightclub was virtually impossible. So this became known amongst my friends as my 'Lucky Dump". And to be honest, I'm not sure, but I swear that the more ghastly it stank, the better night I was in for. I'm convinced it was a DJ with a bowel disorder that invented the 12" Extended mix singles.

I didn't, or couldn't refrain from going on the train, but found the whole process of a wind blowing up my ass a bit startling. And also, I wondered, at what point had Russians started printing their newspapers on some kind of sandpaper?

For the group, the train ride was good ,as we all started to get to know each other a bit more. One of the girls in the group, Treena, was quite punky herself, and it seemed we had a lot of friends in common. And though I was seeing a girl at this time back home, I would be lying if I said I didn't find her quite attractive. But then , to be honest, I was never much of an angel when it came to that kind of thing back home.

So a civilised journey out to Volgograd, where we were met by a coach that took us to our hotel. Here we found no beer on sale, and we realised this was going to be a pretty dry time for us all. We also found over the course of time that it paid to like melons. For no reason that we could fathom, everywhere we went there were melons, and melon juice, and plates of melon. Hell, they even left us a melon each in the hotel room, and not small ones at that. Around this time, the original Pacman game was popular, so I took to carving Pacmen out of the melons and leaving them hidden in the plants that were all around the hotel. I gather that after a week of this the cleaners complained, and no more melons were left in our rooms.

It was on the first night here that the two supervisors called us together in one of the rooms, with a bit of a concern. It seems that they had been asked if we wanted to perform anywhere. Apparently the assumption was that as they sent us a group of dancing Cossacks that we must be some kind of entertainers too.

"What should we do? They are expecting a show", Edith explained, the woman I knew from the youth service.

"Nothing," I said," none of us are performers."

" Well, I have an idea," the other woman, Marian, jumped in. "I do choreography, and I once put a show together that I think we could do here with just a little practice.

"But we are not dancers" someone else called out, to murmurs of agreement.

"No, it's easy..."

"Yes, if you're a dancer."

91

"I don't want to dance"

"We don't have costumes"

"Or music."

"How are we going to follow those Cossacks?"

Marion carried on. " No, this is honestly doable. We performed a sketch once where we did a parody of Morris Dancing. It was really funny, and I can teach you how to do it very quickly."

For anyone who does not know what Morris Dancing is, it is a kind of old traditional English folk dance, that involves a group of men in odd costumes dancing around knocking sticks together, and waving jingly things about. To be fair to Morris Dancers, they are very aware of how it looks, but are usually quite fun blokes who drink an awful lot of real ale afterward. However, to the uninitiated, who might not get that it is some kind of fertility dance, it would look somewhat bizarre and confusing.

And this woman, in what can only be described as a moment of optimism verging on insanity, thought that a group of non-theatrical youths, without the benefit of the costumes which would suggest tradition, would perform a parody – yes, a parody – of something that no Russian would ever of heard of in the first place. How exactly a parody of something that already looks unreal would have worked, thankfully we never found out.

It was quite a strong no from the group, much to Marion's disappointment, and Edith's concern. How, they asked, were they to explain that there was no show to do? Well, I've no idea what they did explain, but the next day we had an agenda given to us of where we were to be taken on trips, and thankfully no show was on it.

It was quite an agenda too. At no point, we noticed, was there any free time, other than when we got back to the hotel. We were to be in a group, and guided by Katya for the whole time there. This was, I found out, standard at the time. We were there to see Russia, but only the Russia that we were allowed to see.

But we did see some great things. One outstanding trip was to a monument to the war, the statue known as The Motherland Calls. I had no idea when we got there just how big this thing was going to be. The statue itself, (and I suggest looking up a picture), is of a warrior woman, and measures 85 metres, or 279 feet, from the ground to the tip of her sword. It was finished in 1967, and was at the time declared the tallest statue in the world. This is no longer the case, but hell, how big do you need a statue to be? We have one of Lady Godiva in Coventry Centre, she of the riding through the streets naked fame. (In fairness, if you see the Coventry girls hitting the clubs on a Saturday night, it seems she started a tradition.) Our statue, however, is of a size that people constantly climb up to put bras on her, or road cones on her head. I guess Brits don't really get statues.

There are also 200 steps leading up to the statue itself, one for each day of the siege of Volgograd, a turning point in The German attack on the Soviet Union. Along the way are various incredible things, monuments, an eternal flame and tombs of war heroes. As you walk towards the statue the size becomes more and more apparent. It is a wonderful testament to Soviet art and engineering, for to make a structure like this is a feat of amazing skill and ingenuity. And the Soviets did seem to be good at making testimonies to themselves.

We were taken to sports stadiums where athletes were trained, and we could see how amazing the Soviet athletics and sports programmes were. We were taken to schools where we could clearly see how wonderful the Soviet Education programmes were. We were taken to some social gatherings of seemingly important local dignitaries, and we could see how friendly and peace loving the Soviet powers were. A music college we visited taught us that the Soviet programmes for the gifted were the best in the world. And so on. In fact, trip after trip, event after event, we had a constant bombardment of the inspiring achievements of the Soviet Union. Hard to believe, with hindsight, we were only a couple of years away from it all ending.

And we ate! My God, we ate. Every single place we went, they laid on a multi course meal of pretty fine things. I always had a bit of an appetite, even though I was a skinny sort of young lad – boy, how that changed in later life – and considered I could eat just about anything. But this was getting beyond doable. As we were taken from place to place, sometimes five or six places in a day, we were given a huge meal. Always with hosts smiling at us, and a feeling that we really would be rude not to eat it. Amongst ourselves, we were complaining that eating this amount was getting difficult, and not really sure what to do. We never really solved that, as such, but on one of the days, me and Treena decided to feign illness. On this day, we had been out, and seen a few

93

things and ate a lot of meals, and to be honest, we could just not face any more food. And the Afternoon and evening activities were that we were to be taken in small groups to host families where we would spend an evening learning, no doubt, about how absolutely wonderful life was in an average Soviet family. Now don't get me wrong, these were all nice people. We'd met some of them in the UK as they were with the dance troupe. And in all honesty, I would have really enjoyed that. But there was no way I could face another meal, and this would have been a huge one, no doubt.

So I pretended I was ill, and Treena followed suit. This caused the Russians some concern, and Katya the guide came to see me and asked if I needed a doctor. No, I did not. In fact, that would have been worse. I would no doubt be taken to a hospital, where I would be shown the wonders of Soviet surgery, and no doubt be given a hearty meal to recover.

By this time, Katya, being only around our age herself, had become quite friendly with us, outside of her job as a guide. In fact, Rob had even taken her out on a date a couple of nights earlier, where I believe they went to a hotel bar somewhere and had a couple of drinks. Rob told us she had seemed very nervous, then eventually confessed that she had something to tell him that might put him off.

"What was it?" I asked him.

"That her parents were divorced."

"And?"

And that was it. It seemed that this was still an issue of great social stigma there, to the point where she felt she had to put it on the table straight away. She was apparently surprised to learn that if we had done a poll amongst our group, there was a good chance about half of us came from divorced parents.

Rob, it appeared, was very appealing to the Russians. In fairness, he was a tall, not bad looking bloke and also, as it was pointed out to him on one of our trips where a farmer on a wonderful Soviet farm we visited that taught us how modern the Soviet programme to feed everybody was, he had a good strong body that could do much hard work. This appealed to the farmer, who wanted to introduce Rob to his daughter, who apparently needed a strong man to work the land and keep her well. In return, she was an excellent cook, and healthy, and would produce many strong children with a husband as big and strong as him. Rob declined. It's a shame, as years later, I went to dinner at his house long after he was married and his wife was a terrible cook, and their strange little child kept trying to eat Lego.

The girls in the group found this offer quite shocking , as did the supervisors, who discussed if they should report this. As to who they would report it to, exactly, I don't think they knew, and as I pointed out, we had come here to learn, not judge, and this was about the most honest incident that had happened to us so far. So Rob went on to be smiled at by many Russian girls, and took the hot guide out on a couple of dates. Good lad.

So I told Katya that I certainly didn't need a doctor, but she needed something to put on a form. I suggested overeating, but there wasn't a box to tick. So I used the old standby of hungover workers across the UK and said sickness and diarrhoea, and that I had tablets with me to cure it, but I needed rest. Treena apparently declared some kind of woman problems, of which no man should ever learn about.

And we were free! Everybody else headed off after lunch to the various hosts, and apparently enjoyed very pleasant evenings chatting about Soviet life, how well they were doing, what their impressions of the west were, and trying to keep as much food down as possible. Me and Treena, on the other hand, went for a walk.

Though a lot more toned down in my appearance then earlier trips, including Israel, I still had short blonde spiky hair, which was enough to attract the attention of various younger people who had very mixed reactions. With some it was stares of anger, with others they came up and tried to talk in a friendly way, but language was a problem. Older people, we noticed, avoided eye contact and went about their business. This little fact alone showed that Russia was changing. Clearly there was a difference between old and young, with the young seemingly more expressive.

We got in a bit of a row with some guys on motorbikes, who really took a dislike to Treena for some reason. She had quite wild hair herself at the time, and I suspect they simply didn't like a western girl with a different sort of look, and felt obliged to cuss us in Russian. However, we stood our ground, and it blew over.

We also found a little fete going on, at the edge of a park we visited. Not unlike a cross between a market and a car boot sale, all sorts of strange little things were on sale, for an incredible amount less than the prices we had seen in the few shops we had been taken to. This was interesting, and here I learned a new lesson. The World does not speak English. Right across Europe and Israel, Communicating was not that difficult, even though it seemed so at the time. There was always someone who could speak at least a splattering of English, if not practically word perfect. Here, no one did. And on top of that, any street signs, or notices, or price lists were in the Cyrillic alphabet, and unreadable to us. Getting around, I found it useful to memorise a street name in what it looked like, rather than what it sounded like. So Smith Street would be Смитх стреет, and I would memorise it as Cumentex cutpeet, so I would recognise it again. This worked, and I used it later on the Moscow underground getting about too.

We then went to a hotel bar, but were told we needed our passports to get drinks, something we could not do as they were kept at the hotel for safe keeping, allegedly. I had also been a bit alarmed about this when it happened on the train, when they had taken our passports and kept them locked up till not long before we disembarked. However, we were clearly foreigners, and the fact we had US Dollars meant that after a bit of negotiation with the manager, we were allowed to buy drinks. In no time at all we had the black market guys hissing at us, but we were well sorted as I had dealt some cash in our own hotel for everyone, and in fact we were finding it a bit hard to spend. Everything was laid on, and things in the shops, what there were, did not really cost that much. The beer prices in the hotels though, I noticed, were not much different to prices back home, but It had been pointed out by Katya that the prices very much depended on where they supposed you came from, and how much they supposed that you were willing to spend. So a bit like London then.

Next day, we made a remarkable recovery, and were off on the next trip. This time to a Cossack farm, or rather a museum built around one. This was, by itself, interesting enough, but I was quite taken by a pair of traditional Cossack leather trousers hanging up. Battered, fur lined, and cool as hell. Even the others jokingly pointed out that they were the trousers for me.

Interestingly, as part of the tour, the guide showed us the remains of an old out building, and quite casually explained that it had been a Cossack tradition to take their wife out to the building for a beating at the start of the week to ensure she stayed good and faithful, then later in the week they done it again to make sure she stayed loving. Well, I'm no interpreter of dance, but I'm damned sure I didn't see that in the love story they performed for us in the Tam-o'-shanter club.

Later that evening there was an opportunity to go out and meet some local music character, which was optional, or to hang around the hotel. The rest of the group opted for the hotel, as they were suffering from the overeating, and needed a break. Me and Treena decided on the visit, as we had had a bit of a respite. In fact, on our crafty day out, we'd hardly eaten a thing, except ice cream. It has to be said that everyone agreed that the Russian ice cream was some of the very best any of us had ever eaten. We tended to get it in parks, where they would usually serve it on a little plate with a spoon, so you had to eat it where you bought it. I've no idea why it was so different and delicious, but if someone had taken us to an ice cream factory and told us how Russian Ice cream was the result of an amazing Soviet achievement, this time we might actually have been impressed.

Hence, just the two of us and Katya headed over to meet this guy, who lived in a small house full of traditional musical instruments, and he could play all of them. He demonstrated, and let us have a go, and told us the history of them, and it was, quite frankly, amazing. We drank tea, and he offered us no more than a few tasteless biscuits, which was a refreshing change. He then told us about the music he wrote for himself and his wife, and how they would perform this for us before we left.

"Your wife?" Treena asked, remembering something he had said earlier. "I thought you said your wife had, well, passed on.?

" She has. But we will always be together in our music. We played together for all our lives, since we met as children. And even death cannot separate love, when two people have lived with passion. Our passion was music. We lived for our music. And we still perform together now, so our passion will live on till we meet again in a faraway place."

You couldn't help but be touched by this, and I saw Treena had a little tear in her eye. Maybe I did too. He walked over to a shelf, where there was an old fashioned reel-to-reel tape recorder, and wound back a tape.

He picked up a balalaika , a type of 3 stringed guitar that he had shown us earlier and pressed play on the tape recorder. As he played, the gentle tones of a ladies voice began to join in, till they were playing together while his eyes left our room, and were clearly looking at distant, loving memories.

Except, she was a bloody awful singer.

I mean, awful. What started off as us being invited into a personal love story ended up with us enduring 20 minutes of something reminding us of a cat in pain. Well, they say love is blind, but I guess it's bloody deaf as well!

However, it had been a fantastic visit, and one I'm glad we did not miss. And also one of the last before we headed back onto the long train journey back to Moscow. By this time, different little groups had begun to form, and we all knew each other a lot better than the journey out there. As a result, we were perhaps a little too raucous, and at one point the supervisor on the train threatened to have us arrested when someone stole a City of Heroes curtain from one of the windows. It magically appeared back. I have no idea who took it, but they clearly had misjudged the Russian sense of pride in their cities and flags.

Rob had disappeared off to Katya's sleeping cabin, and a small group of us gathered in mine. We had been given various books of both classic Russian literature, and contemporary poetry translated into English over the many visits, and we decided to read stuff to each other, in some weird kind of beatnik way. Treena and myself were lying on my bunk, at one point listening to one of the younger lads, Roy, reading out a story he particularly liked. Out of the blue, Treena turned round and began kissing me, and we were soon having a full on snog on my bunk. The others smiled knowingly and made their excuses and left.

Except Roy. That prat kept on reading the story. It seemed that unlike anyone else, he felt no social awkwardness whatsoever. Even when we had pulled a blanket over ourselves, and were clearly not listening to the story about The Cossack and the Eagle that Roy kept on reading. In fairness, we were on a top bunk of 3, whilst he was sitting on the bottom bunk with a small night light on, but never-the-less......

Anyway, we actually had a damned good, if a little cramped, fuck, whilst all the time this lad read out his story. All three of us finished about the same time, which is always a good skill to have, and it was hard to tell who was the most satisfied.

"Well, " Roy asked," Did you enjoy it?"

Treena and I laughed. "Of course. It was bloody fantastic."

"Yep. They sure can write, these Russians."

And with that he turned his night light out and I'm pretty damned sure we heard him have a wank.

VI

We had a pretty decent hotel in Moscow, complete with complementary melon juice, and a couple of days without educational trips. Though we still were to come under the alleged watchful eye of Katya, who by this time had gathered that we were not really falling for the everything is wonderful stories. It was her first time as a guide, and to be honest, you could see the naivety in her waning. At first, she'd sounded as if she was quoting straight from a book, which she probably was. But then, as she began to become friends with us, she told us more about how things really were, and we got a lot of insights.

For example, we noticed that there were a number of older people in parks who appeared to be tidying up bushes. It seems that is exactly what they were doing, as everybody was promised a job, even if it didn't make any sense. We observed this in a number of shops we went into as well. In one department store, where we went to get gifts to bring home, you had to take the product you wanted to a young girl at the counter, who told you how much it was, and sent you to the girl at the next counter who took the money and gave you a receipt. She then passed the goods to another girl standing next to her, who put it in a bag, and handed it to you. You'd think that 3 people serving you would make it a snappy sort of affair, but it wasn't. All three looked at you like you were a total inconvenience to their day, and seemed to take an oddly long time discussing the movement of the goods from one to another.

But you could see there was a decent original principle behind all this. The theory was clever enough, all people equal, all opportunities equal, jobs and housing for all. Except that it overlooked the fact that humans simply don't work like that. People have different levels of ambition, and hence there will always be a hierarchy. Some people are happy to contribute to a group or society, whereas some others only want to take from it. Some will work, some will shirk. Some will be happy with their

99

lot, others never will be. Some will lead, others will want to be led. All of these, and hundreds of other human traits, can overlap, can contradict, and can lead equally to success or failure, depending on health, wealth, and stealth, opportunities or coincidences, and fate. A theoretically equal society would not necessarily be a happy one, and a happy society is not necessarily an equal one, but rather one that recognises and embraces differences.

So it came to our last night, and Rob took Katya out for a meal, which was nice, and as he was my room-mate, it gave me and Treena a chance to carry on with our shenanigans. In fact, we locked him out, so when he returned, he spent his last night on one of the other lad's floors, as Katya was sharing with the Russian woman whom we had brought to translate. This woman, incidentally, did absolutely nothing that I could see. Katya translated, along with one of the girls in the group who could also speak Russian. In fact, she stayed behind for most of the trips, and we would come back to find her getting free manicures, or her hair dressed, or such things, as she played the returning exile card extraordinarily well. So Rob had to sleep on the floor …. I hope it was Roy's, and I hope he read him a long, boring bedtime story.

On getting back to the UK, there was the small matter of my girlfriend, as I had quite taken to Treena. It was OK. It seems she had also been shagging someone else as soon as I had gone, who she went on to marry. Well, that sorted that out then. However, Treen and I lasted a grand total of a couple of weeks after we got back. It was another observation I made about travelling. Like anything else, it's not written in stone and there are exceptions, but in general, relationships that begin whilst on the road do not usually hold up once you get back to "normal" life. The qualities that are attractive whilst out there are not always as obvious or relevant in a day to day life. Of course, that could just be me.......

VII

I had a friend who would travel the world to get a date.

100

I arrived back from Moscow having no job to go to, as I had sacrificed mine to take the trip. However, I wandered down to the job agencies the day after I got back and by that afternoon was working at the main Post office depot in town, clearing the backlog from a strike that had happened whilst we'd been away. This of course meant that all our mail from Russia was still in the system, and that the nice postcards I had sent to my girlfriend would be arriving over the same time that we were entertaining our new partners. Never-the-less, I must have been a good agency worker as they offered me a full time job as a postie, which I took. Already working there was a good friend of mine, Ferret, who I'd been in many home spun shenanigans with over time. In fact, a lot of the old punk crowd seemed to end up at Royal Mail. I think it's because they would take just about anyone who would get up at 4 in the morning and could handle a good hangover.

So in the Post Office canteen one day, Ferret told me that he had been writing to a mutual American friend of ours, Jake.

"In fact, he is all for us coming over there. You fancy it?"

"New York? You bet I do....When?"

With that, Ferret sorted things out with Jake and I booked all my annual leave in one block, plus some unpaid leave, which was something you could do at the Post office back then.

The great thing was, you see, that the way we had travelled around Europe, meeting people from the punk scene or just grabbing hold of anybody remotely punky looking to find squats or even just to get put up for the night, this was in fact a two way street. The same thing happened at home too. Over time, I had put up in my flat a whole host of travelling punks, and later, just travellers, from France, Canada, Sweden, Norway, Germany, and a whole bunch of other places. Some I met at gigs, some in a local alternative pub, others just turned up at the door with an address they had been given by someone I had put up before from their country, or from someone in another UK city who had put me up or vice versa. Travelling to other cities to gigs usually involved finding a place to stay at the start, it was the way we did it, and it worked fantastically well.

Sometimes these house guests would become great friends and we have stayed in touch ever since. Others were great friends at the time, but we lost touch once they hit the road again, and then there were some who

101

stayed a night and have been totally forgotten about. There were also a fair few Dickheads in the mix, who you were glad to see the back of.

In Jake's case, he had been studying in Coventry, and we met him in the Courtyard, a rather well known punk bar in town at the time. He was a great guy, and fell in with the crowd that included both me and Ferret. Towards the end of his stay, I suggested that rather than him paying more rent on his digs, he could crash at mine for a bit, which probably meant he didn't get a lot of studying done.

After we set up a date to head out and see him in New York, I was talking about it in the Courtyard one boozy evening with some friends sat round a table that included Brody, who I hadn't really seen much of in recent times. Though still punk, he'd taken to hanging out more in biker bars, as his relationship with smoking and pill popping had made these the better places for him to hang out. On this day though, I met him having a pint in the courtyard, and naturally we engaged in our one shared vice, copious drinking.

"New York?" he said. "That'd be pretty cool. I've always fancied that."

"Yep. I'm looking forward to it. And it'll be good to see Jake again"

"You know what? I might come along too."

I didn't really take him seriously, just assuming it was the Jack Daniels talking; He didn't really know Jake, and he wasn't working as such at the time, apart from a bit of road crew work for some of the bands that had come out of Coventry during the two-tone days a few years back. Well, that and a helping hand in the distribution of local leisure pursuits out of the biker bars. However, he surprised me by turning up at my door one evening later that week after securing a large loan from the bank, and asking when we were going.

So that was it then. We were off to America.

American customs were nice and easy to clear, though one guy saw us wearing leather jackets and asked us cheerfully if we were in a band or something. Jake later told us that if we had said yes we would have had some heavy questioning about whether we were going out there to work or not. As it happened, I said we weren't which was of course true but the sort of thing Ferret would have said yes to, as he liked to prank people, so thank fuck he kept quiet this time. And it was the States, so this time

Brody's legendary Irish passport was never going to cause us problems, unlike Gatwick airport, where we were taken to one side by the police before we had even checked in, and searched. Apparently, they explained, they had a lot of trouble with youths hanging out at the airport. Well, I guess I should have been complimented, as youth I no longer was. And who'd of thought that a group of blokes carrying luggage and passports might actually be passengers.

British airports over the course of time were to become a source of much amusement for me. Though my hair was to change over the years from spikes to mohawks to braids then eventually skin, and flashes of colour to bleach, I was always – always – pulled out of the queue, or stopped at the Nothing to Declare line to be searched. I guess that customs officers figured that if someone wanted to discreetly and craftily smuggle drugs past them, they would obviously dye their hair blue or something so as to blend in! I swear, I began to notice over the years that some people on spotting I was getting on or off their plane would jostle to get right behind me in the queue, knowing that all eyes would be on my good self. I should have started charging them.

But, as I say, no problems at the other end and there we were in the USA. The real one this time, not the pseudo high street in Trier, Germany that we had passed through before. Though we considered that we were going to New York, Jake's family, who had kindly offered to put us all up, in fact lived in New Jersey, which in fairness was only a bus ride from Port Authority, the largest bus station in America. We had actually flown into Newark airport, so we weren't in New York yet.

We received, it had to be said, a warm welcome from Jake's family. Beds were made up and a hot meal was waiting for us when we arrived. Much TV in the UK at the time, and indeed while I was growing up, was American shows, and they often depicted American family life as a Mom who baked, and those wooden panelled houses with picket fences and large drives. Well, either that or people being shot in New York, which was a tad worrying as we were heading into there soon. And this family home was to us exactly like that. That is, the great house, not the shooting. The street was like every American small town street we had ever seen on TV, and it was refreshing to know that for once our television programmes hadn't lied to us.

It wasn't the only place that looked like it was straight out of a film set. The next day we headed down into New York, courtesy of Jake's Father, who took us on a grand tour. And from the illegal firework sellers in

Chinatown, a busted fire hydrant blowing out water, to the streets filled with yellow cabs and large, gun carrying policemen, this was the New York I already seemed to know. In fact, we had lunch in Chinatown, and it was the best Chinese food I had ever eaten, completely unlike anything I had had back home.

We also went up one of the towers of the World Trade Centre. Now, to be honest, I wasn't really that bothered about going up there. In fact I wanted to go up the Empire State Building. I knew that the WTC was taller of course, but wow, The Empire State? However, in retrospect , having been up that building was to mean a lot when in later years while sitting in a pub back home I was to see the live footage of the towers coming down in the terrorist attack that was to change the world. I even have a patch. Yes, a WTC patch, amongst the many I have accumulated. Bought, probably, in the lobby.

A home cooked meal in the family home, and it was back out to see the same city at night. Jake drove, so couldn't drink, which must have been annoying for him watching us merrily drinking away. In fact, we went into New York City most nights, whilst hanging around the small town of Habsburg Heights during the day, often sitting by the pool in a neighbour's house who had decently told Jake that we could use whilst they were at work.

This of course was unlike most of my previous trips out on the road in Europe. Here we were, sitting by a pool with a fridge full of beer and goodies, and drinking in bars and clubs in New York, whereas before we had been sleeping in bus shelters and seeing if we had enough cash for some hot food. The irony wasn't lost on me and Brody, who laughed about some of the shenanigans we had been up to, much to Ferret's seeming annoyance, as he swore we were idiots for travelling like that. I guess he just didn't get it.

We had found a bar that was to become almost our local, a music venue called the Continental in the East Village. Here, you never knew who was going to walk in and play. There was also a little stage where people could come and do an act for a couple of bottles of beer. There seemed to be a lot of Jewish Comedians who took a turn, all of whom were pretty funny, even though I was probably missing a lot of the references to Jewish life in New York. We were sitting drinking one night when an old, haggard and bald punk looking guy came in, wearing a battered old leather, leopard pattern trousers, and in the company of a much younger and good looking biker type girl. He plugged in his guitar and went on to play some shit hot rock'n'roll and punk.

A few songs in, we worked out who he was. It was Cheetah Chrome, who had been in one of the original New York Punk Rock bands, The Dead Boys. This was quite an eye opener for me. Just sitting in a bar, and one of the legends from the CBGB club, almost the spiritual home of punk, came in and performed about 10 yards away from us. The least we could do was send him over a drink. Well, Brody did, there is no one famous enough, or iconic enough that would ever get a drink out of Ferret. His tightness when it came to money was legendary, possibly more so than even Cheetah's guitar playing.

We got to share a drink with him after the show, where Ferret told him that we had been in CBGB's a few nights ago, and how we were surprised how small it was. Ferret then went on to tell him how he had got off with one of the waitress's, and seemed to think this would impress a bloke who had been at the forefront of the New York sex, drugs and rock'n'roll lifestyle. Cheetah feigned being impressed, but then left pretty quickly on finishing his drink. He wasn't getting us one back then. I guess maybe he had something in common with Ferret after all.

In fact, Ferret hadn't bagged off with a waitress at all. Not even close, though he argued about that for a while to come. What happened was the four of us headed to CBGB's, as no trip to New York would be complete without it. It was a Thursday night, or something, so nobody of any note was playing, though in fairness it could have been a whole group of people who went on to become famous later, as the place was a bit like that.

CBGB's was, it must be said, a bit of a dump. But not in a bad way, like the rock bars of Europe that furnished themselves from the aforementioned central mismatching furniture supplier. Though it did share a fondness for wobbly tables and piss coloured toilets. There were posters and flyers all over the walls and a fairly decent sized crowd, many of whom looked completely spaced out, but oddly no one asked us for spare change. Good luck with that from Ferret. I saw him once lend a mate 50p for some bus fare, and asked for 10p back as it was only a 40p ride. He would also work out the difference if you were drinking in rounds and your beer cost more than his, then ask you for the difference back.

We really had to push him that tipping here was the done thing. In fairness, it takes Brits a bit of a while to grasp tipping. And to this day I have never quite got it, but do it happily as it is part of those peoples living wage. It did seem, however, to make for very cheerful and quick service, which caused a bit of confusion for Ferret, due to his other prominent trait, of constantly being 'on the pull'.

We had arrived at CBGB's and got a drink from the bar. Table service is another thing that I've never really come to terms with. I like going to the bar. I also seem very unlucky when it comes to catching the waiting staff's eye. However, we'd got a drink, while Jake and Brody got a table, leaving me and Ferret looking at the posters and chatting. A pretty waitress came by, and Ferret immediately felt obliged to try to chat her up. Probably by talking about bands he'd seen that might have played there, as we'd not long been to a Cramps concert before coming over to the States.

"So, how long are you guys over here for?"

"Oh, not sure. But we are thinking of heading north."

"Wow. It's nice there. Niagara falls?"

"Probably."

"Go over to the Canadian side. The view is much better there. Anyway, can I get you guys another drink?"

"Oh, yes please. Another bud, thanks."

"And your friend? The same?"

(Reluctantly) "Yes, two buds. Cheers."

The waitress went off to the bar. Then Ferret turned round to me and hissed,

"Fuck off...."

"What?"

"Fuck off...I've pulled here. Go and sit with the others."

"How the hell do you think you have pulled?"

"You heard her...she offered to buy me a drink....."

The penny dropped. He'd taken her asking us if she could get us a drink to mean actually buying it. I was about to explain, but thought it would be funnier not to. And so, she brought us the drinks, and I sat down with the others, so we could watch him. Sure as hell, he stood in the same place and spoke to her every time she walked past, and every time she came back with a bottle of bud for him. At one point he came over and gave us a couple of full bottles, and told us how she kept buying him

106

drinks. Jake had already explained to her when she came to serve us that he was on a separate tab, so come the end of the night, by which time we were all sitting together, she came over with two bills. We happily paid ours, and left a great tip and watched Ferret looking incredibly confused. Brody explained it to him. He threw some money on the table, then threw some more when we laughed and reminded him to tip.

"You guys owe me for two bottles of Bud....."

"Nah. We gave it in tips to the waitress." (laughs)

"Bastards."

"Hey, did you get her number?" (laughs).

"Actually yes. It's on the bill.." (Boy, we laughed.)

That's why if I ever want to go back in time and find out if CBGB's is open by phoning their landline, I'll know to get hold of Ferret's old bill first.

We had indeed decided to head North up to Niagara Falls, and everyone suggested flying, but Brody was on a bit of a budget compared to the rest of us, so it looked like our cheapest option would be the Greyhound bus. Now, that would be another piece of real Americana to experience. But first, a last night out, so we hit some bars in Manhattan, then duly ending up in the Continental as usual,, before heading to a huge Goth and Alternative club in a massive old church called the Limelight. Now this was impressive....Every room, including the crypts, and library rooms upstairs had different DJ's playing different forms of Industrial, Alternative and Indie-dance tunes. I was playing pretty much the same mix back in the nightclub I was Djing in back home, also on a Tuesday night as this was, except my club would fit into one of the rooms here, and each DJ there specialised in one type of sound. It was excellent.

And we met a couple of girls. Well, Me and Ferret did, a couple of Goth girls called Laura and Geraldine. Brody stood talking to Jake mainly, who by this time was looking a bit pissed off. I'd been picking up a vibe for a bit, as he'd been babysitting us really, driving in and out of New York, not drinking himself, and waiting for us on our various shenanigans. Plus, his sister was not really well, and we were three strangers in their house. It was part of the reason we decided to go up to the Falls, rather than outstay our welcome.

We got numbers from the girls, and left the club a bit early, as we were heading off the next morning. We figured on it being about 8 hours to

Buffalo, and we would stay the night there. We said our goodbyes, Jake dropped us at Port Authority, and off we headed. Canada, here we come! But first, of course, a stop at Buffalo.

We arrived in the late evening, and looked out for a hotel. We found a place fairly near the station called the Hotel Lafayette, which looked like it had been quite the place in its day, but that day may have been in better times. The charming fellow behind the counter let us know he could do a room for 3 for $50, which seemed pretty good to me. However, Ferret asked him if he knew anywhere cheaper.

"I do, but I wouldn't recommend them", the fellow replied, looking almost hurt.

Ferret was about to ask where, when Brody slapped him around the head and said we'd take the room. And, in fairness, it was reasonably clean, but the shower didn't work properly, one of the beds was a bit broken and there was a small kettle with no plug. Who cares, we thought, it's just to crash out in, let's go drinking!

We had all agreed to take some smart clothes over to the US with us in case, and we actually co-ordinated. We had smart trousers, white shirts and braces, or suspenders as I learned they were called in the states, after thinking we'd been insulted a couple of times, suspenders in the UK being what the Americans call garter belts. So, clean, looking great, and ready for fun, the three of us hit the town.......

.......and struggled to get in anywhere. We had left our passports in a lock up box at the hotel, and forgotten that being asked for ID is part of the thing over here. So we got knocked back from a couple of swanky looking places we had decided to try our luck at meeting girls in. We'd taken advice from a young lad throwing water out into the street for some reason by the hotel.

"Heyyyyyy" he said, cheerfully as we walked out." What's this, a group of bartenders out on the town?"

"Yep. Know anywhere good?"

"You guys looking for broads?"

He actually said that. I'd heard that in old films, and never realised people would still say broads. He even had the Italian Brooklyn accent to make it sound cool, unless people in Buffalo speak like that too. We told him we were, and headed off to the great sounding places we couldn't get in.

So we were stuck on the other side of town, and decided to try one last bar. It was some run down Irish looking place, but seemed cheerful. The waitress immediately said Hi guys, and asked for ID.

"Look," Ferret said, "We came out without any, and it's all the way back at our hotel. Can you give us a break...Mulligan here will buy you a drink."

She laughed, but said she was sorry, she'd have to see something, even if just from one of us.

"OK....how's this?"

Ferret unhooked a brace, and started dropping his trousers. I think we all stood still in shock, wondering what he thought she meant by showing her something.

But no...There on his thigh was a tattoo of a bulldog, with the words MADE IN BRITAIN, and his birthday round it. I didn't even know he had that.

She burst out laughing, and called the owner, a friendly looking guy, also wearing braces we noticed. "Can I take this? Go on, please...." she asked him, all the time giggling.

"What the hell! I've seen it all now. Hell yeah, you guys are good for a drink here."

So we enjoyed a few drinks, but certainly did not meet any broads, though Ferret insisted that the waitress had a thing for him. We met a few interesting locals who were mainly drunk, but friendly, and had a large bowl of Irish Stew each, then headed back to the hotel. Well, me and Ferret were ready to crash, but Brody grabbed his passport and headed back out. He told us the next day he'd gone to the bar next door, and hit the JD. Boy, he looked rough, even by his usually haggard looking standards.

Niagara Falls was pretty great. A local bus took us out there, and we crossed the Rainbow bridge into Canada. And people were right, it was a lot more impressive from the Canadian side, so good call. We went out on a boat called the Maid of the Mist, all wrapped up in blue macs. Brody said he was feeling pretty rough, and sat down on one of the benches. Most people were standing to get the view. The boat went up and down, and we were showered in cold water, and it was a real hell of an experience.

"Wow, this is something, eh?" I asked Brody. But to no reply. He was asleep. Somehow, whilst having the equivalent of a hundred buckets of cold water thrown over him, and the feeling of being on a runaway rocking horse, he managed to pass out. We woke him up when it was time to get off the boat.

"You've missed the falls."

"Fuck it, I'll buy a postcard.."

We took a little wander around Niagara, which was mainly tourist shops, of course, next to the falls, and looked at the various knick-knacks on sale. Snow globes seemed very popular. I remarked to Ferret at one point how stupid they looked, and why they needed to show the falls in snow anyhow. I'd noticed no matter where I'd ever been, except for Russia, there had always been snow globes on sale. I'd imagine that if there is a tourist shop in Death Valley, they have a snow globe with a desert in it, and the sort of odd, easily pleased people who say, "Hey, a snow globe.....I gotta have that!" would buy it.

A spot of lunch and a beer, and we began musing. After all, we'd crossed the border into Canada, why go straight back? Ferret's view was that we had paid for a room in the Hotel Lafayette that night, so best not to waste the money. Plus, he'd been strangely quiet, I'd noticed. Knowing him from home as I did, I guessed it would be to do with the fact he had a number from the girl in the Goth club, as he tended to be a bit of an idiot like that. Brody wandered off to the bus station, and came back with the news that we could easily get to Toronto.

"It's not far, a couple of hours on the bus, and it's still early enough to get one. No need to book."

"Cool....I'm all for it...."

"Not me," Ferret said, "I'm going to head back to New York."

I was right, he'd got his lovey-dovey head on, and became focused on getting a date with the girl from the club. We tried to talk him out of it, but to no avail. Brody commented that there was probably a direct bus to New York.

"I'll go back to Buffalo first, then head down in the morning."

"Why not just go direct? Sleep on the bus?

"Because we've already paid for the room."

That was Ferret, alright. He was prepared to travel all the way down state as he had a phone number and a crush, but not to lose out on his money for a room.

110

We had another beer, then went to the station. Ferret caught the bus back, and Me and Brody waited for the Toronto bus.

"Shit", he suddenly exclaimed, "Just got to nip back to that bar. Back in a mo....."

"What's up?"

Apparently, he'd bought a snow globe and left it on his seat.

VIII

Brody stole a Frisbee from a Rock Star.

Well, not quite. We arrived in Toronto, it was still late afternoon and the sun was mighty hot. We wished we hadn't got our bags, as though we had travelled light, they were still a nuisance. We decided on looking round town for a room, and heading to a record shop or something to find out if there were any gigs on that night. Well, we fell on our feet with that one.

Walking through town, we saw crowds gathering near what turned out to be the main HMV shop. Naturally we were curious, and joined in the gathering. It turned out that no one less than Alice Cooper was about to play on the roof, promoting his new Album, Hey, Stoopid. I was never especially into Rock Music as such, or rather, what I classed as Rock. It's a subjective topic and no two rock fans will ever agree on what is rock. In fact, I think the expression rock fan is a contradiction in terms. Though they look like a genre-following group, what with the black t-shirts and everything, I found that most of them mainly think in terms of two types of rock. These are (1) rock bands that they like and consider as being real rock, no matter who they are, and (2) rock bands they don't like and consider as being shit for poseurs. No real middle ground there. But yes, I knew of Alice Cooper as he had been around since I was a kid, but I did not really know much of his music until recently. Coincidently his last album had a couple of tracks I had been playing in my club, as many of the Alternative crowd were growing their hair, donning headbands and drifting towards the new Glam Rock sounds spear-headed, seemingly by the likes of Guns 'n' Roses, Motley Crew, etc. Alice fitted in nicely.

And there he was, larger than life, stood on a roof in front of us. Cable TV had become quite a thing over here, which is a shame as he could have had a look at their aerial while he was up there, just in case. Then at the end of his show, which was pretty damned fine to be honest, he threw a few Frisbees into the crowd, one of which Brody caught. Feeling quite pleased with ourselves, we decided on a drink, and found a bar not far away with a whole bunch of rock looking people sitting outside, no doubt telling each other why the bands the other guy liked were shit. In we went, just for just a quick drink, you know, maybe just a snifter of port, or a sip of sherry and perhaps a small beer just to refresh, then we would seek out digs for the night, and come back out.

Well that plan seemed to go strangely wrong. We got chatting to some great people who had some great advice for things to do in Toronto, all of which we forgot. Being so warm and bright, we didn't notice the time go by, until we met a couple of rockabilly girls who told us about a club they were heading to later, and told us to join them. We figured one more drink, then definitely find ourselves some digs, before going on to that club, somewhere called, I think, The Night Gallery. Anyhoo, I have no idea why we didn't look for digs but in the end we were checking our bags into the cloakroom of the club, and enjoying some great music. The girls showed up, and I decided to show off my dancing skills, which was an odd plan as I'd never really had any.

And dance like an eejit I did indeed, to a lot of peoples amusement, and for my finale managed to forget there was a step up to the dance floor, and went arse over tip off the floor, and landed in a heap at the foot of a wobbly rock bar table with unmatching chairs around it, and there I was at the feet of a large, fat gay guy in a blue flowery shirt who drew a sympathetic sharp intake of breath, and said,

"Ooooo....Are you alright?"

Now, even drunk I had a strange flashback moment to the time I fell off my bike in Maastricht, and landed at the feet of a large fat gay guy in a flowery shirt who also asked me if I was alright. I swear, it looked like the same bloke. I nodded that I was OK, which I was, other than my pride, and looked round for my companions who were in absolute stitches of laughter naturally, and began to laugh at myself. I looked at the people sitting around, took a bow, and joined the others.

It did the trick. We were snogging the girls, and got an invite back to one of their flats. And, if my memory serves me correctly, we had one hell of a night. Even if the finer details were a little sketchy.

So, the next afternoon when we woke up, the girls had already left for work, apparently, and left a note saying to eat what we wanted, and they would meet us in another bar but not that night as they had dates, but definitely the next night. Fair enough. We got clean, ate, grabbed our luggage and headed out to find a room.

And almost immediately bumped into a guy we had met in the first bar who called himself Mad Psycho Dave, who suggested we go for a beer. Why not, we thought, it's a lovely day, let's grab a couple of beers, get a room, and explore more of the city. We didn't. We carried on drinking in different bars till late, and someone told us we could get a cheap room just up the road in the nearby Chinatown district, and so off we headed. We didn't find anywhere, and I suggested we head back to where we had been, but Brody said Chinatown couldn't be that big, so we might as well carry on the way we were going.

"Brody, it's the biggest ChinaTown in North America," I told him, remembering something someone had said.

"Nah. We are probably at the end of it."

"Why would you say that? Every sign in front of us as far as we can see is in fucking Chinese! Everyone we pass is fucking Chinese, and there is no sign of a hotel that we can see, because it might only be written in Fucking Chinese. Now let's go back."

Brody seemed to consider this for a moment. Seemed to.

"You don't know they are all Chinese."

That was it, we fell into a bit of a drunken scrap, which ended abruptly with us falling over a little wall, and into some hard, thorny bushes. We pulled ourselves out, laughed at the ridiculousness of it, then wandered back towards where we had come from.

We came to a park, and being veterans of sleeping rough, and also feeling too drunk and too tired to keep wandering around, we spotted some wood near some steps, and began to build a little shelter. By that, we meant propping sheets of wood against the steps in case it rained. We had just finished, and about to put our heads down when out of the dark, a couple of torch beams came glaring at us. It was two policemen.

"What do you guys think you are doing"

We explained. We'd arrived, not got a room, and were going to bed down. We would move on.

"You can't really sleep in this park", one of the policemen explained cheerfully. It was apparently the homosexual gathering point in the wee small hours and they suggested it was not the safest place to be passing out. "But we can help you."

I guess that they thought our lack of a roof over our head was due to a lack of funds as much as stupidity and they took us to a local Salvation

Army Emergency Shelter. They seemed to know the guy at check in, and got us a couple of bunks in a dorm.

"Don't worry about the cost," The cheerful cop told us, "This ones on the Toronto police."

Next day we headed out, thanked the Hostel people, and went and got ourselves a room at last.

"I knew that was a gay park," Brody mused as we had a cup of coffee in the hotel lobby.

"Well, you didn't say anything."

"You could tell. Not one bloke we walked past was wearing a suit, not one. A sure sign."

"FFS, not that again."

We wandered down town, and ended up at the HMV shop we had saw Alice Cooper performing upon when we arrived. Everywhere we had been had been excellent, but we decided we wanted to see if there was anywhere a bit Punkier, or Goth-ish maybe, as most places so far had been rock based. Which, in fairness, was more the norm these days everywhere. So we asked one guy in there if he knew of any good Alternative clubs to go to.

"Er, yeah," he muttered apprehensively, "There's the Lizard Lounge. It's about as alternative as it gets."

"Lizard Lounge, eh? Sounds good to us. Where is it?"

He told us, and we clocked it, had a couple of drinks, something to eat, went up the CN Tower, and back for a snooze. There was a slight nip in the air later, so we donned our leather jackets and headed out. By this time in life, I was no longer wearing studded or painted leathers, just plain old black. Same with Brody. I was getting past the days of dressing in a way that meant I was being restricted as to where I went, but hey, you still couldn't beat a good old biker jacket. Even if it was just a fashionable one.

We weren't sure of the way, so stopped and asked a couple of people including a large policeman, all of whom hesitated before telling us. "It's kinda wild in there", one guy told us forebodingly. "It's an alternative club, you know."

"That's exactly why we are going." I beamed back.

And we arrived at the club, and were impressed before we got to the door. There were Harleys parked outside, and bikers sitting around, some great looking punky girls in fishnets and ripped gear, and loud heavy industrial music pounding from the door. There was a queue going up some stairs which we gleefully joined, passports for ID ready with the glee lasting only till we got to the bouncer at the door.

"Sorry guys. Not tonight."

"What? Why not?"

"It's the leather."

"Ah, come off it," I argued," Just about everyone here is wearing leather."

" I know. You're not wearing enough leather. It's fetish night tonight. No jeans."

Perhaps a little naively and a little late, the penny dropped. Those bikers. A lot of them had those Freddy Mercury type moustaches. And the hot punk girls? Yep. They weren't girls. The bouncer read our faces and grinned.

"I see," I said. "Alternative club means something different here, doesn't it? We were looking for a kind of punk bar."

"No problem, guys," he laughed. Hell, Canadians are friendly. "I figured it was that. Hey, you're all right on other nights, if it's your bag, but meanwhile, there is a late bar just round the corner you might find more comfortable."

We went round the corner, walked in, and got called over by the two rockabilly girls from the other night.

"There you guys are," one of them called over. "We thought you'd forgotten about us."

We had.

We didn't get to go back to our hotel after all, the one night that we actually had one to go back to, but at least our bags were safe. We recovered them the next day, after swapping numbers with the girls, and headed on back to New York.

IX

We didn't get back to Port Authority till late, and we learned what a scary place that could become at night. Beggars everywhere, people offering to carry our bags, other guys telling us they had a cab outside. And no bus to Jake's town till the morning, so we found an all-night bar, and alternated between beer and coffee, as we did not want to get to the house in a shocking state.

We called ahead, and got there in the morning. There was a bit of an air about the place. Ferret had been there all this time, and despite trying numerous times had not got through to the girl from the goth club. Jake seemed a bit off, so I caught him alone in the garden later that day and asked him what was up.

"Look, it's my parents' house. They are not young, my sister isn't well, and they didn't expect three of you. They are finding it a bit tough, and well, I'm working and really can't keep taking you guys out at night. I'm sorry, it's just a bit tricky, but they won't say anything..."

I got it. He was right. Their hospitality had been impeccable and the warmth genuine. So I spoke to the others, and suggested we use the rest of our time and head off. We decided to go the other direction, and head to Florida. So at dinner that day, we informed the family that we had enjoyed every minute, but we had decided to head down south, and due to time would probably head back up straight to Newark to fly home. Everyone was saying no, you must stay here, and are you sure, and we will miss you, but in no time at all the mood in the house was lighter, and instead of going into New York, me and Brody wandered down to a local bar, Monaghan's, that night. Ferret was still moping and trying the number he had, so stayed in.

In fact, being the tight ass with money he was, he missed out. We went in the bar, got a drink, and the owner, a large biker type guy, asked us where we were from, and when we said the UK, he greeted us cheerfully and we found ourselves chatting merrily to him and the other locals. They'd heard some English guys were staying with Jake's family up the road, and they knew the family well. We didn't pay for another drink all night long, and on hearing we were going to Florida, people started making calls for us to flights people, railway people, car hire, etc. Seems the best price was the ol' Greyhound bus again, and we could get one the day after tomorrow. We finally left, after a friendly argument about giving a tip, and told everyone back at the house over breakfast that we had reserved seats, and we'd be off.

On a whim, I called the number of the other girl that we met in the Goth club, possibly to see if I could stop Ferrets moping. Hell, she actually answered! Seemed that the first girl had tried to call, but somehow Ferret had given her the wrong number. Hmmmm. Maybe. She told me to give her an hour and she'd ring back. She did, and we had dates for our last night. They said they would even bring their friend to meet Brody. Poor girl.

The change in Ferret was remarkable. We were apparently taking them to dinner in a Chinese place they knew in queens, and would meet us outside the subway station. Off we went, and had nearly given up after waiting an hour when they pulled up in a car driven by Laura, the current crush of Ferret's life. We arrived in the restaurant, and had a great time, the girls laughing at our various shenanigans, like how we'd all bought the same cheap watch and set the alarm for every hour so we could BEEP in unison, and an interesting incident when Ferret noticed that the girls were eating with chopsticks, and decided to try some. He turned round to a Chinese guy walking past, and asked him to bring him some chopsticks.

"No." came the reply.

"But I want to try them.."

"Not my problem"

"What? I'm politely asking you to bring me some chopsticks."

"No."

"Why not?"

"Because I'm a guest."

We looked round, and sure as heck there was a large Chinese family group sat at the next table, which he went and joined. This really kicked the laughter off. And so it went till the end of the evening. The girls weren't 21, but had told us they knew a bar that would take their false ID, and the plan was to head out to this place afterwards. That was until the bill came. The girls had gone to the bathroom, and Ferret suddenly told us he thought we were being skanked.

"I think they are going to try to get us to pay all of the bill."

"So what?"

"That's been it all along. Their plan"

The girls got back, we got the bill, and Me and Brody both put a third of it on the table. Ferret, meanwhile, worked out exactly what he had spent, and put that on the table to the cent. There was an awkward silence, and Laura ended up getting out a credit card, and paying her share. The girls had fallen silent, and both me and Brody were going a bit red. We quietly left, and walked over to the girl's car.

"So..." Said Ferret cheerfully. "Are we going to that bar then"

"Er, no," the girl I had been with answered, "We have to go. We'll drop you at the subway."

This put Ferret in a sulk, and for the life of him he could not see what had just happened. So he pouted. We were only a few minutes' drive from the subway and pulled up right outside. Me and Brody, in the back with our two dates that were no longer dates, said polite goodbyes, and were getting out, when I saw Ferret who was in the front about to get out the car, when unbelievably, Laura leaned over to kiss him. And he missed it. He got out, muttered goodbye, and the girls drove off. Well, that was Ferret. He travelled halfway down a continent, called constantly, finally got a date with the girl, then wouldn't throw in $15 or so for her meal. He also blamed the girls for leading us on. I didn't tell him that Laura had tried to kiss him. I thought that would be funnier on the plane.

We were headed to Daytona Beach, which Ferret had heard of as they run some quite famous beach races there, or so I'm told, sport or cars not being ever on my radar. Well, it was a hell of a trip on the Greyhound, though a great way of seeing places, especially after we started getting more and more south and were not just looking at free-ways. The drivers changed from time to time, and we noticed a change in how they were, especially the more south we got. The stops we made got longer and longer, and we learned that "You have 45 minutes here" in reality meant however long the driver fancied. It paid to go with the flow and you didn't really have much of a choice.

Ferret to driver at rest stop. " 'Scuse me, what time do we get into Jacksonville?"

"About 7 or 8. Or maybe 9. Who knows."

"Can you be a bit more specific?"

"You boys on vacation?"

119

"Yes. Yes we are."

"Dun't really matter whut time y'all git there then."

We missed the connection to Daytona.

However, we found another bus going to Miami. It had spaces, but we had to buy new tickets, much to Ferret's annoyance. We had a bit of time, and had a wander around Jacksonville. Seemed that that laid back attitude spread to the shops there too.

Ferret to guy in store. "I like this t-shirt...Do you have a larger size?

Guy on stool beside the counter. "Probably."

Silence.

"Er, can you get me one?"

"I could. But that'd mean gittin' up and going in the back to look. And I'm not really in a mind to."

"Oh. OK. Thanks anyway.

Ferret didn't get the T-shirt.

Passing through the smaller towns , we couldn't help but notice that as you got out of the centre, the housing got poorer and poorer, and also blacker. We would hear of the poverty divide in some places over here back home, but we could actually see it now. Yet sometimes the centres looked very picturesque. There was at that time inequality in regards to wealth back home too, but I'd never really seen it on such a large scale. Usually in the UK, as you went out of town, the suburbs would be more affluent as you reached the countryside, but then the scale of places is completely different here.

And we finally arrived. And boy, were we the English guys abroad! We got a pretty cheerful motel called the Si-Si, the weather was fantastic, and so after checking in we showered up and hit the beach straight away. We were wandering along by the sea, when I spotted a couple of seriously well-built surfer looking guys running down the beach toward us at some speed. What was this, I wondered?

"Hey....Hey guys" they called as they neared us, sounding cheerful and friendly enough.

"Hi?"

"You guys English?" (did the pasty pure white skin give it away?)

"We are..."

They looked at each other smiling, with a 'we knew it' look about them. "We thought so. Do you have any drugs for sale?"

Not sure what rep the Brits have here, but they looked both surprised and disappointed when I told them that we did not. Brody looked both surprised and disappointed that he had none to sell them. They chatted, and then took their bronzed, muscular bodies off for another run in their search for narcotics. We took our sun-blindingly white skinny but with podge's bodies off for a paddle.

And you know, we had a great time down there. We found some great music clubs, even catching a show by Buddy Miles one night. We had all got a bit more money left than we had originally thought we would have, mainly due to Jake's family's hospitality, and sleeping on buses and hostels by accident. The waitresses in some of the bars were possibly some of the most beautiful women I had ever seen....

Brody and Ferret seemed to develop a passion for exploring surf shops, of which there were plenty. However, at no point did it occur to either of them to actually try surfing, but they did both leave with matching surf shirts. I believe Ferret also had a snow globe with a plastic surfer catching a wave inside it. We spent the best part of a week there, and not one of us caught even the slightest hint of a tan. We even secured a date one night, and went out and bought matching Hawaiian shirts, which at the time we thought would be hilarious. We never found out, as the girls didn't show up, and we told Ferret to throw the phone number he had away. Then we took the long coach back to Newark, and it was home, sweet home.

X

I can't remember exactly when as a kid I stopped going round to my friends' houses and asking if they were coming out to play. I'm also not sure when the bikes got locked up in the shed, to be hardly used again, and instead we would meet up to do other things that we no doubt considered very grown up, but were in fact really just the tail end of

121

childhood. But the change happened at some point as we were growing up, and so it should.

The journeys around Europe had been during a kind of carefree period of my life that drew to an end as responsibilities crept into life. I'd experimented with youth politics, worked hard, and just followed the flow till I'd ended up at the Post office. I had no real interest in any kind of career as such, (well, maybe a wee yen to run a pub one day), but the Djing in the nightclub was still going strong, which I loved, and I was quite happy to walk around posting letters, till without realising the influence of my more recent journeys, began doing union work as a rep, all the time still managing to get up to no end of shenanigans in between

But the seed had now long been planted to get out and see even more of the world. Part of the desire to travel has got to be the urge to explore. We may not be going into the Amazon, or deepest Congo, but never-the-less we are still heading out into the unknown, and that is one of the most exciting feelings you can ever have.

To this point, without realising, I'd always travelled with friends or colleagues, and though we had great shared experiences, I was realising that being together 24/7 with anyone can get tense, and no two people take the same interpretation of the shared experiences back with them. For some, it was just a bit of one-off fun, others use what they have picked up wisely, maybe even seeing the world a little bit differently. And some, like me, can hardly wait to be out on the road again.

I'd often mention this urge to go heading off again, and plenty of friends would always say, Hey, let's go to Spain, or, I'll go back to America/Russia/ Amsterdam with you. But I think I'd reached a point where at the back of my mind I knew that I was going to stop calling for my friends and asking if they were going out to play. I didn't really want to revisit the same places again. Or rather, I did, but knew there were plenty of other places I wanted to get out and see, even if I didn't know where they were yet. So it was time to put on my big boy pants and get ready to head out alone. And realistically, it was only ever going to be a matter of time till something turned up.

Part 3
A Foreign Posting

I

I was a year late for work once.

It was only a matter of time till something turned up. I was still working at the Post office, along with Ferret and a few other good friends and was renting a house in my usual stomping ground of Hillfields in the city. I still DJed, went out for all manner of shenanigans on the weekends, and ticked by quite nicely. But there was a little niggle in me, an itch that needed to be scratched, though not the type I brought back from Amsterdam. And then, looking through a music paper one day, an advertisement jumped out at me.

Bridge the World. I liked the name alone. I read on, and it was a company that specialised in putting round-the-world flight tickets together. Round the world? The whole one? This was it. It showed a few examples and the one that stared at me was India, Nepal, Thailand, Malaysia, Singapore, Indonesia, Australia, Hawaii, Los Angeles then back. The route could be tweaked and twiddled, but why on earth would you want to do that? I phoned up and made the enquiries, and it was not as expensive as I thought it would be. (I'd taken the 'From £whatever' with a pinch of salt). Of course, it meant saving money to actually

123

survive out there, and we were quite the spenders on beer on the weekends! So, I hit the overtime at work, big time.

This meant covering post rounds when other people were on holiday, or off ill, and in all weathers. It wasn't a problem. Some days I would be tired, and ready to go home and then someone would say, oh, North 22 needs covering, and I'd be out there delivering again. All the time, I would be pushing letters through doors and thinking, every letter a mile. Every letter a mile. Every letter a mile. It worked. I tucked the money away, till I figured I had about enough to keep me going for a couple of months, then phoned up the charming Australian girl at Bridge the World, and booked my tickets. As before, I took all my annual holiday allowance together, and booked a couple of months unpaid leave, which they gave me reluctantly, but gave it to me never-the-less.

Whilst doing this extra work, I took up with a girl from Birmingham who promptly moved herself into my house and seemingly didn't believe in working for a living. Within no time at all she was planning what nicer part of the city we could move into, which would apparently be no problem as I had saved up a lot of money. The fact I was heading off round the planet just seemed to go over her head and she just said we'd move when I got back. I gave up explaining that the money was for travelling and let her carry on looking at the property guide in between her favourite afternoon TV shows. She also had what could be called a strained relationship with telling the truth about anything, so it came as no surprise that when I told her that I had ended the tenancy on the house, which I had told her I was going to do from the start, that we had a blazing row about where she would live. I told that if she got a job, she could carry on living there, but I couldn't pay the rent for months on end and all the bills, etc., while I was gone. This was, she told me, simply not an option. Apparently, she went on, I knew the reasons she could not work. In fact, I did not. But over the next few days a list of rare ailments, health problems, sexism, stress problems, anxiety problems, a bad back, one leg shorter than the other and numerous other reasons emerged, just short of alien abduction. Though she may have said alien abduction, I'm not sure. The answer to her problems, she explained, was simple, I would have to cancel my holiday.

Holiday. Out of everything she said, calling the adventures and shenanigans I had planned out in my mind a holiday was the worst of the lot!! I guess, technically, not being at work and going abroad could be seen as a holiday to some, but hell, that wasn't it. That wasn't it at all. I was going to explore, to learn new things, to see crazy places and people. In no way did I see it as a holiday, which I associated – and still do – with beaches and bars and bath towels. So we argued every day and the reasons for me not to go got more desperate.

"I'm surprised she hasn't tried to say she's pregnant" Ferret said to me and some of my friends on the post in the pub after work one afternoon. "It's about the only thing she hasn't bullshitted about yet."

I got home, and she announced that she was pregnant. Well, finally she was out of bullshits.

II

You only really need a good toothbrush.

I did my last day at work, the girl moved back with her parents, I moved my possessions to my Mum and Dad's respective houses, who by this time were divorced but still friends, and packed my stuff. I'd picked up an army kit bag, and stuffed it with new shorts, shirts, jeans, smart clothes, travel Iron, towel, and an incredible amount of other stuff that I knew that a good traveller would need. I wisely decided on a little bum bag too, for my passport, travellers cheques, flight tickets and oddly, a little travel toothbrush that folded in on itself that someone gave me. Though the advert had read it was a round-the-world ticket, it was in fact a whole bunch of individual one way tickets. In later years, with the coming of the internet, virtually anyone can organise this themselves and you probably could with a lot of phone calls and time back then too, but the agent ensured it was the cheapest tickets to everywhere, so there were a lot of night flights and such. My first flight was fairly early, but luckily not too bad, and anyway, who cared.

And come the night before, out I went for one last night drinking with the lads for a while. You know, a snifter of port, or a sip of sherry and perhaps a small beer, just to refresh. However, it didn't seem to go quite like that, instead we got incredibly drunk, and I was barred from one of the regular clubs we drank in after we got in a bit of a brawl, and crashed at my friend Bok's house as arranged as I'd handed the keys to my house back to the letting agent. Over the night we had the usual shenanigans: it seemed Ferret fancied some girl, but she wasn't interested, Dan complained that him and his girlfriend were arguing all the time and he was thinking of finishing it, and Bok was cheating on his wife. Oh, and everybody's job sucked and they were thinking of getting another one, so I was to let them know when I was going on my next journey after this, as they were jolly well coming with me next time.

I missed the coach. I have no idea how, I was sure I was on time, but it was gone. This left me in a pickle and a hell of a panic. A few phone calls, and another friend came in his car and drove me down to Heathrow. I just about made the check-in. I was running through security, and put all my bits on the conveyor, but somehow managed to leave behind the quite expensive camera I had bought especially for the trip. Well, this was going bloody well, wasn't it.

There was a little compensation, though. A rather sweet looking girl, with short hair and the sort of glasses that give off that 'I look innocent but I'm hot as hell in the bedroom' kind of impression got chatting to me on the plane after a mix up with the seats. Seemed she was travelling alone to India too, and we went and got something to eat together at Moscow airport, where we had to change. Well, we changed but it hadn't and the food was no great shakes: but I decided to have a pint of Guinness.

"Do you drink Guinness then?"

"Nope, not at all. I'm not really a drinking man" I lied.

"Why are you drinking it then?"

"Well, according to everybody, the best pint of Guinness in the world is supposed to be served here, at Moscow airport. It's to do with the water it's brewed with or something. Even Guinness has it top of their list of the best places to drink it. So I thought I'd see for myself."

"Really ? And is it better?"

"You know, I have no idea. I don't know what it's supposed to taste like."

I hadn't really thought that one through.

We'd got talking to another girl, a white girl dressed up in some over the top Hari Krishna clothes heading out to find herself. Which, as it turned out, was a sight I was going to see quite a lot of over there. We were all close enough to chat to each other on the plane and at one point decided we would share a cab down to the centre of New Delhi and look for digs. I was to later learn about the lonely planet and Rough Guide books that were the backpackers bibles' back then. But at this point, none of us had any idea that these existed, so we just decided to find a hotel.

Well, that was the plan. Naturally, it went wrong and my bag never came off the plane, which caused me to panic yet again. The girls waited with me and I went to all the unhelpful kiosks, only to be told to come back tomorrow when it might have arrived. Maybe they thought it would buy its own ticket and catch me up?

So I found myself in India, the furthest I had ever been from home, with a bum bag that luckily contained my documents, including my vaccination certificates, the clothes I was wearing and a toothbrush. A little bit worried, we caught a cab, found a cheap hotel, and arranged to meet up in the morning, as it was quite late by now. The bed was crawling with insects, the shower didn't work and I had no clean clothes. Yet it didn't matter. I was in India, I was on the road again, and on that single day the Post office, the girlfriend, the lads and everything else seemed to fade out of my mind and it felt like I'd stepped onto a plane at Newark, USA, and got off at New Delhi.

I did go to the airport the next day, but with no luck. I filed a lost property report, wrote a letter to my insurance company, and never heard from either ever again.

I've seen people freak out over lost luggage over the years but I found I learned a valuable lesson about 'stuff'. I picked up a cheap small bag, a couple of t-shirts, and some underpants. Now they were a treat. I could only find what struck me as 50's or 60's style huge white cotton undies, that I remember drying on the fireguard with the other washing when I was a kid. Well, beggars can't be choosers, and to be honest, they were quite comfy. Between my little knapsack, and my bum bag, It took me no more than a couple of days to realise that I had, in fact, been liberated. I simply did not need any of the other stuff I had brought. Once the annoyance of losing it wore off, which was surprisingly quickly, I found that I was really quite happy about having very little. It was to be a long way down this trip before I bought proper clothes again. Instead, for the next few months I lived in shorts and t-shirts, rinsing them out at night and they would be dry in the morning. For the rest of my life, I never put anything in an aeroplane hold ever again and I never took more than I could pack in a bag that I could carry onto a plane.

The Hari Krishna girl headed off on her search for herself the next day, and me and Sharon, the first girl from the plane, picked up a few more waifs and strays by hanging around an area called Connaught place, a kind of business centre that also contained a large park and a market. There was Mark, an Australian guy, Freddy, another English girl who had brought the heaviest bag in the world, as she filled it with books assuming, wrongly, that she would be on her own a lot, a Frenchman called Francis and later Joey, an Irish chap from a small village, who had never been out of Ireland before, but had decided to head off to India to find a wife.

Like Freddy and myself, we all learned a lesson about luggage I think. She had thought that as she was travelling alone she would have lots of time on her hands, so would need lots of books to pass this time. In fact, all of us in this little crowd had never travelled alone before, so we all had our ideas and misconceptions of what it would be like.

Unless you want to be, you are never alone when you travel. Most travellers and backpackers tend to arrive in certain places, where an ever changing community of like-minded and interesting people would thrive and intermingle at any time. So long as you are sociable enough, you will fall in with a group of people remarkably quickly. And for that small moment in time, you are the greatest of friends, you look out for each other, you have each other's backs, and you have the absolute time of your lives. Then, especially in the pre-internet days, you swapped addresses so as to write but probably didn't, and agreed you'd all meet up again one day, which you also probably wouldn't. Then you went your separate ways on your travels and arrived at your next destination and would be sitting in a cafe and find yourself talking to another traveller because your omelette went to his table by mistake or something, and soon you would be with your next crowd of the greatest friends you ever had.....

We'd moved from the hotel we'd started in and had found ourselves a youth hostel. By this time nearly all youth hostels around the world were available to all ages, but we were only allowed to stay for a maximum of 5 days for some reason. But it was a good starting base. We hung out near the park, which was nice, but also meant an incredible amount of entrepreneurs constantly coming over to us. There was a guy, for example, who offered us a Cup of tea. I said yes, and he came back, 10

128

minutes later with a china cup and saucer. He waited while I drank the tea and then went off with the cup. Another guy would come up with one banana for sale. This went on a lot, with various odd items, including one sandal once. My favourite though, was an old Sikh who came up one day with a little notebook in his hand and told us he was the best at his job. We asked him a couple of times what that job was, but instead of telling us, he kept showing us the book. So I had a look, read the glowing reviews from happy backpackers, and said to him,

"You clean ears?"
"Yes sir. I am the best ear cleaner in New Delhi."
"But you clean ears?"
"Yes sir."

Well, sometimes the sense of the ridiculous gets the better of you and I decided it was time for an ear clean. So, he produced a set of instruments that I'm sure were about as sterilised and hygienic as you'd expect in a park, then proceeded to take his time and used long tweezers with cotton wool and scrapers, and other strange unknown things to thoroughly clean my ears. He told me there was a lump of really tight hard stuff in there and that it would cost more to take it out, but the fear of a perforated eardrum kept me off that one. Strange thing was, I really enjoyed it. It was a very relaxing and pleasant experience, apart from the fact he kept showing me lumps of dirt he'd allegedly pulled out. I was a bit sceptical about that, I'm sure my ear isn't actually that big. So, I paid him, wrote a glowing review in his little book and went on to believe I heard things a lot better that day. I also went on to be the target of every ear cleaner in the city after that too. I would be standing looking in a window and suddenly become aware of someone peering into my ear next to me. All of who could apparently see this lump of tight, hard material in there, and offered to get it out urgently. I knew this was part of the game, but even so, it was said to me so many times that the next time I went to the doctors about something unrelated after I got back home, I asked him to check, just in case. He assured me that there was nothing stuck in my ear and asked if I'd been talking to the ear cleaners in Asia.

We eventually moved into a place with a couple of shared rooms, and discovered the joy of rooftop drinking. The nights were warm, the roofs were flat, and we'd sit up there with beer or wine and chat a lot at night. Other travellers would be on other roofs, and sometimes we'd invite people over or be invited over to theirs. One night we were sitting with a couple of American guys who were over here as environmental economists. On asking what that was, they explained that they were there looking at the economic impact of America on the country. In fact, up to now, every American I had met there was seemingly there to look at the impact of America on something or other and the conversation would usually drift on to America's influence on the world and such. I couldn't be bothered listening to it again, had an early night and woke up at a stupidly early time.

Unable to go back to sleep, I went for a walk. It was about 4.00am and as I hit the main roads, everything was busy. I stopped by a vendor and bought a cup of char, which was tea brewed up with milk and sugar already in it and wandered around. I hadn't done this so early yet, and was in for a taste of New Delhi that wasn't as sweet as the other experiences so far. Lying on the floor in all directions were the poor. The really poor. Like I'd never seen in my life. They were asleep, sometimes as families on worn out blankets on the street, and in some of the carts I'd seen the market vendors using. Some of these people were like living skeletons. Around them, other people were going about their business, setting up stalls or whatever, seemingly oblivious to their plight. I guess you don't see them after a while. I was very taken aback. This was a vast amount of people, along many streets. I walked back along there later and they were gone, and it was business as usual. There were carcasses of animals to be butchered lying on the floor where earlier there had been humans barely existing. I had no idea where they all went. Where they would go to spend the day. I still don't.

We'd head out to various things to see, with the intention that we should really go to the Taj Mahal. One of the must see sights, it is only about 3 hours on the train from Delhi. We picked a day, and went to the station, where I figured I could pick up a ticket to Kathmandu while I was there. I was already realising that the time I had given myself for this trip was going to be tight. I'd imagined whizzing from place to place, taking in everything I could, and picking up the obligatory embroidered patch. I had not, in my naivety, figured on hanging out with new friends, and simply relaxing on rooftops. Relaxing, in fact, hadn't been in the plan at all. The station was manic, with people jostling all around the couple of ticket kiosks. An official looking man came up to us and said there was a special air conditioned office for tourists only to buy tickets. We liked the sound of that, and up the stairs we went . This would be much better.

This was much worse. We were pleased to see that there were only 9 people in front of us. Only myself, Sharon and Mark had gone down, as we were going to get the tickets for the whole group. And it was indeed air conditioned and quite posh compared to the mosh pit of the downstairs station. However, we got our first taste of Indian bureaucracy in action. We'd already observed when checking into places the endless filling in of forms, all handwritten and in triplicate. Even with only 9 people in front of us, it took 2 ½ hours to get to the desk. 2 ½ hours!! They had moved into the computer age, which in India meant putting everything onto numerous forms on the PC, and then filling out the usual triplicate paperwork by hand anyway. It also seemed that I had got a third class ticket, which I was assured by the others was a pretty bad idea.

Next stop for me was the bank to cash a travellers cheque. I told the others I would catch them up and popped into a bank, where I figured that I couldn't go wrong with American Express. But the first bank said they could not cash it, and so did the second one I tried. It was someone in the third bank that told me I could only cash it in the American Express office, which I then had to find. When I got there, they filled lots of forms out in triplicate, then put it all onto computer. I stopped for a bite to eat by a little stall on the way out and got talking to a French girl who was travelling across by motorbike. She was staying in a small village near Delhi, and asked if I fancied seeing it. I did, and off we went. It was fair to say that things went well and I didn't get back that night. Sharon had all the train tickets to Agra, so I caught a bus back the next day intending to catch the group at the Station. However, the bus stopped about halfway back and the driver went to sleep. A car eventually pulled up and another driver got in and told us the first feller had been drunk, so he would carry on. I was melting, and hadn't brought any water, but some little kid on seeing the stationary bus turned up with bottles of coca cola to sell at a rather high price. I didn't even haggle. In the end, I completely missed the others, so I decided to go by myself the next day.

Well, that was the plan, but the girls had decided that they were going to travel south together, so we had a bit of a party for them after going for a meal in quite a posh hotel. We were having a ball, and lots of waiters were standing at the table too, joining in the laughter as we shared tales of our shenanigans and at one point I mentioned buying underpants.

"And do you know all I could get?" I said, and pulled a pair out of my little bag, which I had brought. Everybody roared with laughter at the sight of the giant white Y-Front underpants. Everybody, that is except the waiters, who just looked at each other bemused, clearly not knowing why we were all falling about. We all realised at the same moment exactly what underwear they were all wearing right then.

Freddy reluctantly agreed she should shed a lot of her books, we drank a lot of wine, and we all woke up quite late, and feeling rough but had an afternoon breakfast with the girls before they went, so no amazing temple for me.

In fact, I never got there. Something always turned up. My original whistle stop plan was to see a couple of famous things in each country before moving on. The Taj Mahal was the first one. It is an incredible place, built to house the tomb of a 17th century emperor's favourite wife, and eventually himself. I wonder what happened to his not so favourite wives? I mean, did he build smaller, less famous tombs or did he just get the co-op to make the arrangements, like my Grandad did with his wife? It must have been a bit annoying for the others, watching the work coming on.

So there it was. I'd totally messed up the first part of my plan, and yet I was not, in fact, too concerned. There was a curry house back in Coventry called the Taj Mahal, so I joked that I would just go there when I got back, so as I could say I'd been. Oddly, I in fact did just that, but the food wasn't anywhere near as good as we were eating out here. There were plenty of postcards with its image on sale everywhere and if I really wanted, I had seen a quite detailed snow globe on sale so I knew what it looked like. And I can confidently say that the Taj Mahal is indeed the most splendid mausoleum in India that I have never been to.

Come the day before I was planning on heading off, I sat on a roof drinking wine with Joey, the Irish guy who had joined the group. Joey was the epitome of an Irish farmer, with the whole red faced ruggedness going on, the laid back attitude ,and he had been wearing one of two pairs of flannelled Indian pyjama suits that he had had since we met him. He had thought all Indians wore pyjamas on the street and wanted to blend in, even though most people we saw did not do that and he stood out like a sore thumb, especially as he wore a grey flat cap. It was, though, actually quite acceptable to wear pyjamas if you so wished, and he had even located a guy on the street round the corner who washed them for him every two days. In fact, I found out that pyjamas were actually brought to Europe from India by the British and Portuguese and the word itself derived from an old Persian word, the Persian Empire having also once ruled great areas of what is now India.

I liked Joey. He had an interesting perspective on the world. We were talking about passports one time, and how they were all European ones now. He offered his take on Ireland, Britain, and EEC.

" 1169. Since 1169, we fought and we died for our independence. And what did we do when we got it? Gave it to Europe, and we've all got the same bloody passports again anyway."

"I haven't got enough time" I said to him, that last night, reflectively.

"To get to Nepal?"

"Not just that, but yes, that too. I can get there, and rush through, but that's about it. Look at being here. I'm bumping into people who are travelling across just India alone for about a year. I have a few months to go around the world. Sure, I can see stuff, but what about this type of thing? Just sitting around, doing very little."

"You could just not go back? I gave up my job to come out here and look for a wife."

"How's that going?"

"Shite, to be honest. Not what I expected at all. Love the country though. But I'm heading on somewhere else to find a wife next, I think. Time to move on."

"Thailand? Somewhere like that?"

"No, I like the Indian women. Very beautiful. Somewhere I can meet one of them, I think."

"Pakistan? Bangladesh?

"No, Scotland. You get a lot of Indian women in Scotland."

Others came up and down on the roof over the evening, and I mused over my dilemma with everyone, sound-boarding off them all. I finally knew what to do and went down to the airline office the next day and changed my ticket from Kathmandu to Bangkok, for a ticket from New Delhi to Bangkok instead. I realised I had buggered up with time, and figured that I needed to drop one country in order to see more of the others.

Ticket changed, the remains of our group headed off to the Red Fort, in Old Delhi. Designed and built by the same architect and for the same

Emperor as the Taj Mahal, it had not fared so well. At some point the Persians had looted it on defeating the Mughal empire and then the British had dismantled a lot of the marble after an uprising. However, it had an impressive history, even if a lot of it was what seemed to be piles of rocks.

Walking around Old Delhi, the extreme poverty was more obvious, and the colourful bustle from where we were staying was replaced by a more desperate busyness. I was taken by the fact there were open urinals on the side of buildings where you just peed in public, with no shelter. I felt obliged to do this. A keen photographer, Mark's attention was grabbed by a man on the street with an old Victorian style box camera. He insisted we got a couple of photos taken, so he could watch the guy in action. Sure as, the feller took the photographs and developed them right there using a couple of built in drawers somehow. This was before digital and you had to drop your film into a photo shop or, oddly, a chemist to get your pictures and it took about a week, so it was pretty interesting to see this ancient instant technology. I still have the picture.

Francis was leaving, as his girlfriend arrived from France, and they were heading off to Goa. We were all about to go our separate ways in any case, and I was next. So we had a last night on the roof, and shared a couple of bottles of the local Rosy Pelican beer we had taken too, as my flight was in the early hours and I was heading straight up there. Those drinks lasted for hours, those drinks lasted for a moment. I decided to catch a rickshaw to the airport instead of a cab, the little black and yellow three wheelers that cost next to nothing to travel around it. It wasn't the money, I wanted to soak up the feel. The driver was reluctant, but I gave him the bulk of the money I had left, which was quite a sum in local currency. The air tasted disgusting as pollution was a real problem here and before getting out of the city, which was perpetually busy, we came to a roundabout where an elephant had sat down but the bloke riding it could not get it back up. It blocked the way for a while, but this was India. I smiled all the way to the airport, stopping only to spit the crap in the air out of my mouth once in a while.

I'm probably supposed to say that in hindsight I should have spent my time actually exploring India rather than just being based around Delhi: and indeed that would be very true. But in fact, I was also incredibly excited to be moving on and that feeling I'd experienced before, about heading into the unknown, was as thrilling and mind tingling as it could be. I had met a fantastic group of people and the whole time had been amazing, and yet it was only the start of this adventure. Indeed, some great shenanigans had been had already, but the world was waiting.

I was sure I was really travelling now and my confidence was up. Because in the couple of weeks immediately before heading out, I would be lying if I said I hadn't begun getting nervous and wondering if I'd done the right thing. It just seemed so damned scary, so hugely out of my comfort zone and the idea of facing it alone was dawning on me as it drew closer and became real. But as in any new, scary situation that we all face from time to time, I swallowed my nerves, dived in, and realised, Hell yes, I can do this. I can and have!

II

I once had no idea where on the planet I actually was.

I arrived at Bangkok airport, with no idea whatsoever of where I was going to go once I got out of customs. All I knew was to make sure that the taxi driver put on the meter wherever I was going. It doesn't take long before you realise that happy , smiley helpful taxi drivers at most airports are to be avoided at all costs. Always go for a miserable looking one, you are then at 50-50 that you will not be ripped off. I was reasonably lucky, the guy spoke good English and asked me if I was going to Khao San. Now, if there is one place known to all travellers and backpackers, it is the Khoa San Road, but not, at this time, to this eejit here. So I thought he was trying to tell me his cousin had a hotel till after much confusion he told me it was a place full of hippies. Many hippies. And so the Khoa San Road it was!!

My first impression was a huge WOW! Market stalls, small shops and travellers and yes, beaded hippies everywhere. This was fantastic. I walked along till I saw a sign in a small window saying rooms to let and went in. I found myself in a small hotel with a tiny counter and an elderly

Chinese lady at the desk. I booked for one night, at what I think was only a couple of quid in the local Baht. I got a small room with only a bed, a sink and a chest of drawers, but it seemed fine. There was a shower on the floor above that I used, as I seemed to have a kind of greasy sweat all over me, but then it had been quite a flight so I was bound to be a bit sticky.

It turned out that in Thailand, you can never really get rid of that strange sweat. Even straight after a shower, you feel like there is a layer of very thin greasy stuff on you. You just kind of get used to it. I had a nap and went out to explore. I found a little bar, had a couple of beers and then went back to my room for a good sleep. The sink made it perfect for rinsing my clothes at night, and they would be dry by the window in the morning. Or afternoon.

I felt refreshed but incredibly hungry. It occurred to me that I hadn't eaten since Delhi, so first things first. I saw a little garden cafe that looked nice, and looked at the menu. This is when I realised that I had no idea whatsoever about Thai food. The English translations were not a lot of help as being brought up on Irish cuisine meant potatoes. Any potatoes. Mash, boiled, roasted, chipped....There was no meal that did not involve a spud. Well, not till my mother managed to make a Spaghetti Bolognese once, which surprised not only herself but all of us too. This was spaghetti, but not the usual Heinz in tomato sauce. It was a radical move on her part, and we ate a lot of it after that. At least the spaghetti needed boiling, which was her primary cooking skill. She did try to do corn on the cob once. But after an hour and a half of her sticking a fork in it while it boiled, and not getting the familiar soft and mushy feel that equated to our vegetables, she gave up, threw them away and decided they must have been bad ones. We never got corn on the cob again.

I did recognise omelette and rice however, though that struck me at the time as a most unusual mix. Rice was the stuff that went with curries that we got from the Chinese Takeaway on birthdays. My Mum had tried doing rice a couple of times, but it usually took the non-stick of the cheap pans we had. I still never trust wild rice, as the black bits still remind me of that. But today I was hungry, and I ordered my breakfast and a cup of coffee. A waiter came out with what looked like my order and promptly put it down in front of a young traveller sitting at the next table, who smiled and told the guy he thought it was for me.

"Cheers, mate..."

"No problem," he said, in an Irish accent, "I think we all look the same to them."

I laughed, and he came over and joined me at the table.

"Name's Johnny"

"Mulligan. Or Rich. Take yer pick."

We got chatting, and it turned out that he'd been on the road for a good number of months. You could tell; when his breakfast came out, it sure as hell looked more appetising than my plain omelette on a heap of boiled rice. He also had a flyer that someone had given him for some kind of club nearby that was on later that evening and asked if I fancied it. I did indeed. So we arranged to meet up in a bar in his hostel, and we'd go from there. We had a couple of bottles of beer and went our ways till later.

The club turned out to be some kind of live music bar, but with no band. Anyone could get up and play. Nobody was doing this though, but we got talking to a couple of Dutch guys who were also staying at the same hostel as Johnny. And that is where I got my first taste of Mekong Whisky. One of the Dutch lads ordered a bottle, some cola and 4 glasses, and we shared till it was gone. I'm not normally a whisky drinker, but this stuff was not bad. In fact, it became the staple drink of choice most nights after that, usually a shared bottle with a group at a table in some bar or other. This first night though, the Dutch lads were heading to an all night club in the centre somewhere, and Johnny got talking to a Thai girl who came in and seemed to know him. I decided to head back to the Khao San Road.

Which is when I got lost. I thought I knew the way, and it wasn't far, but somehow I took a wrong turn I guess and found myself on a street I completely did not recognise. As I walked along, It occurred to me that not only did I not know how to get to the street where my digs were, I didn't really know where in Bangkok the street actually was, as The lads had said they were going to the centre, so I supposed the street was not in the centre. That chain of thought continued and I realised that if you showed me a map of Thailand, I would not be able to put my finger on Bangkok. Not even a guess. This was followed by considering that if I had such a map, say a map of Asia, I would not be able to pinpoint Thailand with any confidence. So that was it then. I was lost. Really lost. Not only did I have no idea where my hotel room was, I had no idea where on the planet I was, let alone how to find the street. And do you know what? I smiled. And then laughed. This was quite an incredible feeling...I couldn't actually be any more lost than I was at this moment.

I got a good couple of minutes of joy out of this, till I turned the next corner and found myself back on the street.

The Khao San road never sleeps. It is perpetually busy, and changes by the hour. There was a little travel agents along from my hotel, which I noticed that at closing time put all their leaflets and brochures under the counter and became a little bar instead. We used this a few times. And there was a shop near my hotel that sold nothing but towels, sold by a young Thai girl that was one of the prettiest women I had ever seen. I went past it a few days later and suddenly it was a shop selling bootleg tapes. Actually, bootleg anything were quite common here, including video tapes of current films, lots of which got played in the little bars and cafes. A lot of our days were spent sitting around in these places watching newly released, or not yet released movies, in a strange paradox of being totally relaxed and unwound in a place that was incredibly busy and loud.

And of course, the Mekong Whisky. Within a couple of nights, a small crowd of us had come together. There was Simon, an Australian guy making his way home. Then Erik, a Norwegian who seemed to have endless money. Turned out that his job was cleaning something to do with nuclear reactors. The pay was tremendous, he was only allowed to work so many days a year, and though he didn't, I like to think he had a sort of green glow. Then the two Dutch guys would join us on and off. One night we began drinking the whisky, moving from bar to bar, till night turned to day. Then night again. And so on. Time seemed to mean very little here, and at some point I left and went back to my room.

I thought I was dead. I honestly thought I had died. I came round in my room, feeling somewhat fuzzy. Worse than that, I was paralysed. I was lying on my back and could not move a muscle. I couldn't even turn my head at first. As the gravity of this sank in, I began to get a feeling of fear sinking in. I went to call out, but my throat was bone dry and nothing

138

came out of it. So yes, it passed through my mind that I was dead, and this was how it felt. I hoped to hell I was wearing my shorts as I'd like to be found with at least a bit of dignity. Then a couple of muscles started to twitch slightly and I concluded that I wasn't dead but possibly in a lot of bother. I realised eventually that I could rock slightly and as I was on the side of a very narrow bed, I figured the noise of me falling off it might attract attention. So after a bit of rocking, I indeed fell off and landed with a huge thump on the bare floor.

It did the trick. No-one came, but my body jerked back into life, albeit a slow and unsteady form of it. I pulled myself up, and splashed water all over me. It came out in a conversation later that Mekong is brewed with some kind of local stuff that is a natural amphetamine. Drinking steadily, you get to that Happy pissed stage, and don't get too forlorn or angry pissed. You also don't seem to get tired. Having had three days on the stuff, and only nibbling on bar snacks, I guess I had basically exhausted myself. Interestingly, many years later, I read up on this, where many forums and the like contain people who state that this is an urban myth, and Mekong is just a cheap nasty local whisky. Others disagree. I am in the latter camp. Sure, it was cheap and nasty, and you needed a fair amount of cola to drink it, but let me tell you, it's the only alcohol in the world that I have ever drank that stops me getting tired after a good session on it! Make of that what you will.

After a long shower, I went to find coffee. It was mid-morning, and I found Erik sitting in the lobby of my hotel, watching a Mad Max video.

"Heyyy....you're alive...We haven't seen you for a whole day, we were worried."

He was grinning as he said this.

"Mate, I thought I was dead. Where are the others?"

"Pah, all asleep I guess."

I ordered two espressos and drank them fairly quickly. I could see Erik watching me as I drank. "You're a funny colour."

"I feel a funny colour. And you're probably green. "

"You know what would sort that out? A bottle of Mekong. Let's go up the road and get one. It's on me."

"What? Are you fucking mad? How can you have that stuff for breakfast? I need to eat. Let's get food instead."

We went to the first cafe we came to, and I ordered a couple of things off the menu, even though I had no idea what they were. Erik again watched till I had finished.

"You ready for Mekong now?"

"Fuck off," I laughed.

Erik ordered Mekong. I may have had a glass.

I was with Johnny in the estate agent-come-bar a few nights later when the girl he had been talking to in the club on the first night came in with a friend and sat by us. It's hard to tell age with some Thais as they seem to have a youthful look about them, but I'd put the friend in her 40's, so a good bit older than I was then, but attractive in a hard life kinda way. Anyway, over the conversation I realised that they were in fact a couple of hookers. It seems that when a lot of the girls who work the PatPong red light area begin to get a bit older, some of them drift to Khao San, where there were always a lot of budget travellers with a lot of drink in them to entice. And so it was that me and the older girl went on to another bar later, after Jonny left with his, ahem, friend, where she proposed that I come back to her room.

"No, not for me, thanks" I said, more through nerves than morals (of which I never had a great many of to be honest.)

"You sure? Good time...."

"Yes, thanks, I'm OK." But out of curiosity I asked her how much it would have been.

"140 Baht. Good price.

It was. A bit of maths made that about £3.50 in pounds, which was cheap even back then.

"Ah, there you go," I said. "Good price, but I only have 145 Baht till tomorrow, and I need to get some food." I said this just to not seem impolite

"I get you food. Have food at mine."

"..Er, yes, but I honestly want another beer or two. Let me get you a beer."

"We have beer at mine too. Beer, food and sex."

To be honest, there was no real arguing with that. I tried to think of a reason to turn down Beer, food and Sex, but absolutely nothing whatsoever came to mind.

And she was true to her word. We got to her digs, which seemed to be in some kind of complex just off the street, and she ordered two meals in a cafe underneath. I figured the meal must be about 40 Baht, and another beer was 10, so by the time we went upstairs to her room the sex was going to be about £2. Bloody hell, I'd spend more than that on a drink for a girl in a pub at home before she'd say she was already meeting someone!

In her room, she took her clothes off, except for a suspiciously large pair of panties. Now, everyone is aware of Bangkok's reputation for Ladyboys, so being already naked on her bed, I decided to forgo tact, and put my hand where her balls would be just in case. Nothing. Not so much as a stray testicle, so I went ahead and had a pretty damned fine night. I woke up at some unknown time, though it was still a bit dark, desperately needing the toilet. There didn't seem to be one. Maybe in the corridor? I tried to wake her up to ask, but there was no shifting her. I pulled on my shorts and sandals and went outside, but the door shut behind me and I was locked out. I could see no toilet, either, and by this time I really was about to leak. However, outside each door there was a bucket of something that looked like clothes soaking, though I have no idea why. I thought it rude to piss in her bucket, so her neighbour's one got a top up. I swear it had a head on it. Or, like Erik's green glow, it didn't but it is more fun to remember it like that.

I left, and bought a t-shirt for about 50p on a stall, and went back to my room and slept till the afternoon, before heading out and finding the others watching a video of Patriot games in a cafe, and sat down with a coffee, aware that all eyes were on me, and big grins on all the faces.

"Well, well." Simon eventually said. "Word on the street is that you were seen going off with the girl from the towel shop last night"

So that was it. Somehow, a rumour had gone round that rather than the aged, though generous hooker I had been with, someone thought they saw me with the amazingly pretty girl from the towel shop.

"So," He carried on. "Good night then? We called by your hotel earlier, and they said you hadn't come back till this morning and were asleep. C;mon, tell all."

I thought about this. These were my friends, and it's wrong to lie to your friends. Also, not fair on the girl from the shop who was oblivious to this. That gorgeous, sweet, pretty girl with the amazing body and astonishingly attractive eyes. These guys thought that a girl like that would go home with me. Should I tell them that actually an old hooker bribed me quite easily with beer and food?

"You betcha I went home with the towel girl," I said, winking. "And what a night, lads."

Loud cheers and raised glasses, and I was king of the gang for a day.

I like the expression that Simon had said. 'Word on the street'. It was very apt as there was a feel of community along the road, and you got to know everyone quite quickly. Some stayed there longer than others. It was now occurring to me that I'd been here for a while now and hadn't really left the street, apart from a few trips down the side streets. This wasn't uncommon, apparently. Everything you needed was here, and it had the coolest vibe I had ever known in my life. England was becoming a bit of a distant memory, more distant than it should be in real time, but I was discovering that once you get out on to these places, out on the road on your adventures, time seems to work differently. I'm sure there is a very rational and dull explanation for it, but who cares, it's a strange and wonderful thing, and you don't notice it till you try to work out how long you have been away.

In any case, it was time to explore a bit more. Johnny was waiting to get a ticket to London, and his money was running low. He was trying to get money transferred and was having a lot of trouble. It kept getting sent back, as the bank couldn't seem to handle getting Irish Punt's being sent. He said this was a recurring problem. Another couple had joined the group, an English guy called Mark and his girlfriend, Heidi. I couldn't get these two. While the rest of us were in the standard well-worn shirts and shorts, they would come out of their hostel every day and night in immaculately clean clothes, jeans or skirts, Ironed tops, and spotless trainers. We couldn't figure out how they did it.....Maybe they found a travel iron in a lost luggage sale in India?

But they had booked an excursion along the Chao Phraya River, which struck me as a good move. I already knew I was going to be changing the dates of my flight from Singapore and that I probably wasn't going to get back to the UK on my arranged date, but was feeling less and less concerned by this So I went on the two day trip with Mark And Heidi, and thoroughly enjoyed seeing something that wasn't the Khao San road. Though I didn't see an elephant. I would have liked to have seen an elephant.

I got talking to an interesting young English guy on the way back. I'd seen him on the street, and nodded hallo on the boat, so we ended up chatting. I was learning that a lot of people you meet on the way have an interesting backstory. In this feller's case, he'd inherited a big wheel on a fairground from his Grandad, and it was the income from that paying for his travels. He'd never seen the wheel, someone was paid to operate it, and probably took a hell of a lot more than his pay, he speculated, but didn't mind so long as his money came through.

He told me that a couple of days earlier, on a whim, he'd spotted a flyer in his hostel asking if people would visit foreign nationals in local prisons, as they didn't get to see many people. He'd visited an old boy from Yorkshire who had been caught drug smuggling and was serving a sentence longer than he would probably live.

"So why did you do it?" he asked. You don't look like a drug smuggling kind of bloke."

That was the point, the old feller explained. He'd never done a thing wrong in his life, but his wife had passed on, he didn't really see his grown up kids or grandchildren, and felt lonely, so he took a huge redundancy from work, retired a couple of years early and eventually headed off to see the world. Some guys persuaded him that no one would ever suspect someone like him, and told him how much cash could be made. On a whim, he decided to do the first criminal thing of his life and got caught. Hence now in a Thai Jail.

"That's shit. You must regret it so much."

"Actually, no," The guy said. He got his pension sent to the jail, which was worth considerably more than it was at home, and the way the system worked, he could afford a nice single cell, and better meals. Even beer. He'd made friends there, and could have a Thai girl come and visit him once every fortnight. He was, he had decided, far better off and less lonely than he'd been at home. He did appreciate the backpackers coming to visit though, he explained. The only thing he really missed was Coronation Street, and liked it when he got the odd update now and then.

By the time we got back, Johnny had finally got his money transferred, and booked his ticket to London. The two Dutch guys turned out to be DJs, and had secured a spot in a bar/club called the Hippydrome, which was another venue just off the street. We all headed down and they did an hour, and were pretty damned good. We were, naturally, all full of beer and whisky, and were not really surprised when Simon told us that he had been talking to the owner and apparently a band was supposed to be playing in his other club up the road but had not turned up. Simon helpfully told him that we were a band, and we would play for 600 Baht. So we staggered onto the other club, oblivious to the fact that we weren't really a band, and found ourselves in a place that had instruments already there, as many places here seem to, and discussed our set.

It was already quite busy, and we were introduced as a top band from Australia called the Wallabies, (FFS) and took to the stage. Simon picked up a guitar, and played the opening chords to Sweet child of Mine, to a rousing cheer, and I started hitting the drums, which probably sounded terrible as I'd never played them in my life. This left Johnny to sing, and he had assured us that he was known as a bit of a singer back home. However, he failed to say he only knew Irish folk songs, mostly in Gaelic, and began singing some such weepy ballad whilst Simon played, and I banged along to our Guns 'N' Roses opener. And so it carried on. Living on a Prayer, La Bamba, Brown eyed Girl.....It didn't matter what Simon played, Johnny sang a slow Irish ballad. Maybe at first people thought we were being ironic, but that didn't last and the manager told us to stop. No one actually booed, but it was very quiet and less busy.

We also did not get 600 Baht.

I bought myself a bus ticket to Penang a couple of days later. Reluctantly, it was time to move on. I had felt really at home on the Khao San road and towards the end had even gone and seen a bit more of the city. And what a great crowd of people. Still, there was a world to explore, and the road was calling. The guys came down the bus station with me and we had a last bottle of beer before I left. But not, as Erik suggested, a bottle of Mekong. Good to leave on a high note. After all, how many people can say they played with the Wallabies Live in Bangkok?

III

That had been a long, hot and sticky bus ride. I think it took about 15 hours all told to reach George Town, the capital of the island. There were a couple of rest stops along the way, where I got talking to a couple of girls from the bus, one Scottish and one Aussie who were both on the same mission. They didn't know each other, but were both working in

Bangkok, and nearing the end of their visas. The way round this was to go over the border, then come back with a fresh stamp, hence giving them more time. We all got on pretty well and decided to book into a cheap hotel in the China Town that the Scottish girl knew of.

What a clash of cultures! There are 3 ethnic groups in Penang, the largest being the Chinese, followed by Malay and Indian. In fact, talk to any taxi driver or such of one group, and they will almost certainly complain about the other two. But, from a travellers point of view, this made for some amazing places to eat and a buzzing place to visit. I got a room and the two girls decided to share a room next door. The room wasn't too bad, it had a shower, but I figured I'd go and find a hostel the next day. It was cheap, but I already knew I was staying out longer than I budgeted for, so it was time to get economical. I had breakfast with the girls, who then headed back to get their visa stamps. It was quite an interesting looking place, but I found it a bit of a comedown after the Khao San Road adventures. I booked into a hostel for a couple of nights, and headed down to a place a couple of guys knew in the evening. It was a large outdoor bar, very laid back and chilled out, and full of various travellers and backpackers. I bought a bottle of beer, got talking to a few people and then came across for the first time what was to be the bane of my travelling life; The twat with the acoustic guitar.

You can be sitting having a great time somewhere, drinking, whatevering, partying and then in he comes. The bloke who takes his guitar round the world with him as a form of contraception. You are not aware he is there till you hear that all too familiar sound of him tuning up. Whenever I'm travelling and hear that sound, I now find that the hairs stand up on the back of my neck. The whole kick ass atmosphere is about to be brought down, for these guys only know slow miserable songs. Even if someone asks them if they know a really good belter of a song, they will do the slow miserable acoustic version anyway. Everyone is usually too polite to tell them to fuck off, and to be sure, a little crowd of naïve eejits will sit and listen and clap. This encourages him to tune up again – for they seem to need to do this between every song – and ruin another classic. It is also a guarantee that if you are getting on great with a girl, and all is going well, that he will play the very song that was her and her ex's 'that song'. She'll get a bit teary and you know you are about to be friend-zoned.

145

The only saving grace this time, though I didn't know it of course, was that Wonderwall hadn't been written yet. It would be worth checking hospital records to see how many times they have had to remove the fretboard from the arses of acoustic guitar players who know all the words to Wonderwall. Instead we got American Pie.

So that set the mood, and I wasn't really feeling the place, so I headed back to my digs. After a bit of exploring the next day, I decided to cut short my stay here, and bought a ticket to Kuala Lumpur. The night before leaving, I got drinking with some Australian Paratroopers, who were stationed in Butterworth, a nearby barracks town. They told me that I should change my bus ticket, as there was a big party coming up, but I decided to catch up on my time and carry on. So no great adventure here, but a nice place to visit. And eat. I ate a lot.

It was about a six hour bus ride to Kuala Lumpur, but the bus was air conditioned, so not too unpleasant. On getting off, there were young Malays giving out flyers to anyone who looked like a backpacker, including ones for hostels. I found one I liked the look of and booked in. There was a bar in there where I found a few good drinking companions, and was about to settle in there for the night when a young Canadian lad decided that we were to go to some clubs he had heard of. So showered and shaved, off we headed for a night on the town. This is where it first occurred to me I may need to purchase some jeans soon, as I was still wearing shorts whilst my companion was dressed in smart jeans, shoes and a white shirt. We caught a cab, and listened to the Indian driver complain and warn us about the Malaysian Chinese till we got to the first club on the list where I was indeed the only person wearing shorts, I noticed, even though it was hot, but luckily we were outside.

However, in the next place people were dressed even smarter and though nothing was said I felt very out of place. We had started chatting to some local guys when a pair of attractive women came over and took quite a shine to the Canadian who was in fairness a pretty decent looking chap. Gorgeous as they looked, it was clear that they were actually two transexual women. Not that it mattered as I looked like an out of place hippy who they ignored and my friend looked like, well, he had money. One of the local guys whispered to me to be careful, we were playing with fire here, but my friend seemed undeterred. A couple more drinks, and he asked the girls if they wanted to join us going to the next club, which they accepted.

146

However, another one of the local guys seemed a bit embarrassed, and hesitantly told me that I would not be allowed in there dressed as I was. I had had a feeling that had been coming. My new friend said we could head to a bar instead, but I told him to go on, it was my fault, and I'd be fine. I caught a cab back and listened to a Chinese driver complain and warn me about the Malaysian Indians, then I hit the sack.

Next day I was sitting in the common room / bar area of the Hostel with a Kiwi guy and his girlfriend chatting about all sorts of important nonsense when the Canadian emerged from his room and joined us.
"Did you get back OK?" he asked.
I did," I answered, wondering if he couldn't see me sitting here looking OK.
"You are never going to believe the thing with those two girls."
"The Ladyboys?"
"What? You knew? How long did you know?
"From when we met them."
"Why the hell didn't you tell me?"
I laughed. The others were grinning too. "I thought you knew as well" I said, quite truthfully. "I just assumed you were OK with it...Hell, who am I to judge."
"Do you know what fucking happened?"

Ah, good. It was time to sit back comfortably and enjoy the next 5 minutes. I told him to hang on to the story, as we were only drinking coffee and this was clearly going to need a couple of bottles of beer for the full listening experience.
So, beers in hand, he told us how he had been dancing in the club with one of the girls, and she started dancing quite intimately. He was paying for the drinks which were quite pricey till near the end of the night when she asked him if he wanted to get a room in a small hotel next door. He naturally agreed, and then she asked him if he'd like the other girl to join them as well.
He couldn't believe his luck and by this time being quite drunk no penny was dropping about these girls' careers. He paid the bill and went to the room with the girls, and one of them suggested he take a shower first, which in fairness was never a bad idea in the humid nights. He came bounding out the shower to find the two girls naked on the bed

with huge erections pointing right at him, and a pair of handcuffs attached to the headboard.

Genuinely taken aback, he tried to explain that he'd made a mistake, and it was his fault, but the girls got quite angry and told him he still had to pay them as he'd had their time all night. And then, I guess, the next penny finally dropped, and he started to argue, only to be warned by one of the girls that she was a kick boxer, and the other one threatened to pull a knife out from her bag by the bed. He decided to cut his losses, paid them quite a sizable amount of Malaysian Ringgits, then caught a cab back. I'd like to think that the driver complained about some race or other, but he didn't mention it.

That sure beat all the tales of nice things people had seen whilst out sight-seeing, so we laughed accordingly and he was king of the gang for the day.

Now, you get quite street wise to all the scams and rip-offs that dubious locals will try to pull on you whilst on your travels, which can often reflect poorly on the rest of the locals which is of course totally wrong but there are a lot of these people about. I'd like to say I was too wise to fall for any of them and indeed I was pretty sussed in regards to dodgy people anyway, but here in Kuala Lumpur I got my first – and last -sting.

I had been thinking how everyone I was meeting was pretty great, but they were always other travellers apart from bar staff who I always got on with, even at home. With this in mind, I had been exploring the city by myself, which is some job, as it is immense! There is a lot to see. An awful lot. Sitting in a small outdoor cafe having a coffee, a young Chinese guy at the next table started chatting, after asking where I was from. He told me a few good places to visit, a few good bars to frequent and mentioned that his sister was going to study in London. I told him I didn't really know London so well and he told me he was a bit worried for her as his parents were getting her a visa card and it hadn't come through yet. He even showed me a picture of his sister, a pretty girl, of course. He also casually mentioned that he wasn't sure what a visa card looked like, and I showed him the visa sign on my bankcard.

After another coffee, he asked if I wanted to meet his family, which of course was a warning sign, but bear in mind that everyone had been telling me how hospitable the locals were and I really wanted to meet a few non-travellers. So we went back to his house, a very respectable town house on a nice street. Had it been some dodgy district I would have walked there and then, but everything seemed fine.

We went into the house, where his mum (?) was friendly and made tea and snacks. His sister was, not surprisingly, out but would be back later. It was very pleasant and quite soon his 'uncle' arrived, a business suited Chinese with an expensive watch and a briefcase. This is where I cannot believe that I could have been such an idiot! To this day I am angry with myself and always will be. Uncle Angel (Seriously) told me how he worked in casino's around the world and trained croupiers. He also offered to show me how to play Blackjack but not for money of course. After a few friendly games, Mum brought more treats and beers and poor old Uncle Angel got a call off someone and looked worried.

He had a rich business associate coming round as he'd set a game up but the other guy, a young rich hippy whose Dad owned hotels had just called to say he couldn't make it. He then confided in me that they were going to rip off the businessman with a scam they had, He explained it worked as no one suspected a Chinese and a European to be working together. He showed me how it worked, and went to coax me in. After all, he said, it's not your money, it's all mine, and you have nothing to lose. I also suspect the beer was not all it should be, as normally I'd have made my excuses and left, but suddenly the other player was there and we were round the table. Uncle Angel was the dealer, which was the basis of the scam. The game went on till we reached a point where we- or rather I – was looking at $US48,000 on the table, and I had an unbeatable hand. At this point, and only this point, the guy said that he needed to see my money, as I'd used Uncle Angels up to now. I had nothing else to say, except that I only had cheques, and pulled out a £100 travellers cheque.

Because by this time I knew I was looking at a pantomime. Uncle pretending to sneak peaks at the other guys cards, the whole body language was wrong, and I found myself wondering just how they thought they were going to get money off me. I had clocked a couple of heavy looking things around the room, and made sure there was enough beer in my bottle to stop Mum clearing it just in case, but I guessed the weapons would be a bit heavier than that. The 'victim' politely said he didn't take travellers cheques, and I agreed he was wise. Uncle told the 'victim' we were just going to confer for a minute, about him giving me credit.

"What are we going to do?" He asked, as if I was an expert on this. "We stand to gain 48,000, but I only have 40,000 dollars in the house. (And yes, they were playing in US dollars.) Do you think you can get $8,000 to meet him now? We can split the winnings 50-50."

"I just simply do not have it," I reiterated. "I don't think I've ever had that much."

And then my new friend, the lad from the cafe who had been sitting there all the time piped up and said,

"But don't you have that visa card?"

Got it. That was the one. Except it wasn't a credit card, as he had obviously thought, but merely a cash card I had to primarily use when cashing a cheque, as this was often needed back then. It did make withdrawals, but only in a few cash machines. These were still quite new back then. And so I pulled it out.

"This?" I said. "This is just a cash card."

I saw the look Uncle gave the lad, and it was not too pleasant. But they continued the play act. Uncle Angel told the Victim that I was good for the money in cash tomorrow, and we could carry on the game then. He got us both to put our cards in an envelope and sealed them, with us both putting our initials on the seal. We arranged to meet at the house tomorrow. I shook hands, went to visit the toilet, which I knew was downstairs then legged it out of the back door just in case, and ran down to the main road and flagged a cab.

The driver was a Malay, who went on to tell me how you can't trust the Chinese and the Indians.

Naturally, I had no intention of going back there, but strangely, once I had realised what was going on, I too had played along as the naïve backpacker which, to be fair, I had been. It also occurred to me that there was a lot of money and my squiggle on an envelope, and at one point in the cafe the lad had casually asked me which hostel I was staying at.

So I got some sleep, and decided it was time to move on, just in case. The hostel was literally 5 minutes from the bus station, so I got up early, and went to the safe drawer behind the desk in the reception, as I had bought a cheap camera in Bangkok and had a good few photos of the various friends I had met there. It was gone. And it seemed my key fitted about 4 other drawers too, as I checked, including one that had four passports in one guy's name. The film I took in Delhi was still there. I guess the cheap knock off of a brand name camera hadn't been such a good idea, and so my memories would be just in the little notebooks I would keep and the patch I had bought.

I went straight to the bus station and caught the first bus to Singapore. With hindsight I guess that they were no doubt more likely to be looking for another mug, but at the time I wasn't sure. And anyway, I'd seen most of what I wanted to see, so it wasn't really an issue. Of course, it was probably the most illegal $24,000 that I never won.

IV

I travelled round the world and bumped into 3 people I knew.

I knew I really only had a couple of days in Singapore, so had to make the most. I had a flight date for Indonesia, and didn't really want to push the dates back any more. Actually, that's not true, I wanted to forget the dates all together but there was still that niggle of common sense that told me I had a job to get back to. Like the angel and devil that sit on your shoulders, except there was a hot angel with devil horns and a party dress singing down one ear and a kind of bland, non-entity whispering stuff I didn't like in the other.

I met a couple of Swedish Backpackers on the bus who said they knew of a pretty good Hotel and decided to tag along. Most of the bus ride though I spent reading an old paperback of one of The Saint novels, about the glamorous globe-trotting spy Simon Templar, which I found surprisingly good. One good thing about planes, trains, buses and such trips is that you get to catch up on a lot of reading. There is nothing better sometimes than to read a page, look at the passing scenery, read a couple more pages, scenery, pages, nap, that type of thing to enjoy the journey. This I was finding more and more; That the journey itself, the actual travel was as important as the destinations. In fact, sometimes it is worth taking the slowest way to get to a place and enjoying the experience. This is especially true of trains, where you can soak scenery up in comfort. Interestingly, though, I rarely read on ferries. I really would rather look at the sea.

151

We arrived, and bumped into a kiwi guy at the bus station that the Swedes had met before. He told us about an even better Hostel for just 7 Singapore dollars a night and off we headed. The place was clean, with basically just mattresses on the floor, a bar, and a hell of a mix of travellers. First things first, so a shower and shave were top of the agenda. The showers in the last couple of places were not going to win any plumbing awards, so this felt like heaven. I Sat in the common room and a whole group of folk, encouraged by a couple of Finns, were getting ready to go out on the town, and invited me along.

This was my first experience of drinking with people from Finland. Can those guys drink! I have always felt I could pit myself against anybody in a drinking competition, but I think I may have to concede defeat in regards to most of the Finns I have met over the years. And so it was this night. We were a mixed bag of Finns, Swedes, Austrians and a couple of Danish Girls. My plan had been to save some money here and just sight see, but that went out of the window. At some unknown time we staggered back to the hostel after one hell of a night and I was woken up about 7.00am by an alarm clock and a voice telling me they had to go now. I opened my eyes as best I could and found myself lying on my mattress with an arm round one of the Danish girls. She got up and pulled her clothes on. Hard to remember that this was a crowded dorm.

"Oh....Ok....Already?"

"Yep. Plane to catch. Remember that Losmen I told you about. Don't forget. See you there. Running so late." She blew me a kiss.

I just kind of watched the two girls grab their backpacks and leave. I waited for a hazy memory to come flooding back to me. It didn't.

One of the Austrians on a mattress next to me said Good Morning and told me she seemed like a nice girl. I considered this.

"What is a Losmen?" I asked him.

" A kind of guesthouse in Bali, or anywhere in Indonesia. Is that where you are meeting her?"

"I have got no idea."

I never saw the girl again, nor did any memories come back. Damn.

I couldn't see my shorts, but had underpants on, so I went to the toilet in the corridor outside. A couple of girls were out there and started laughing much to my bemusement.

"Nice pants," one of them giggled.

152

Ah. Yes. I had totally forgotten that I was still wearing the ridiculously oversized white cotton Y-Fronts that I had bought in Delhi. I had gotten used to them, but they were not going to win me any fashion prizes.

I took a little wander through the city around the Hostel and got a spot of breakfast somewhere. What an amazingly clean place. I'd heard that about Singapore, but it was impressive to see. I gather that they even have chewing gum as being illegal, something I wholeheartedly agree with. There also seemed to be a fair amount of green places about, intermingled with some amazing architecture. The people seemed to be in a hurry going about their business, and oh good lord, the stickiness. It seemed even worse than the last two countries even though I thought I was kind of getting used to it now.

After a pleasant day exploring, I headed back to the hostel, just in time to find the Finnish guys getting everyone motivated to head out again. Another shower, and ready to go. This time our shenanigans took us to the nearby Geylang district, one of the red light areas. A little seedier than the rest of the city I had explored, it still had a nice vibe to it and the beer was cheaper. We were sitting outside a little cafe bar, laughing at something - possibly my underpants stories - when I heard someone call me.

"Mulligan?"

I looked around, and there at a table outside the next cafe was a small group of people, one of whom I immediately recognised as Karen, an Australian who had been working as a barmaid in one of the clubs back home I had been Djing in.

"Bloody Hell" was about all I could think to say. So naturally we sat and had a couple of beers and a catch up. Oddly, a couple of months before I left we had been chatting in the club about me heading off and she had told me how she was hitting a few countries on her way home soon too. We kept meaning to get her address in Australia, but never really got round to it. So here we were, of all places, on a little street in Singapore - Someone should have written a song. Eventually her group headed off, and we moved on to some pretty loud party bar that the Finns had an instinct for finding and next thing I remember it was morning, and one of the Swedes was kicking me on my mattress to wake me up as I had a flight to catch. I'd apparently asked him to do this if I wasn't awake.

153

I lay there for a minute or two, then the same two girls from the morning before walked through our dorm and started laughing again. I was lying on top of my sheet wearing only my underpants that I swear were now getting even bigger and whiter and Y-Frontier. On that note it was time to dash, I yelled 'bye to everyone, and just got a bunch of grunts and weary waves. I cannot remember any of the people in the crowd's names, I had no camera to get a picture, their faces are long gone in my memory, but hell, that was one of the best bunches of people I have ever met, and I have an embroidered Singapore patch to prove it.

V

It was a nice flight over to Bali, one of the islands in Indonesia and whilst on it I decided to have a holiday, so to speak. From what I had gathered there were going to be some pretty glorious beaches to be found, so why not just soak up some sun. On arriving at the airport I saw there was a little tourist information booth and I decided to see about these Losmen I had heard about. Hey, maybe I'd even bump into the Danish girl again. However they seemed intent on selling hotels instead, though I noticed that the prices were remarkably low anyway and figured why not treat myself. Hence, I got myself a nice chalet in a rather flashy place next to a pool for the week, and they even came and picked me up. I found myself at Kuta Beach.

It didn't seem quite as sticky here, which was a bonus. I dumped my little bag in the chalet and wandered back to a small market I had spotted on the way to the hotel. It was time to finally replace my shorts and t-shirts with some new ones, as these old faithful's had been rinsed and worn for way too long. Prices were dirt cheap too, so I disposed of the old stuff and walked to the beach after a fantastic shower, feeling quite refreshed. And to top it off, I spotted a woman doing plaits on the beach. When I headed off on this adventure, the spikes and colours were long gone, and I now have short cropped hair, except for some long coloured plaits at the back which by now were getting like mini-dreads and any colour in them had washed out. So, after a relaxing hour with the very silent woman, I had fresh plaits, held in with beads and found that I now felt like a totally new man.

The beach, however, wasn't that relaxing. It was indeed beautiful, and when I first sat down looking at the sea I thought it was absolute heaven till 30 seconds later when someone came up trying to sell me beads. Or bracelets. Or sunglasses. It could have been anything, because that was it, it never stopped. The vendors coming up were relentless. Coming here without doing my homework, I was not to know that Kuta, where I was staying, was in fact one of the Australian holiday makers main destinations, effectively what Benidorm is to Brits, except with a much poorer population to whom the tourists are just walking dollars. And who can blame them? I gave up after an hour, and found a beach bar that was cheap, and I still got a great view of the sea so I just relaxed there till I headed back.

On returning to the hotel, I noticed it had a swimming pool in the back garden area, so I went out for a swim. They immediately opened up a bar beside it, and assigned a young waiter there, even though there was only me. I felt sort of obliged to buy a drink and chat to him. He told me his name was Tony, which I found hard to believe, and that he could look after me while I was there.

"Don't order from the menu or the bar" he advised. "You just call me. I do you a special price on everything."

He continued to tell me about a few things he could get me, such as discounted taxis, tickets to clubs and that there was a local Gin that he was particularly keen on getting for me, and that he could bring it to my room, but I wasn't to tell the people at the bar. I hadn't tried any local spirits yet, so after the fun with the Mekong in Thailand I decided to give it a go. I gave him some money, which seemed a bit steep by prices here, but what the hell, I'd found in Russia that these black market guys can be pretty helpful at taking shortcuts.

I had a bit more of a swim, which felt good as I'd had no real exercise in some time and went back to my chalet and switched on the TV which proved pointless as there was just an odd sort of variety show in the local language playing. It was about half an hour later that my door knocked and there was Tony's voice whispering to me.

"Mr Rich. Mr Rich. Here is your gift."

Well, not much of a gift at that price, I amusedly thought to myself, but opened the door and found Tony giving me a thumbs up and a very pretty local girl in a short dress next to him. She walked straight in and Tony winked and left.

"Hi" She said, through a huge smile. "I'm Jinn."

Well, that was quite the surprise. There was, of course, only one thing to do, so Jinn stayed the night. Apart from her obvious skill set, she was a really nice girl who spoke a fair bit of English. She did offer to be my girlfriend for the whole week I was there, for what seemed to me a remarkably low price, but I decided against that idea. She feigned disappointment in a smiley kind of way, and we enjoyed the night together. At least, I did and she appeared to, which possibly was down to a large tip I gave her as I felt a bit guilty. I'm guessing this wasn't the kind of tip my ex-wife had meant I should be giving locals, when she was moaning at me way back in France, but I'm sure she would be proud that I had listened to her and took her advice. Come the morning, my companion left, and within moments Tony was at the door asking if I wanted anything else for later. I politely declined this time. Hell, I hadn't even found out what the local gin tasted like. Well, not with tonic, anyway.

I did meet up with the Swedes again on the beach who recommended that I come by their hostel that had a great bar. And the week was pretty much taken up with sitting in that little beach bar by day, aside the odd day catching a bus out- including one day Tony gave me a motorbike ride to the main town, Denpasar – though another town up north, Ubud, proved quite interesting. It seems Bali is a mainly Hindu island and province, unusually for Indonesia which is on the whole a Muslim Majority. This was reflected in a lot of the craft work and art that you see. The evenings I would have a swim, then head to the hostel to relax. I did try going for a wander down the beach at night once, hoping to get some peace from the vendors, but after being approached 4 times in as many minutes by young Balinese men offering to vend themselves, I abandoned that idea.

I did catch the sunset a couple of times though. It was, I must say, a joy to watch. Sometimes you could see little fishing boats silhouetted against it, which only added to the effect. I watched a German guy one evening try to film the sunset with a video camera. He had it on a tripod, and

156

stood patiently with it till the final moments. He was probably there about 20 minutes, all told, when, just at the end, a vendor walked up to the camera and with a big smile, unrolled a painting right in front of it, blocking the view. There was a lot of swearing. I get that these people are making a living, and tourists have money to spend, but in all honesty how could anyone think that that was going to sell a picture?

Back at the hostel, I became pretty good friends with another Swede who had joined the crowd, who I recognised from Singapore. He was yet another Dance DJ, and had a few interesting plans ahead. I was beginning to realise that being what was classed then as an "Alternative" DJ was making me a bit of a dinosaur musically speaking, though we all had respect for our respective music's and crafts. He did tell me that he had some photos of some of the people I had met in Singapore and would forward them to me when he got his films developed in Sweden. I never got the pictures, which would have been a long-shot to be honest, but a year or two later I was watching Top of the Pops, or some similar chart show on TV, when a Swedish Dance act came on performing a massive hit they had around Europe. And what-do-you-know, there was the DJ Feller. Seems his plans went pretty well.

So a little holiday had been had, but not the easy beach and swim kind of thing I'd hoped. I'd certainly recommend the Indonesian Islands to anyone, but maybe not Kuta. Great for party bars, which on this occasion I hadn't really been wanting to do, but though beautiful, not a beach to relax on, which I had on this occasion I had actually wanted. But I'm glad I took a shenanigan break, so to speak, as things were about to change.

On my last night, I'd gone back to my chalet after a few drinks with the guys at their hostel, which may have been a heavier session if it hadn't been for the arrival of some twat with an acoustic guitar who tuned up and began singing Hey Jude. That was my cue, and in no time I found myself stretched out on my bed, relaxing. There was a knock on the door. It was, as I guessed, Tony.

"Mr Rich? You go tomorrow? I looked after you, yes?"

Actually, he had come good on tickets for a couple of good places, so I agreed he had, and slipped him some money as a tip, which seemed fair.

"Ah, thank you Mr Rich. I will miss you. Can I get you some beer or anything, to help you relax before your plane?"

I thought about this. Did I want anything?

"Well, actually, Tony, there is something I could do with."

"Yes?"
" I fancy a bit of Gin……"

VI

I'd always fancied Australia. Maybe it was just the media image of it we would get, but there seemed to be a ruggedness and honesty about the country and the people that caught my imagination. In fact, I wasn't to be disappointed on this. Me and the lads had once had an Aussie night out back home a couple of years back, when Jake from New York was still in Coventry. Myself, Jake, Ferret and another mate called Dave had headed over to Birmingham dressed in remarkably bad cliché Aussie clothes. Army trousers, bullet belts, Doc Martens, string vests and all wearing one of those seaside hats with "G'day Sport" in large letters and corks hanging on bits of gold string off them. Except Jake. He wasn't up for that idea. Wise man. We went round a number of pubs talking in bad accents, and trying to impress girls, which oddly it did. We got in a fight with some old boys in a more local-type boozer, because they apparently hated Australians, so we kept the pretence up anyway and much to my amusement culminated in meeting some girls in a goth bar called The Barrel Organ, who bought into our story. Well, most of our stories.

"Are you from Australia too?" One of them asked Jake, who was in a leather jacket and jeans.
"No," He said in his broad New York Accent, "I am not."
"Where are you from then?"
"New York"
"What, in America?"
"Yep. That's the best New York!"
"No you're not. You don't even sound American."
"WHAT? I am from New York. But you believe that these idiots are from Australia?"
"Well, yes. Look at them, you can tell. Hey.." she called out to her friends, "This bloke says he's from New York."
"You're not from New York," another one of them said.

158

Ferret interceded in a bad Aussie accent. "He's always saying that, Sheila"

"You see," the first one carried on. "I told you that you weren't from New York."

Jake gave up and went to the bar and ordered a drink.
"You one of the Australians then?" the barman asked.

But this time, here I was for real. As we touched down in Sydney, I felt that familiar feeling of excitement of course, and nervousness, but was quickly impressed by the two customs officers who were joking about, and one asked me to punch the other one in the face as part of some ribbing they were doing. Now, having had so much trouble with customs guys in the UK, the idea of doing that was quite tempting, but probably would have brought a quick stop to my travels. But I liked the attitude and the quick glance at my passport, and off I headed to the tourist information area where I was delighted to find a whole corner marked 'Backpackers'. Here was a bunch of leaflets for different hostels and – ingeniously – a bunch of telephones and a board with a button for each hostel. I picked out one called the Backpackers Village, picked up the phone, pressed the button and someone took my name and said they'd be there shortly to pick me up. Sure as, within about 20 minutes, me and a Canadian guy, Chris, were on our way in a battered old minibus to an equally battered hostel that left a lot to be desired, but was pretty cheap at $10aus a night or $50aus for a week.

The hostel, like many others in Sydney, was in the Kings Cross district. A pretty rough, sleazy kind of area but teaming with all sorts of life. There were a multitude of bars, clubs and strip-joints, small businesses, and a maze of dealers and aged hookers to pass in-between. I liked it; sort of reminded me of my own district back home. First couple of nights me and Chris explored a few bars. The second night he disappeared to the toilet, didn't come back, and when I saw him in the hostel the next day he said he'd got chatting to some girl and went back to hers. Lucky swine, I thought.

On the third day he announced that there was not enough life in the hostel, and was off to look for somewhere better. The room had been a four berth, which we shared with Hasiff, an Asian-English guy, and Leonardo, an Italian lad. To be honest, it wasn't a great loss. I'd become used to finding my fellow travellers to be generally decent and fun

159

people, but though I couldn't put my finger on it, there was something about the bloke that rubbed people up the wrong way. I did keep bumping into him in a couple of the better bars around the district though, such as O'Malley's or the Goldfish Bowl. By now I also possessed a pair of jeans and trainers, as despite the heat there, a lot of places seemed pretty strict on dress codes. Chris had met a few other guys in his new Hostel, the Down Under, who I got to know as well. When out at night, I tended to drift between these guys and the lads from my hostel who now included Dieter, an older German guy who took charge of cooking. Each room had a little cooker thing, rather than the hostel having the usual communal kitchen. Though looking at the place, that might not have been a bad idea. It was now becoming the norm for me to cook rather than eat out. That had been cheap in Asia, but I was aware of my budget going down. I wonder did the people that invented packets of pasta, instant noodles or rice and cheap ready meals realise that they would be sustaining Backpackers on their journeys around the planet forever? They deserve medals.

Then I caught a break. I realised that the date had come round where I would have been travelling back to the UK the next day from Los Angeles. However, here I was. I also knew that my money was way less than I had planned on, as I kept extending my time out here, and I wasn't even too sure how much I had left. The traveller's cheques had long gone, and I was drawing money from the bank. However, probably due to the technology of the time, the machines would not give me a balance. I was thinking about this on the way out to get some milk one day, and happened to glance at the little notice board in the lobby of the hostel, to find that someone had stuck up a handwritten notice offering $45 a day for work and a phone number. I gave it a call. Though many backpackers and travellers arrive in countries with all the right permits to work, there are plenty that do not. So there are always people going to offer a bit of cheap cash-in-hand work to the latter group. I had never originally been planning on working on this trip so had not even thought about permits, though to be honest I believe I just fell outside the age to get one at that time in any case.

The man on the phone said he was doing a pick up the next morning outside the Kings Cross Tube station. I dutifully turned up, and got in the car with himself and another lad. It seemed we were going leafleting and that if I wanted, there was work every day. We reached an area, he gave

160

us a little map with where we would be covering, asked us if we'd be OK as it was a lot of walking and told us where he'd pick us up. I nodded and told him I'd be fine.

Of course I would be. The irony was not lost on me. Here I was, halfway around the planet, due back at work pushing letters through people's doors in the UK by the end of the week, but instead I was here, in Sydney, waiting to have adventures. And the first one was to be walking around the streets pushing things through people's letterboxes. Hell, this sure beats being a postman!

However, it kept me ahead. The money per day went up when we had a bunch of leaflets to deliver. Though used to walking in my job, the heat was certainly not something I was good with. Plus, a couple of months of no exercise and a lot of drinking had begun to catch up. However, I stuck with this for a few weeks, and was beginning to get acclimatised, when one morning the man didn't turn up, his phone number was dead and we didn't get the money for the day before. However, I'd got more money than I started with, so I couldn't complain. Other than a bit of sunburn.

Well, with nothing to do that day, I took a wander down to Sydney Harbour. It was not far from the hostel, but I hadn't actually gone down there yet. If not in Kings Cross, we'd tended to wander to a few bars in a district called the Rocks, which was a pretty cool place to drink, and seemed a great place to meet girls, though none of us had managed to bring any back to our dorm, or "The Room Where Travellers Go To Die" as we liked to see it as. Though on occasions when meeting up with the lads from the other hostel, we'd notice Chris disappear after a while, and tell us the next day that he'd met some girl, or a barmaid, and had gone home with her. There was a lad called Robbie with them that finally said what everyone was thinking one night.

"So... Seems Chris has gone off with one of his imaginary women again."

Everyone laughed.

Another lad, Mark, carried on.

"Has anyone at all ever seen any of these girls, or him actually leaving with one?"

"Nope."

"No."

"Never."

No-one though could figure out where he actually stayed as he wouldn't come back in the morning. It was also a mystery how he got out of bars with no-one seeing him leave. But then, my friend Ferret back home had been good at that, though that was usually because it was his round.

Anyhow, ended up down Sydney Harbour, to find there was some kind of event on. It was busy, there were all sorts of little performances and playing right in front of the Opera House was what I believe was a military band. I had a wander round, and stopped to watch the band play. I was debating in my mind whether to travel up to Ayers Rock, see a bit more of Australia, cut out Honolulu and fly out of Los Angeles after a quick visit, or fly out to Los Angeles this week, cut out Honolulu and maybe try to greyhound Bus across the states, and get my ticket changed to fly back from New York. Either seemed good, or the other option was to fly to Honolulu this week, quick visit there, quick visit Los Angeles then home. It was while I was thinking this that the band suddenly struck up a rousing rendition of Waltzing Matilda.

There are, I was learning, moments when you just let the universe tell you what to do. So standing in front of the iconic Sydney Opera House and listening to the most Australian song in the world being played right in front of me, I found myself smiling as it seemed pretty clear what to do. I was going to see a bit more of this wonderful country, and as for the money, well, I'd just put myself in the hands of God and Fate, and something would turn up.

Well, It looked like both God and the Devil wanted me to stay here. I went for a couple of beers around the harbour area and got chatting to a Canadian girl I'd been bumping into a few times on my nights out. She was on her own, as her roomies had headed up to Darwin, and we decided that as I was celebrating we should go on a bit of a binge. We were absolutely drunk out of our skulls and the last thing I remember was drinking in a quite nice bar in Kings Cross called the Beefsteak and Bourbon, and nipping down to my hostel to get my passport so I could get some money. I have no idea why I thought I needed my passport, as I was using my card, but I did it anyway. The girl was gone when I got back, apparently she'd been sick on the floor and asked to leave, so I sat and had another beer.

Unfortunately, the next thing I remember was waking up in a hotel room that I did not recognise, with no cash or passport. Luckily, I did still have my card though. Having no idea how I got there, I figured I was in trouble if I still had to pay, though to be honest my thought process was not that clear. So I went out past the reception desk, where the girl at the counter asked me if we were checking out. Who the hell were 'We'? I said no, not yet, and rushed outside to get my bearings. I really had no idea where I was. I wandered around for a bit, till I spotted somewhere I recognised, and got back to my hostel.

"Y'know, you probably had to pay in advance," Hasiff advised. "And even if you didn't, you may have had to leave your passport at reception. Which means that the cost of that room is going to be far less than getting a new passport."

He was quite right. So we wandered back to where I vaguely remembered where the hotel was, but I was clearly vaguer than I thought. We could not find the hotel, or any hotel in fact around there. I was beat. I had lost my passport, so I wasn't going anywhere for a while. So it was police reports, then the British Consulate, who then gave me the address of the British High commission which was in Canberra. It was here I had to post the application to, because though it's easy to forget, Sydney is not the capital of Australia.

It wasn't a major problem, though. I went to a bar a couple of days later where I knew the Canadian girl done the odd shift to tell her about my plight and see how she was, but they told me she had phoned up that morning to say she was heading up to Darwin to catch her mates up and had left them a bit in the lurch. So I volunteered and got a bit of cash-in-hand bar work for a couple of weeks which came in pretty handy. The bar was a bit of a rock bar, but the furniture matched and there was no piss coloured paint in the toilets. Clearly there was an opportunity here for a rock furniture franchise. There was, however, a regular, a fat rock guy in a faded Genesis T-shirt who leaned on the end of the bar most nights, so it was getting there.

I held the fort, so to speak, till my friend got back and resumed her job. The manager said he'd let me know if any other shifts came up but I wasn't going to hold my breath on that. And no need, it seemed. My passport came through which got me thinking about my options again, but on the same morning Hasiff came into the room with a bit of news. By this time our little group had expanded to a few others in the hostel, and we'd been hopping off to places such as the Blue Mountains together, and getting along pretty fine. I didn't see much of the other crowd by now, as people split up and went on their own journeys, or got work.

"I have been talking to some bloke," Hasiff informed us, "who is recruiting people to sell stuff for Barnardo's, the children's charity. You travel round on a bus, and get free digs, and earn commission. He's going to be in O'Malley's tonight if we want to go down."

"Fuck," I said, "That sounds almost too good to be true. How long is it for?"

"All the way to Christmas. We'll be selling toys. Commission on everything we sell."

We all agreed this sounded like a great idea, and with free travel too, so we decided to go down and see the guy that evening.

"There's got to be a catch" I mused, "There always is."

"Well, we do have to dress up as Elves."

And so it was that I found myself part of a group of Santa's Helpers and indeed I had to dress up as an elf. But the deal was real. We were told that we were self-employed, and so responsible for our own taxes. Which explains why they recruited a bunch of backpackers in a pub who were never going to pay taxes. We were to travel around in a mini bus, with another person driving a huge van full of toys alongside. We got a room in a motel for the night paid for, including a breakfast. Everything else we paid for ourselves. Then, in the morning, we bought however many toys from the van we needed at a fixed price, and either sold them for the recommended price or above, or could sell them back to the van at the end of the day.

We were not, it turned out, selling for Barnardo's at all. There was a deal that for every dollar sold from the van, Barnardo's got a 1 cent donation or something like that, but their name was plastered all over the literature. The guy running the team also got commission on the van sales.

And then there was the elf costumes. In all honesty, that may have looked good on some of the team but I can honestly say not me. I was a bit older than the others, had the beginnings of a beer gut, a short mohawk that Hasiff had recently shaved in for me, and a labret piercing that really wasn't too common over here then. In fact, Martin the team leader did confide in me a couple of weeks later that he had been a bit pissed on the recruitment night and when I turned up for the bus the next day was going to knock me back except for the fact he was worried that

164

the rest of our crowd would leave too, leaving him 6 people short. I didn't take offence. I really was a shit elf.

To prove Martin's worst fears correct, on the first day I really failed abysmally. We went about selling, walking into shops and businesses in a busy little town and I managed to sell one toy lamb. Cost from van, $3, sold for $3.50. Grand profit of 50 cents. Still, I got a room and a breakfast. I genuinely thought I had made a huge mistake and thought of heading back, but the next morning I was buying from the van and had my toys laid out on the floor when some of the women from the motel came out and asked what we were doing. I told them it was for Barnardo's and it was toys for Christmas, and they got pretty excited then started buying lots of stuff off me. I'd had a bit of ribbing off all the others about the one lamb sale, so looking at their faces as I sold nearly everything I had laid out was a joy indeed. In fact, I had made nearly $100, and bought some more toys for the rest of the day. And I hadn't even put my stupid costume on yet.

I definitely did not start off as a natural salesperson, but soon began to pick up the ropes. We were covering lots of ground over New South Wales, starting with the Sydney suburbs, then expanding out. We would hit either industrial estates or shopping centres by day, and do the door-to-door stuff in the evenings. I found myself in my element on the Industrial estates. I found not looking remotely elf-like to be quite the advantage. I developed a certain type of plod as I walked into a small place, or better still up to a group of blokes sitting outside eating or smoking. They would look at me coming towards them with a look of mockery or mild disgust till I got up to them, pulled my elf hat off and said in a self-depreciating way,

"Yep. I know. I'm a friggin' Elf."

This would usually do the trick. I would get a couple of jibes off the men, then someone would ask what it was I was selling. That's when I could bring up the Barnardo's connection and how the stuff was pretty good value with Christmas coming up. If I knew I was doing the estates, I made sure I had very "Bloke Friendly" toys. We had some stuffed Gorillas and lions which I made sure came out of the bag first. I also had a couple of very nice girls dolls, which I would bring out last. These were actually really great dolls, and were quite expensive to buy off the van so most people avoided them. But I found that once a group of men were looking at the toys, the ones with daughters would jump at these

165

dolls if you got the timing right. And in all fairness, they were a pretty fine toy. Once business was concluded, I'd make another couple of jokes at my own expense on being an elf, get a bit more friendly ribbing and be on my way. Everyone was happy.

The shopping centres I was never so keen on. Some of the others thrived on these, but I never liked walking into shops and such. We didn't have a licence to sell on the street, which we were constantly reminded of by the police if we stood still for more than five minutes. However, I got round this a bit by constantly having an open sandwich packet and a small empty flask I carried around. I would sit on a bench, and be 'Stock taking' and if asked, tell the business centre manager, or police, or warden that oh, I wasn't selling, just checking my stuff while I had lunch. I would have to move on then of course, but would have sold a fair amount by that time.

One day I was with another one of the team, a Canadian guy called Kelvin, and it began to drizzle with rain when we decided we did actually want a bit of lunch, so we stood in a doorway to eat our food in the dry. Now, a lot of the shopping areas over there, I noticed, had doorways between the shops leading upstairs to what could be rabbit warrens of small businesses. An attractive young woman came out, and told us we couldn't sell there as we were blocking the way for customers. Assuming she was a hairdresser for no other reason than that there seemed to be a lot of little salons in these upstairs places, I apologised and quite genuinely explained that we were not selling, just having a bit of lunch out of the rain.

"Ah, no worries then. Come and sit in our waiting area if you want, you can have a coffee or something too. It'll be more comfy, and not block the way."

That was pretty nice of her so we followed her up and sat down in front of the reception desk as she told the more mature lady behind the desk why she had brought us up. The Lady put the kettle on, and we made ourselves comfy.

It was, it turned out, a brothel. Apparently quite legal there. As we sat there eating, one or two other guys came in for appointments and were clearly puzzled by us. I guess if you go along to such a place and there's two blokes sitting next to each other in Elf Costumes with big bags of toys, you're going to wonder how much we were actually paying, and for what exactly. We ended up having a couple of coffees and a glass of wine, and the working girls, in between customers, would come out and nearly all bought something. The girl who invited us in was quite the character. She was a Kiwi, who had done a lot of travelling herself. She chatted a lot and even gave me her parents address in New Zealand in case I got out there but on the strictest of instructions that we said we had met her working as a waitress. Giving out family addresses was surprisingly common in Australia and New Zealand it turned out, mainly because they really do seem to have a strong travelling culture over that way. I never got to take anyone up on it, but am quite confident that a warm welcome would have ensued.

There were good and bad days with the selling, but I was beginning to get a fair bit of money put to one side. On Martin's advice I had opened a bank account there and started putting it away when we'd reach a town. We did go out when we'd reach a place with a decent bar or club when we had the odd day off, but generally we would just hang around the motels at night which was fine as there was a pretty good bunch of people on the team and we made our own amusement quite well. We started around the beginning of November, and by the time December came round, I knew I would have plenty to fund the rest of my trip.

At this point I had really not been keeping in touch with back home at all. In fact, I really didn't have a clue when, or if, I would be going home. I'd drifted into this kind of nomadic mindset that I hadn't expected, my original plans of things to see on a short trip had been left behind, and I was extraordinarily happy about that. Perhaps the happiest I'd ever been in my life, or so it seemed in the moment. I had no house to go back to and I'd clearly made my choice on whether to stay in this beautiful country in the sunshine, making enough to get by, or go back home to being a postman on the Foleshill Rd in Coventry, delivering mail in the cold and rain. Home was both physically and mentally a long, long way away, and didn't really seem like home at all. At this point, Australia was.

One thing was for sure, this was a really good way to see a bit of the country, though from a sales point of view that could be a double edged sword. The Sydney suburbs, though pretty much a collective of small towns in themselves were lucrative, but just towns nevertheless. As you got further out, the towns were smaller and more interesting looking, but the low population made selling harder, even though the reaction to us was pretty friendly. We came to one such place that turned out to be a twin town of Coventry, Parkes, named after Henry Parkes who had been one of the politicians responsible for uniting the various states of the country into one federation leading to the eventual commonwealth of Australia; but he had been born in the Canley district of Coventry before heading out to New South Wales with his wife. He worked his way up from scratch there and was also a leading advocate of the abolishment of the transportation of prisoners from the UK to Australia. This was probably very wise, for though he wasn't to know it, if it hadn't been abolished, half of the modern Canley district would now all be over there. We managed to use the connection to somehow get me on the local radio station, and we had a pretty good couple of days!

I loved the travelling between towns too. Once you got out of the suburbs there was this bare, but rugged scenery, just large areas of nothingness. The impression was that of the old wild west. So much so that there were even cowboys out there. A couple of times we saw men in that type of gear driving livestock across the flats. Even pulling into little rest stops, you realised you were in a very different Australia to the cities.

The line-up of the team changed from time to time, as people left and we pulled new people in. Usually by Martin driving back to Sydney. A couple of new English guys, Noel and Dominic had joined the group, and were a pretty fun couple of blokes. They both also liked a good drink, which made them OK in my books. There was one occasion Noel particularly impressed me. We pulled into a rest stop that seemed to be a garage / bar / truck-stop / sheep shearing station. We had been driving a while this day, as tended to be the case the further out we got, so Martin suggested we take an hour to eat, and stretch legs, etc. Me and Noel decided to get a drink in the bar.

It is a moment I regret that I had never got round to replacing my camera. When we walked in, it was full of huge, rough looking guys who couldn't be more cliché, with cut-off work shirts, or singlets, and yes, one even had a hat with corks. We were in our costumes, and walking in was a real piano stopping moment. This bar was spit and sawdust, and though it didn't, I like to think of it having those saloon doors from the westerns.

"What do you two Poms want?" The barman enquired, assuming we were Brits before we even spoke. We ordered two Schooners of Tooheys, a local beer I'd got to like in Sydney. A Schooner is about 2/3 of a pint, and the Aussie Standard at this time.

168

"What the fuck are these idiots?" one of the large men in the bar called out. We just smiled and sat down.

We had a beer, aware of all eyes looking at us, then thought sod them, let's have another. I went up to the bar, and Noel said he'd be back in a minute, nipped off to the minibus and came back with our bags of toys.

"What the F**K," I thought.

I didn't have to wonder for long. He took a sip of beer, pulled a stool out to the middle of the bar, stood on it and made an announcement in his loud, Manchester accent.

"Gentlemen," he began, "We may look like a pair of Pommie idiots, and indeed we are, but we are here bearing gifts. Christmas gifts. Who's for saving a bit of money this Christmas?"

My first reaction when he jumped on the stool was we were probably going to get killed or at least badly beaten, but this indeed worked. It did go quiet for a moment, then someone called out,

"Whatcha got?"

I looked over to the barman and to see if it was OK, he gave the nod, and we started putting toys on the table. I noticed that Noel had the Gorillas and lions on top too. Nearly everybody wandered over, and asked the prices, and we started having a bit of a laugh with them, talking about the British National Elf Service, and how we were a long way from Gnome and such like. The guys were pulling out rolls of dollars from their pockets and chucking it down like confetti and saying they'd have that , that and that for so much, which we would hmm at, then agree, as they were offering more than we would have asked in most cases.

Then there were the dolls. I had one of the really nice dolls, and as soon as one man bought it for his daughter, the others asked if there were more. I ran out, grabbed the keys to the van and brought the whole lot back. And sold every one of them. Noel went back to the bus, and asked a couple of the girls still sat on it how much they spent on toys that morning, said he'd pay them back with a bit of commission, and brought their two bags into the bar, one each. The guys were still peeling money off rolls, all buying bulk and offering a price we'd take till we had sold out completely. One of the guys bought us a drink, which we had, then we got a shout it was time to get on the bus.

And that would have been the picture. Here was this dive of a bar, full of great big tough-as-nails Aussie farm workers and truckers, but now all

169

surrounded with cuddly stuffed animals, dolls, Christmas hats and other assorted goodies. As we left, the blokes all shouted out 'Cheers' and 'See ya, mate,' and everyone was happy. In fact, when we got to the next town, the pair of us decided to take the evening off and go to a local bar in the hope of meeting girls, as we both agreed we had been on the road a while, and some female company would be nice. We got incredibly drunk, and met two large girls who looked like they could take out the tough guys back at the bar with one hand tied behind their backs. Stuff happened, and we never spoke of the rest of that evening ever again.

Truth be told, I was not a great salesman. Most of the others were taking far more than me. Then again, I was a bit lazier. Sometimes doing the door-to-door in the evenings people would say they didn't need any toys, but I could come in for a beer if I wanted. You can never underestimate the friendliness of the Australians, and for all their ribbing about the Poms, they always made me feel pretty welcome there. It was one such evening sitting in some guy's garden drinking as he showed me a number of Harley Davidsons he was putting together, as part of his retirement fund that I realised I'd had enough of selling and the costumes. I also knew I'd built up a good fund to carry on, and the urge, that never ending desire to hit the road and explore even further was kicking in. The next morning I had a chat with Martin, said goodbye to everyone and caught a hot sticky bus ride back to Sydney.

It was about a week before Christmas. I got a bunk in an 8-berth room in the Backpackers Village, and found a great crowd in there already. There was Joey and his girlfriend Ange, Phil and Ben, the Manchester Men, A couple of Dutch lads and a weird Indian Guy who we called Gandhi. Everyone did. He had apparently lived in this room in the hostel for over 4 years. 4 years! When he was asked why he lived there – as he had a job, though we never found out what it was – he said he loved the company. There was nothing about Sydney he couldn't tell you.

Walking down towards O'Malley's one day, a bloke came running across the road straight at me, calling me to hang on. He came right up, looked at me and asked,

"Are you the Postman from the Foleshill Road in Coventry?"

Startled, I told him I was and he looked incredibly satisfied.

"I knew it," he went on, "I told the others it was you. Good seeing you, mate."

And off he went. I had no idea who he was, or who the others discussing me were, but I class him as the second person I "knew" on my journey.

The day the Dutch guys checked out, Hasiff checked in with another lad from the Santa's helpers, as they had decided that they had all made enough, and the venture ended. So come Christmas day we somehow managed to rustle up a Christmas dinner for the 8 of us on the two-ring and a grill contraption that passed as cooking facilities. Fed and happy, we all headed off to Bondi Beach, with slabs of stubbies – little bottles of beer – on all our shoulders. All along the beach, thousands of people had rigged up sound systems, mainly in the back of vans, and various national flags could be seen flying around the place. It was a fantastic atmosphere. I would have to say it was one of the best Christmas days I ever spent in my life. Walking round in just shorts on a hot day, drinking with my current and temporary best friends ever, and enjoying the whole rave atmosphere. Dance tunes played everywhere, and we partied hard!

Apart that is from poor old Hasiff who managed to get punched somewhere along the way. And, as I unfortunately came to expect, off some English guys. It wasn't to be his worst event in his Christmas calendar though. That came on Boxing day, when we'd carried on drinking some bizarre whiskey someone brought to the hostel. I had never really got on with Whiskey, apart from the Mekong in Thailand, but got absolutely slaughtered on it and lay down to die on my bunk, a top one above Hasiff.

And so it was I didn't wake up till I felt Hasiff prodding me from his bunk, and calling me.

"Mulligan! Mulligan! Are you awake?"

He asked me that about 3 times before I acknowledged where I was exactly, and grunted down at him.

"Did you take a drink to bed? Have you spilled beer all over the mattress?"

There was a panic in his voice, and as I was coming round I began to realise why. I was soaking wet. And no, I hadn't taken a drink to bed. The embarrassment of what I realised I had done had me considering lying, but I decided that wouldn't hold up.

"No mate. I think I may have pissed the bed."

Hasiff groaned. Poor lad had been out cold too, and didn't realise till he woke up that both him and his sleeping bag were soaked. This was not helped by the thinnest mattresses known to mankind, so a trip to the launderette on me was the next job after a shower. The sight of him sitting up with piss wet hair and his bruised nose has stayed with me to this day. How we laughed. Well, me and the others did. Not so much Hasiff.

Which brought me to the last day in Sydney. Me, Phil and Ben had decided to head up to Ayers Rock via Adalaide. Our plan was to climb the rock, which is in fact the largest Monolith on the planet, on New Year's Eve and see the New year in up there. I was sitting in the room with the other lad from the Santa team on the day after boxing day waiting for them to come back from the laundry, (I, of course, had done mine with Hasiff's sleeping bag) and he was looking a bit forlorn.

"You know what," he said. "I get some money sent through tomorrow. I've got 10 cents till then. 10 bloody cents! What the hell will I do with that?"

I thought about this.

"You know the best thing to do? Throw that 10 cents out of the window. You're right, it's worthless, and frustrating you can't get anything with it. Throw it away, and you will have nothing at all, and you'll feel better, as you'll know you actually have nothing."

He threw the coin out of the window, sat for a bit then agreed with me.

"You're right. Having nothing feels better than having a useless coin. Cheers."

I was still congratulating myself on my wisdom when Phil and Ben arrived back from the laundry, eating Ice creams, and ready to go.

"Hey," Phil said. "Look, McDonalds are selling 10 cent ice creams."

We said Goodbye to the lad while he glared at me and we left. I suppose I really should have given him 10 cents, but then, he had said he was happier with nothing.

We were travelling by Greyhound, and the trip to Adalaide was horrendously hot and the bus was full so no sleep really. We spent a couple of nights there, and it was, to be fair, a nice place. I used some of my new funds to get new clothes, even a bush hat and sunglasses! It did occur to me that at no point had I seen a kangaroo, which was a little disappointing. Still, plenty of time left. It was also notable how the desert

172

got redder as we neared our destination, Alice Springs, The closest town to the Rock.

It was good to start seeing some different kinds of things. We saw a Willy-Willy, a kind of desert whirlwind at one point. And Spinifex grass, so sharp that you cannot touch it. In fact, the Aboriginal people had used it for spearheads, and the plant itself for fishing. And wild camels. Yes, that surprised me. My understanding is that the camel was used in the pioneer days to open the country up, as it was much more suited to the job than horses. As they got released in the wild, they thrived in the environment.

Arriving in Alice felt great. It's one of those places everyone has heard about, and just sounds….Well, great! And clearly plenty headed out there, as we were snowed under by people dishing out leaflets for hostels and hotels when we pulled in the bus station. We settled on a place called Toddy's Backpackers, just outside the town, that proved to be quite a find. $7 a night each, our own chalet, a swimming pool, shuttle to and from town and an all-you-can eat barbie for $6 every night. And clean! Hell, we were used to room 8 at the digs in Sydney, where the dirt was holding the place up. This was bliss.

New Year's Eve came, and we did not climb Ayers Rock after all. Instead we caught the shuttle into the town centre and partied the night in instead. We learned the hard way to use the shuttle bus. First day there, we decided to walk into town, as we could actually see it from the hostel. We were warned not to, but did so anyway. Only about a quarter of a mile, but by the time we got there, we were nearly dead from the heat. I had never known heat like it, and was absolutely not prepared at all.

And here was that thing about drinking and hot weather again. We spent the whole of New Year's Day by the pool, dehydrated and exhausted. And still the heat! There was a little fridge by the pool, and in between sips of beer, you'd put the can back in there, or the can would go hot. Not warm, hot. Leave it out long enough, and it would be too hot to touch. Hence the wise device known as a cooler, a kind of polystyrene holder that you held your tinny with.

Another thing we noted was that places had signs up advising a cover charge, but didn't actually charge you to go in. A bar owner explained that that was for the Black fellers, as he called them, to stop them coming in. This tallied with signs we had seen on the way up, and saw again once we left, stating that anyone caught buying drink for Aboriginals would be barred from the premises. This originally struck us as totally outrageous and we wondered how it was legal. But we were to learn that at that time, this was in conjunction with the tribal elders, as alcoholism was rife in many of their communities. Popular opinion that we heard a lot was that there is something with the enzymes due to their genetic make-up that makes them more vulnerable to alcohol dependence, but the more likely reasons were poverty and the harsh lifestyle. Certainly you could not deny that there seemed to be a fair amount of obvious folk with serious alcohol problems sitting around, some of whom we found out lived by a dried up river nearby. It was said that if you saw that river flow more than 3 times in your lifetime, you must be a native.

I also had a bit of reflecting to do. Coming out of a bar on New Year's Eve full of cheer, I had decided to phone home. There was a public phone box which oddly had a coin jammed in somehow and was giving free calls to anywhere. Word had gotten round and so there were a few people in front of me, and when it got to my turn I phoned my Mum first, who didn't answer, then my sister who was not in. Instead I had a quick chat with her husband, who told me that the girl from Birmingham I had been seeing had, in fact, actually had a baby.

The thing was, all the time I had been out here, I hadn't rang home once. This wasn't being rude, but without realising, somehow I had disassociated myself from my life back there, and though I'd always meant to call, I never really got round to it. Nor even think about it. In the meantime, it seemed, the girl had been in touch with my family after a period of time to declare she was actually pregnant after all, much to their surprise, and if truth be told, probably much to hers too. And the baby, a boy, had been born just a few days before this call. Of course, no one could get in touch with me as there was no way of knowing where I was, and this was the first time I'd spoken to anyone. So I had another son.

It was about the 4th January, well after our original plan that we finally did the climb. Or the walk up, whichever way you look at it. Ayers Rock, or Uluru to give it the Aboriginal name, is 348 metres high, and yet the bulk of it is underground. And it's not alone. Alice Springs is the nearest town, but even that is over 200 miles away. We had taken a dorm at a nearby resort geared up for just this sort of thing and booked a tour. Hence, we also got to see Kata Tjuta, or the Olgas, a formation of rocks about 16 miles from the rock. Both are visible from each other. Both are also part of the same Aboriginal stories. The tour also got us a walk around the base, and seeing the sunset, which we were told can involve a number of colour changes. It didn't, it stayed red, but was a great sight anyway.

The next day, we got to do the climb, setting out very early to beat the heat. It made very little difference, but we were half way up before we began to flag. We were, it had to be said, remarkably unfit. We also were the only bunch that decided to take cans of beer up as well as water and a little cake to celebrate once on the peak. However, after a remarkable amount of huffing and puffing, we finally got to the top. And it was worth every tired, sweaty step. I literally felt on top of the world and there was this red desert spreading out as far as the eye could see in every direction. It was quite frankly one of the greatest moments of the journey so far. We stayed up there soaking up the awe inspiring view and enjoying the feeling of sheer wonderment for as long as was reasonably possible. There was a visitors book at the top to sign, too. We did this, and got the photos of course. I'd bought a cheap camera in Adelaide especially for this. Then we opened the cans of hot beer and managed to drink them with the cake as we looked around reflecting on it all. Reluctantly, we knew we had to head back down, which was a lot easier. Bizarrely, I heard someone say to their friend that it was a pity there wasn't a tearoom or café up there. Yes. That would be a nice trip for the staff every day. Mind you, there were plenty of places at the resorts all around, and plenty of souvenirs, of course. I'm pretty sure you could even get a snow globe.

We were off again the next day. We were heading out of The Northern Territory and on to Townsville, in Queensland. The journey would take a few days. We stopped off at a camel farm, where I rode a camel for the first time. I'd been on a horse before, but it didn't have the ability to turn its head right round and look straight at me like I was some kind of idiot. Still, a good experience. All the more so, as when I was getting back on the bus, I finally saw some Kangaroo's, bouncing along the way they do. Hey, I'd climbed Uluru and saw kangaroos! What could possibly be better?

The Great Barrier Reef, that's what. From Townsville, we went to a place called Magnetic Island, which had a great Backpacking vibe, and got ourselves booked onto a mini cruise out to the reef, that included snorkelling. However before arriving we had been stuck on the

Greyhound a lot, but also some interesting stop offs. A bit like the Greyhound I took with Brody and Ferret on the way to Florida, there was a very laid back air about the drivers.

We called in at one place, a small town, and he decided that we had a couple of hours to kill. It was one of those small wild west looking towns we were getting used to seeing. We could see only two bars/hotels and went into the one that looked marginally less shabby.

Getting to the bar, we were the only white guys in there, the rest being rough looking Aboriginals who certainly looked us up and down. The exception was a little old white woman behind the bar, who stood about 5ft tall, and looked like everyone's favourite Grandma. As we looked at what was on tap, a huge Aboriginal in a bush hat and cut off army shirt walked up to the bar and asked for a beer. The Woman just looked at him, then in a voice like mini thunder said,

"You. Yes you. You owe me a fucking apology, dontchathink?"

"Last night? Yeah, I'm sorry, Mary."

"Sorry? Sorry? Sorry my arse. What have I told you about fighting with knives in this pub? You don't fight with knives in here. You fight with your fists, or you take your fucking knives outside. You understand?"

"Yeah, I am sorry, Mary, but he…."

"No excuses. No knives. You got your knife now? Give it here!"

Humbly, the guy handed a pretty big blade over.

"Right. You get that back when you leave. Now then," She said, looking over at us. "What can I get for you three fellers?"

We paused. Then Ben said, "Just three beers please."

Deciding it would be a swift beer, we stood kind of quietly at the bar: however the large guy started to talk to us.

"Poms, eh?"

"That's us." (How do they always know?)

He turned out to be a pretty decent bloke, even though one of the first things he did was to show us a 5 dollar bill and tell us how she was our queen, not his. I mentioned that I didn't really know her anyway, and we had a laugh, and a couple more beers and he told us that a lot of people found they could scrape the image of the queen off the new type bills, as they were a kind of plastic. Apparently, the law stated specifically that you couldn't deface the Queen's head on paper money. So lots of people leaning towards republicanism had taken to scraping her Majesty's head

176

off, as plastic wasn't paper. A kind of pointless victory, I thought, but he seemed very happy about it.

So we got to go out to the Great Barrier Reef. The boat took us out to a kind of fixed platform where you could swim from. Phil And Ben hired diving equipment, as they both had a diving licence, but I was merely snorkelling. Well, I say merely. The first time I went in, I was almost immediately in awe. I had always been a big fan of Sci Fi, and especially Star Trek. It was interesting to see how most sci fi depicts other worlds, usually as a rocky kind of place with strange cities in the middle of nowhere. One particular niggle of mine with Star Trek especially was that on every planet they would beam down to, it didn't matter how advanced their space programmes were, no one had invented the car yet, meaning everyone seemed to walk everywhere. The backgrounds in Sci Fi usually seem to depict a whopping big moon or other planet in the sky to show it was alien.

Here was the real thing. I was in an actual alien world! I've always been a pretty good swimmer, and right from school could swim underwater for quite a length of time. I put this down possibly to never having smoked, and playing brass instruments (badly) such as the trumpet and French horn. So I was able to swim around and explore pretty well. And this was indeed going into another world. The colours, the fish, the giant clam, the coral itself. I was absolutely bedazzled. I knew I needed something to record this, so went back on board the boat and purchased a disposable underwater camera. I think it took 24 pictures, then you took it to a chemist to be developed. I still have them, and though awful pictures by the standards of cameras that were to come, they still show the striking colours.

In fact, the lads told me later that their cameras were pretty good, but once you got deeper than where I was snorkelling, the colours began to get lost anyway. I didn't realise how long I was out there, I had become so mesmerised by the whole wonderful scenery down below. At one point I realised that I was the last person out there, and everyone was waiting. I also realised later that I had managed to get my first sunburn, something I'd managed to avoid for the whole trip so far.

We spent the next couple of nights on the island, relaxing and lazing around in hammocks. It was incredibly peaceful and a well-deserved break from the hecticness of the last few months. And then it was time for us to go our separate ways. I was heading back to Sydney to catch my next flight to Honolulu, the lads were going on to Darwin. I'd have loved to join them, but by now I knew it was time to carry on exploring. I figured on one night in Brisbane, just to break up the bus journey. It proved a wise move.

I knew how much I had in the account that I'd opened there, but had still never been able to find out how much was left in the account that my original bank card was for. This proved very frustrating. I had even gone into a Lloyds bank in Sydney, but they told me it was a separate company, and they couldn't find my balance out. I knew I'd pretty much depleted it, but wandering around the town at night, I gave it a go in a cash machine, to see if anything was left. I figured that if I asked for the maximum I could work my way down. It was $100. And the machine gave me the money, but still no balance. I tried the same thing the next morning at the bus station, and got another $100. Now this I hadn't expected.

I had got back to Sydney by the next day on the overnight bus, and managed to take yet another $100. I decided to do this till it stopped letting me, and sort the consequences out when I got back to the UK.

I had two days in Sydney till my flight and so booked myself into a different hostel this time, where some of the guys told me they were going out to one of the suburbs by the underground for a jelly wrestling night and asked if I was in. I was. One last good night, I thought, might as well leave Australia with a bit of a splash.

We went out to wherever it was, had a good few drinks, watched a few half naked girls wrestling in Jelly and headed back. I enjoyed it, but it was very 'city' and the last couple of experiences were still at the front of my mind so it seemed a bit humdrum by comparison. There was a broken door stuck open on the train, which surprised me that it was still running. I was soon to find this handy though. Coming back, I was bursting for the toilet, and could hardly wait to get back to Kings Cross Station. It got a bit too much though, so at one point I told the others that when we left the next station, I was going to pee out of that open door. And sure as it pulled out, I did just that. It even went into a little tunnel.

Unfortunately, the other side of the little tunnel was actually Kings Cross, and we passed by lots of people with me still taking a pee. So I managed to piss over a whole row of people till the train, or me, stopped, whichever was first.

Well, I got my wish. I left Sydney with a bit of a splash.

The next morning I found myself at Sydney Airport with a very puzzled looking customs official. He looked through my passport a couple of times and said,

"You haven't got an entry stamp?"

"Yes, I know, I lost my passport here. This is a replacement I got over here."

"Ah, right. Just think, you could have been here for years. We'd have no idea when you came in."

I have no idea if that would have been true or not. But it didn't matter. I'd loved Australia, I'd stayed way beyond what I had originally planned, and felt it was a country I could enjoy living in, but at this moment in my life it was time to move on and explore somewhere else. That feeling was back and I could feel the excitement building up as I boarded that plane to Hawaii.

VII

I went all the way to Honolulu to find the worst fridge known to mankind.

It had been a long flight, though enjoyable as there were not many people on board and I had a row of seats to myself. I was able to stretch out with a blanket, watch a movie and have a coffee or a beer at leisure, then get some sleep. It seemed I had also gone back in time somewhat, due to the oddness of crossing the international date line.

There was even a hospitality bus for just $6 which would drop you off near where you were going. Luckily, a guy on the bus recommended a place he knew, so I found a place to stay pretty quickly. It was a backpackers hostel, but in the middle of a cheap housing project which was unusual, however it served its purpose. I was surprised to see that the owner was an English guy, Wayne, who on hearing my accent asked if I liked Guinness.

"I've had the best in the world at Moscow Airport," I told him truthfully.

"I've heard about that. Is it much better?"

"No idea. Probably."

Anyway, he said he fancied a Guinness later, and no one else here drank it, and even if they did, the one bar he knew that sold it was off the backpackers usual beaten path. Well, it struck me as a plan, so we popped out there later on. He suggested that if I answered the phones to take bookings during a certain few hours in the morning I could have my bunk for free, which struck me as a fine plan too. After a few pints, we headed back and sat in the office, which was a kind of communal room by default. As ever there was a pretty good crowd there, including a couple of young American lads, Matt, a big Australian surfer type, and Koka, a pretty hot Korean girl. That wasn't her real name, she said, but people struggled with her real name so she used her nickname instead.

I had gone out and picked up some cheap beers and was about to put them in the fridge that first night when everyone looked panicky and shouted at me No, No, Don't open the Fridge!! They looked relieved I hadn't opened it.

"Yeah. It needs a bit of a clean." Wayne explained.

A few of us went out the next day to look at Diamond Head Volcano, and decided to walk. Somewhere along the way we got completely lost, and ended up back near the hostel. So more office socialising, with every newcomer being warned not to open the fridge on pain of death. Later that evening, I decided to make a call to home, to find out the situation regarding the child, and let them know I was on the last bit of my shenanigans, but didn't want to take the piss with the office phone so went out to find a public call box armed with a bunch of change. I did indeed find one, complete with a bit of a queue, called my sister's number and pushed a load of change into the slot.

"Hi, sis"

"Hallo?"

"How's it going?"

"Hallo? Hallo?"

"Can you hear me?"

"Hallo? Is anyone there?"

With that she put the phone down. And not one coin of the change came out. Annoyed, I turned round to push the door open, except there wasn't one, so I fell out of the kiosk in a heap right in front of everyone behind me in the queue.

And there he was. As he always was. A Large fat gay guy, this time in a yellow flowery shirt.

"Ooooooo", he said, as always. "Are you alright?"

"Yes, fine thanks," I answered whilst getting up and conceding I had lost any dignity I might have.

"You fell out of the phone box, eh?"

"Yes. Yes, I did. Thank you."

It was nice to see that the Large fat gay guy was Polynesian now.

At some point over a meal that a bunch of us went out for ,I got together with Koka and the next few days were spent taking bookings in the morning, seeing some interesting stuff with her and the others in the day, and sitting around the office with a few beers at night. The bank machine had finally given up on giving me money, but I'd accumulated a fair bit, which I stuck in the account I had set up in Australia. We went out again another day to walk to Diamond head, but this time got hit by some

181

unseasonal rain, and headed back. Damned elusive volcano. On the second last day, I was answering phones when the others came in. They'd got up early and caught a bus out that way. It was well worth it, it was quite impressive, they said, and they hadn't woken me up as they knew I was on phone duty. I hadn't even taken a single booking.

Then it was time to go. I was a little sad to be leaving Koka, but of course we promised to write, knowing we probably wouldn't, and changed phone numbers which we knew we would both lose somewhere. We all had a great Mexican meal out the night before I was off, and came back to the office to sup a few beers. Wayne had even got a couple of cans of Guinness. Like the night we went out, I didn't have the heart to tell him that I didn't really care for the stuff much. And so it would have been a great chilled night out if not for one thing.

Someone opened the Fridge.

It was a young Welsh lad who had just arrived, and came in as we were all laughing about something, walked straight up to it with a microwave meal and asked if he minded him using it as he opened it.

"Noooo, Don't open the ....."

Too late.

Holy God, what a smell. There were some little bags of squishy stuff in there and a kind of black stuff growing all over it.

"Fuck, Fuck, Fuck" was the most used word of the moment, as we scrambled to open windows and doors or just escape. We left the room for a good 15 minutes, but still the smell lingered.

"Why the fuck don't you get rid of that fridge?" Matt asked Wayne.

"Just needs a good clean."

I caught a taxi to the airport the next day and the driver decided that it was a good idea to pick other people up along the way and divert until I got to the airport and missed the last call for the gate. And here is where I saw a difference in myself. At the start of the trip, when I missed the coach to the airport in the UK, and then my luggage hadn't arrived, I'd been in a bit of a panic at the time, worried that everything was going to go wrong. The heart had raced, and I had been frantically wondering what to do. But after so long on the road, I now knew that these things crop up, and you just fix them, and worrying won't really get you anything but an early coronary.

So I had a chat at the desk and they fixed me up on the equivalent flight to L.A. the next day. Nothing to do then but head back to the hostel, where everyone was in the office, and laughed as I came in. Matt was just on his way out to the airport, so we said goodbye again.

As luck would have it, the three girls sharing Koka's room were also leaving. Though we'd got together for a bit, being in two full and separate dorms had meant we hadn't actually consummated the relationship, so to speak. So I asked Wayne if it was OK to book the 3 beds in that dorm myself.

"Too late." He said.

"Shit. Already booked?"

"Yep."

"That's a shame."

"Not really. Koka booked them when you came back" he grinned.

Turned out that night that it was the best damned plane I ever missed!

VIII

I wisely caught the bus to the airport the next day, and sat back comfortably on the plane, feeling somewhat content with life. It was to be a long flight but I'd got a good book on the go, the smell from the fridge had finally left my nostrils, and if I'm being honest, my balls were feeling pretty much drained so relaxing on the plane was no problem. In fact, what could be better? The window, that's what. After we took off, I looked out and had an absolutely splendid view of The Diamond Head Volcano. They were right, I thought, it was pretty impressive, then I nodded off.

Finally, I found myself in Los Angeles. I actually had a couple of flyers for hostels that I had gathered up in Sydney, as the lobbies in the backpackers there tended to have flyers for hostels all over the place. I had narrowed it down to two. There was one in Venice Beach, which sounded very nice, and I'd been told by a good few people that the

Venice Beach area was a great place to stay. Instead, I took option two, which was in Hollywood. I just liked the sound of Hollywood.

I think it was fair to say that Hollywood was not the great and glamorous place the name conjures up in the mind. In fact, It was fair to say it was a pretty run down sort of district. I had taken a taxi to the hostel on arrival, and found out they were having their own Karaoke night with free beer, so didn't bother going out anywhere else that evening. Which is how I came to meet the third person I knew along the way, a punk guy from a nearby town back home who I knew from gigs and the club I worked in. I met him in the communal room in the hostel.

"Mulligan!!" he exclaimed when he saw me. " I don't believe it!"

"Hey…. How's it going? How long have you been out here?!

"That's the thing. First day. And two nights ago I went up to your night in Busters Nightclub for a sending off shenanigan and asked where you were. Your mate who was Djing said that you'd fucked off round the world last year and no-one has heard from you since."

"Well they'll see me soon. This is my last port of call for a while."

"Do you know the funny thing? When your mate told me that, I told him that I was heading off round the world and if I saw you I'd say hallo, obviously as a joke … .But as you're here, Hallo."

We laughed. This was his first stop and my last, and here we were having a drink in the same backpackers.

Except that it turned out it wasn't quite the last stop. I caught a cab down to Hollywood Boulevard the next day, and explored a bit. I had a look at the stars outside the Chinese theatre and got a snap of the Hollywood sign, of course. I also found myself on the corner of Hollywood and Vine, which struck me as pretty cool, as it's been mentioned in a fair few punk and New Wave songs, so naturally I found a bar as close to the corner as possible so I could start stories off with 'I was sitting in this bar on the corner of Hollywood and Vine' but unfortunately not a single shenanigan happened. The story would end with 'And I had a drink' which would be wrong as most shenanigans would -and should - generally start with that.

Back at the hostel, they were having another free beer night, something that quite baffled me but I wasn't going to complain about. I got chatting to a German girl who told me that they were selling tickets at the reception for a trip to Mexico the next day for a pretty reasonable price so I figured that it would be better than trying to explore Los Angeles which is quite frankly huge, plus I'd never seen Mexico.

So off we went and had a thoroughly great trip. We stopped at Mission Beach, San Diego on the way for a while, before crossing the border into Tijuana. I didn't even have to show my passport, though they were pretty strict about that on the way back. We spent the whole of 4 hours in Mexico. Still I figured that if I had a local drink I was entitled to buy my embroidered patch, and call it a hit. It was, in fact, an interesting 4 hours. Though just what seemed like a tunnel ride from San Diego and a bit like Bali in regards to touts trying to sell you stuff, you could really feel the difference in the countries. The architecture changed, the people, the smell in the air. I had begun to realise that even when you take a short trip to a new country, your senses are working overtime, and you don't realise just how much you are taking in.

You generally realise just how much you took in later, when the place comes up in conversation, and you start reeling off facts, and observations, and you have memories and images in your mind of what you saw and smelt and felt that you hadn't realised. I had learned that no journey is too short and that when people say it's hardly worth going, to take no notice of them as it most certainly is, and you will get something out of it. In this case I was happy that one of the things I got was a bit of a snog with the German girl on the bus on the way back, but we could put that down to a vast amount of tequila she managed to knock back over the border.

Two days later, I was on the plane flying back to the UK. It was a long flight, and certainly I found myself reflecting on the things I'd seen and done. From a family of 5 on a motor scooter in Delhi, to losing my luggage and having nothing. The craziness of the Khao San Rd, my huge mistake in Malaysia, meeting people I know, ending up being an elf, raving at Christmas, the smell of that fridge…. And the people! Oh, lord, that amazing procession of fabulous and amazing people that I'd met along the way. I had been gone for all my life. I had been gone for no time at all. It was either or both and it didn't really matter.

And then I was home. It was a Saturday. I caught a train back to Coventry and called my Mum to ask if I could stay a while as I had no home just yet. But before heading there, I stopped into the Courtyard pub, where the alternative and punky crowd all drank to see if any of my friends were about. I'd only been there about an hour when they began to arrive. There was much back slapping, and I asked what had been happening. It seemed Ferret fancied some girl, but she wasn't interested. Dan complained that he and his girlfriend were arguing all the time and he was thinking of finishing it, and Bok was cheating on his wife. Oh, and everybody's job sucked and they were thinking of getting another one, so I was to let them know when I was going on my next journey after this, as they were jolly well coming with me next time. So pretty much the same then.

"So tell us what you've been up to."

"You know, lads. Just a few shenanigans."

On the Monday, I went down to the McDonalds in town near the Post Office at 9.00am because that's where I knew the lads from Royal Mail would be having a breakfast as they finished their rounds. It is one of the odd quirks of the British workforce that the better you are at a job, the more you get punished for it. In the case of postmen, if you were quick on your feet, young, fit and good at the job you would obviously finish your post round quicker than someone older or slower or just not as good. So the managers would try to get you disciplined for finishing early if you came back to the depot, regardless of the fact that people had received their mail at the earliest possible time. Hence, my own group of friends there met up in McDonald's for a coffee before heading back after the first post, as there were two posts a day back then.

After much back slapping again, the lads persuaded me to come into the office canteen which struck me as not a bad idea, as I thought I could find out when I officially got sacked so as to do whatever the hell I was going to do next. I was having a cup of tea when one of the managers came in, saw me and came over.

"Well, Bloody Hell. The Wanderer returns."

"Yep. Good to see you."

"Run out of money?"

"Pretty much."

"Do you know that you still work here?"

So the bombshell was dropped. He explained to me that when I didn't come into work, or notify them of absence for so long, the procedure was that they had to give me 24 hours' notice to contact them or my services

186

were terminated. Of course, I had told them I had given up my address, and landline as it was then, so they couldn't give me the notice.

"Bottom line," he said, "I have just seen you and am giving you that notice now to be back within 24 hours. If you turn up tomorrow morning in your uniform and at your sorting frame, you will still be working here. Look, you'll probably get the sack, but it will take a couple of months to go through, and I guess you could do with the money in the meantime."

So the next day, I was back in uniform, and delivering letters. I went through the discipline process, and they ended up calling it a 5 year serious offence. They wrote this on a card and filed it somewhere for presumably 5 years. If I'd have come back on time, and not decided to stay out, I'd be doing the same thing but would have missed half the planet.

The money in my bank I found? I'd obviously not been paid, but had still been getting the monthly bonuses as an employee.

So I kept delivering, but in my heart I knew I needed to get out there again. It just didn't feel quite right here. Remember Mulligan, I told myself, every letter a mile. Every letter a mile.

Six months later I walked into the manager's office and requested another six months off the next year as it was time to go to Africa.

PART 4

The Lion, the Bitch and the Warzone.

I

I was invincible. As the weeks went by after I got back, I discovered two things. One was that I now truly believed I could do anything. My confidence levels in myself were at an all-time high. I guess after you conquer the world, the sky isn't the limit any more. A mate was moving in with his girlfriend, so let me pay the rent and stay in his flat in case it didn't work out. I had my job back and my imagination was going everywhere with plans to travel more and more.

The other thing I learned though was that I was struggling to fit back in. I had noticed on earlier journeys that difference in how time runs differently. I think this is due to the fact that your mind is geared up to be stimulated and learn from new experiences. This would have been a survival trait. On the road, everything is new, so you are constantly stimulated. As a result, you feel you have been gone a lot longer than you really have, as you have often had more experiences in one day than you would in a week or probably even a month in your day to day life. You feel older and wiser when you get back, but in a wonderfully enlightening way and find that you are still looking for that stimulation, but probably not encountering it. Which is where I found myself. I was ecstatic at first to get back with the crowd, see everyone again and tell all my new stories, but you could see their eyes start to roll after a while, and they would go on to tell me the same stories that in my mind happened many, many years ago, even though it wasn't as long as it seemed. I even walked past the club I'd been barred from the night before I left, and the doorman said Hi, and told me I wasn't barred anymore. I'd kind of forgotten I was.

I also made contact with the Birmingham girl and met up with her and met the baby. She brought her boyfriend, who she was marrying. I talked to her about paying maintenance, though my Mum persuaded me to buy her goods in kind instead, so all the food, nappies, clothes, etc. When I put this to the girl, she muttered fine, and I never saw her again. It turned out that the child was being brought up by his Grandparents, not herself after all. I did write to her Dad, but got quite a sharp letter back telling me where to go, which I suppose from his angle I deserved. In later years the lad made contact and we went on to build up a relationship, which was a pretty decent outcome all things considered.

Eventually I began to drift back to normal and fun shenanigans at home ensued, but my mind wasn't totally at home. My mind was still out there and I found myself planning all sorts of trips until my eye was drawn to an advert I saw in a magazine somewhere. Africa Explored.

I had broken the barrier where I'd left the comfortable net of my friends looking after each other when we went away and ventured off on my own, using my wits, learning from mistakes and discovering who and when to trust others or listen to my own instincts. I knew that every time you come back from travels and adventures you come back a slightly different person and that the longer you were away the more influential upon yourself these differences became. I hadn't gone off round the world on any kind of voyage of discovery, or seeking myself, or any such deep sounding concepts. No, I'd gone looking for fun and shenanigans, and the self-discovery came pretty much by accident. And though I had been incredibly nervous, and yes, scared, when that plane to India and beyond became real, I knew on my return that it was time to explore somewhere a bit more mysterious and hell, I knew nothing about Africa.

Apart, that is from what my parents told me as a kid, which was very little. Everyone, they seemed to think, was starving all the time. This knowledge was usually passed onto us when we didn't finish our food when we were young.

"You eat that up" my Mum or Gran would say "Or I'll send it to the starving children in Africa."

Then, when our teensy little stomachs could honestly not manage any more potatoes, they would whisk the plate away and announce that right, that's it, it's going to the starving children.

At the time, I really couldn't see the threat there, even though it was clearly meant as one. It struck me, in fact, that it sounded like a pretty fair plan. I had too much food, the African kids were starving, so surely sending them the extra food was a good thing? In fact, for a while as a young child, I began to deliberately leave a bit of food even if I was still hungry so that the poor children could have some. I wasn't really sure how it got there, or what state the gravy would be in, but it seemed like the right thing to do. I was incredibly disappointed when I realised that it all went in the bin, and that I'd forfeited some pretty decent home-made chips (Cooked in lard, too) after all. I did express my dismay about this to my Mum and Dad when I learned the truth, who decided that I must be pretty stupid for believing that in the first place. Like the Santa Claus thing.

"You must be kidding" was the manager's reaction at work when I made the request for six months unpaid leave. "Tell you what, we'll get back to you about that."

They did, the next day and told me that my request had been refused.

"Don't worry, Mulligan, knowing you, I'm sure you'll get out to Africa one day."

"Oh, I will. I'm still going. I just thought it would be good to have a job to come back to."

"You're still going to go? Even if you lose your job?"

Though hard to understand, the urge to explore was too strong to worry about my job, there would always be another job when I got back.

"Yep. No offence to the place. But I'm definitely going"

One of the managers with a reputation for being a bit of a hard ass came by my sorting frame the next day.

"Mulligan. You've got your time off. Make sure you come back this time!"

Apparently, I found out later, it was him that went in and pleaded my case. Well, what do you know? Either he had an itch to travel he hadn't scratched yet, or had had a bit of a past we didn't know about. Either way, I jumped with joy and began working and saving as much as possible. Finally, I booked a place with the Africa Explored Company, which was run by, unromantically enough, a bloke in Wales. It seemed they ran converted Army trucks crossing the continent. It was a way of travelling called overlanding, which I had not heard of before, but seemed a pretty decent way to cross into the unknown. The adventure I booked was to begin in Dover, with the truck heading through Europe, crossing to Morocco, then travelling through Algeria, Niger, Burkina Faso, Ghana, Benin, Nigeria, Cameroon, Central African Republic, Zaire, Uganda then ending in Nairobi, Kenya. There was an option to carry on through other countries out to Victoria Falls, but I figured by then I'd have enough knowledge of all things African to continue on my own at that point.

Eagerly I awaited the day, doing overtime and taking extra DJ work on at night, sometimes finishing in a club at 2.00am, and back in the Post Office by 5.00am. Still, every letter a mile…

Then it went totally wrong. My ticket was booked and paid for, time off secured, when I got a call from the guy who ran the company. It had all kicked off in Algeria, and travelling through there was, in his opinion, a no-no. There was, it seemed, no way of going around. I'm guessing independent travellers could risk it if they wished, but as a company he wasn't going to risk paying out if his passengers got shot, which in fairness is a pretty reasonable concern.

The money back was offered, of course, but an alternative he suggested was he could put a few of the different routes they used further south together, but you'd have to make your own way to Nairobi to start, where he had trucks finishing the expeditions from before the issues in Algeria had escalated. The civil war had been going on for a couple of years, but in September of 1993, The GIA, a jihad group called Groupe Islamique Arme, had begun killing foreigners, and set a November deadline that all foreigners were there at their own risk. By the end of the year they had killed 26 foreigners, and most of the others had left the country. This, of course happened whilst I was merrily posting letters and looking forward to my adventures. That was it. No spare food off me for starving Algerian Guerrillas, that was for sure!

There was no doubt in my mind that I was still going. Looked like it was the jumble of trips then. And a month later, out I flew to Nairobi, Excited, carrying very little luggage, and once again the memories of home seemed to drop away. And it was like I had stepped on a plane in Los Angeles, and gotten off it in Africa. Let the shenanigans commence.

II

The guy who ran the company suggested carrying a copy of the Africa Explored booklet, so as to identify others from the trip at the airport. I didn't bother, but spotted a couple of other people wandering around with them, so by the time we arrived in Nairobi, a small group of us had formed and found ourselves with a day to kill in the city. Another group from the expedition had also got together and hired a minibus for about £12 each, whereas we had decided on an overnight train to Mombasa, which is where the trucks would actually be leaving from. All this info was in the very handy, though badly photocopied, booklet we had been sent. The train cost £17 each, included 2 meals, and was a sleeper too, no less. Well worth the extra fiver, I reflected. Before leaving, we went up the conference tower, and whilst sitting in a park a friendly fellow came over chatting to the group, and offering advice on what and what not to do in Nairobi. The others, mainly studenty types, chatted away to him, while I decided to have a sleep. I pretty much knew what was going to happen.

Sure enough, one of the others woke me up and told me that the bloke was getting really weird, and nearly crying about how he needed to finish his studies, and how hard it was as education was expensive there. In between this, he aggressively told other touts to go away from the group.
"Give him money."
"He hasn't asked for money. He just says how hard his life is. But he's getting more aggressive. He might be a bit unstable."
I sat up.

"Thanks, mate. You've been pretty helpful. But we gotta go now."

I gave him a few Kenyan Shillings, amounting to about a quid. He looked disappointed, but wandered off. Seemed I'd been out cold for about two hours, and it was time to get to the train station.

"I thought he was just being friendly. He seemed really nice at first, when he came over. He said he likes to practice his English when he can."

"Get used to it." I told them. "You're going to get a lot of this. Tell them politely to go away, and don't engage."

I could see they didn't really believe me. They'd learn.

On arriving in Mombasa, we caught a taxi to Tiwi Beach, where we would find, we were told, the trucks for the expedition. We were also warned by the taxi driver not to walk from the beach to the main city if possible, but to use cabs. This, it turned out, was not just the driver securing trade but was in fact pretty sound advice. Muggings on tourists who stray off the busy paths were quite common it seemed.

We found an area with a number of the converted trucks parked up. It seemed that there was more than one company based there, and ours had two trucks parked together. We wandered up and found a small, tough looking Kiwi guy called Ron cleaning one of the trucks. He turned out to be our driver and possibly the most miserable person I'd met since arriving here. He took our names and chucked us some tents.

"How do you put them up?" one of the student lads asked.

"You a student?"

"Yes…Engineering."

"Well, Engineer the fucker up then. Just use your big brain. Oh, and it's two to a tent."

"What if you are here on your own?"

"Make a fucking friend."

To be honest, I quite liked him straight away.

We found a pitch on the beach near some other tents. I shared a tent with a young Australian girl, Rhonda, in what was and what remained a purely platonic arrangement. She was a naïve sort of girl in some respects, yet had been travelling solo for some time, and getting by OK. She also had what was possibly the most annoying squeaky voice I think

194

I'd ever heard. It's these little traits in people that I was to learn make a lot of differences when you travel 24 hours together.

Which is how the expedition was to be. There were 20 of us plus Ron the Driver and his girlfriend, Emma, an English girl also working for the company. We were a mix of Brits, Aussies, and Kiwi's on our truck, but the other bus – a word the drivers all seemed to hate - seemed to have more of a mix. The truck was converted so that there were two long benches down the back, which opened up into lockers where our luggage, the tents, and food all went. It was mainly open, but a canvas covering would go over it in case of rain. We all threw into a food kitty every so often, and we'd stock up at various places along the route.

This was to open up learning about the ways of many small markets in the different countries we were to pass through. In the more tourist areas the trick was to haggle. Now, you could tell that the vendors knew that tourists love to go home and brag about their haggling skills, so they had perfected the act of seemingly being beaten down, and looking defeated by the tourists' obviously superior haggling skills no doubt developed after years in Waitrose or Tesco. So everyone was happy. However, the genuine food markets which were not particularly for tourists seemed to embrace a culture where the fact you were a white outsider clearly meant you had money, and they told you a high price and stayed there, even as others bought products beside you. The trick was to wander around enough stalls till you found someone who realised that you were about to buy a weeks' worth of his trading in one go and that doubling his profits that week was better business than us wandering off. We always found such a place.

We spent the best part of a week on the beach waiting for various people to arrive. There was a little food place there where you could get a decent meal for about 90 UK pence, still expensive by Kenyan prices, but handy enough. The beach was a pretty nice place though, so plenty of swimming and what not. You just had to be careful about going too far from the designated area. At two points at each end of the beach, there were turrets, like lifeguard stands, except the guys had rifles. If someone tries to mug you on your side of the beach, they will shoot. If you walk past them, you are on your own.

We heard about a German couple a few weeks ago that had gone for a walk past these guys and been butchered by machete, seemingly the weapon of choice around here. This, as we had just arrived, seemed a bit daunting. However, as the Expedition went on, I began to hear a lot of

195

stories about things that happened "just last week". Most involved machetes and death. I can't truthfully say all these things didn't happen the week before, but my guess is they are all true stories that have become warning anecdotes. Such as the group that got in a fight with local Masai after camping off a designated camp spot on their territory, and one guy was killed and needed to be strapped to the roof of the truck for a week to get to a city, whilst his distressed girlfriend was in the truck too. Another was a guy who pissed off the local police and they found him murdered in his tent the next morning and the police wouldn't come out.

By the end of the week, we had decided that the rite of passage was what we named the follow through club. Contrary to certain opinions, the reason we get bad stomachs abroad is not so much to do with low hygiene, or bad food, but simply that we take in new bacteria and such that we are not used to. Though ice cubes are usually to be avoided in places where you cannot drink the tap water. One by one after the first couple of days, we all would experience that sudden feeling, and it was touch and go whether you made the toilet facilities or not. In fact, there was no shame in telling others on the beach that you had just shit your pants, and were going to your tent to change. I saw one of our lads, a 6ft6 beanpole of a bloke called Dave running to the toilet one afternoon with one of the weirdest, leggy runs I'd ever seen. Unfortunately, he didn't quite make it, and exploded a days-worth of crap out of his baggy shorts just as he reached Rhonda coming out of the toilet, who at just under 5ft had a particularly unpleasant experience. She didn't really speak to him for a couple of days, but with her squeaky voice, that was possibly a small mercy.

The night before we were due to leave, I was sitting with some Irish UN soldiers based nearby in the little café/ bar area on the beach when a group of stunning African girls arrived, who the soldiers knew. A few drinks later we were all paired off, and one girl, a veritable Amazon of a woman with the smoothest of skins and breasts to die for came with me back to my tent. Rhonda was in there, and I asked her to nip out for a while.

"Mulligan" she whispered, even though she was right next to me and my new friend. "I think these girls are hookers."

" I think you're right and don't really care." I whispered back. She left the tent and zipped it up. I was just taking my shorts off when the tent zipper started to open, and a packet of condoms were thrown in, which somewhat ironically bounced off my old man. After some fun shenanigans, the girl left to go to the toilet and didn't come back. Not a problem, but I did see her leaving another tent two down from me in the morning. I never found out if she had another proposition when she left, or came back to the wrong tent and some guy had the best surprise of his life.

It turned out that there are a huge number of campsites, designated spots and truck stops all over the continent where these sort of vehicles and expeditions would arrive. So though a kind of beaten path, a lot of these places would have been impossible, or at least very difficult to arrive at or even find if you were travelling by hitchhiking or train. Or even your own car as the people who drove these trucks had an excellent knowledge of these routes, and didn't share that knowledge freely. They knew places that were not particularly prominent in any of the rough guides or whatever. We headed back towards Nairobi, where on the second night we stopped at a restaurant called Carnivore, where you got a plate of roast potatoes and they came round serving all sorts of meat, from beef and goat and working up to Zebra, Crocodile, Hartebeest, snake, etc. Nothing endangered though, which is no doubt a good thing, unless you had a real hankering for a panda sandwich or something. There was a nightclub attached, where we went dancing, and the lads were approached by another group of very attractive African girls. I had a couple of drinks with a girl who was really funny, but politely declined her offer to come back to my tent. After all, my hard earned money was for exploring, I decided, and so had an early night instead. I saw one of the other lads at breakfast who told me the girls all went back to the tents, so some of the lads had to sleep outside and got chewed to death by Mosquitos (Which was to become a way of life.)
"How much were these girls charging?" I asked, chuckling.
"What? Oh no, they weren't hookers. They were just all out partying."
I stopped chuckling and kind of swore.

The route we were following took us through part of The Great Rift Valley, known to some as the cradle of humankind. Now, there's going back to your roots, but this sure couldn't be beat on that score. This was where we first began to encounter the Maasai, the semi nomadic tribes people so associated with Kenya and Tanzania. The Maasai were not

197

originally native to this area....They were, and still are, a warrior race that conquered their way south from North Africa, till they settled in these areas. As they judge wealth and prosperity on cattle, these lands proved invaluable to them.

They have over time learned to exploit the tourist trade, especially in the sale of souvenirs. However, this is usually in the form of clothes or jewellery and at no point did I see a Rift Valley snow globe, though it could be that I just didn't look hard enough. Whole Maasai villages see armies of tourists on trips organised from local hotels every day, and have gift shops at the exit of the village with extortionate prices. However, they are a beautiful, tall race of people, and with the distinctive red robes and native bling, they give a glimpse of the Africa we think we want to see.

This is where our driver came into his own. These overland guys tend to avoid those sort of places, and instead know of small villages where for a small fee, we could park outside, with the blessing and safe keeping of the villagers. And here, whilst parked, you could, if you were lucky and language skills allowed, get to talk to some Maasai villagers, though they always had an eye on selling you something. However, one recurring thing we learned was that they did NOT want their photo taken, even if you offered money. This was a different situation in the more tourist friendly villages, I gathered. In fact, if you so much as tried to point a camera their way, they would giggle and laugh, but disperse and turn their back on you and hide their faces. I tried to get a couple of crafty ones, but wasn't ever quick enough. After a short while I didn't try or ask. After all, I began to remember how infuriating it was as a punk with coloured hair back in the day when walking through town, and tourists would gather round and start taking photos. I should have realised straight away to respect their wishes on that particular one, but hey, maybe those tourists back home saw me with the same admiration I had for these people? Hmm.

These stops were leading to us camping outside the Maasai Mara game reserve, where we would be hiring the white open top safari jeeps and a driver for a couple of days. 1,510 km square of beautiful, wonderful land. Entering a game reserve for the first time, it's hard to disassociate from a safari park at home at first. You realise that instead of bringing the animals to a small area of land, they have designated massive areas of land where the animals already are. And what animals!!

The thing to remember – and which causes a certain type of tourist to get worked up – is that this is most definitely not a safari park or zoo. So there is no guarantee exactly what or when you are going to see the wildlife. This is where you begin to grasp the size of the area you are in. But the drivers can track, and will do their damnedest to make sure you get your money's worth. Because that money is what helps keep these places going. And they are needed, to fight back against development and poaching. It's a sad fact that the wildlife go about their business, unaware of the dangers to their species. They are neither angry with, or grateful to humans in regards to their future. And the very last animal of any species will take its last drink one day, and die, never knowing that millions and millions of years of its evolution and survival has just come to an end for rapeseed oil, or burgers, or a nice coat, or even a snow globe.

We'd been driving maybe half an hour when we spotted our first herd of Elephants. This was it -This was the real thing. As a young lad, my parents had taken me to the long gone Coventry Zoo, where a lone Elephant lived in a small concrete enclosure next to a camel in the next enclosure. I thought it looked a bit sad then, and in later years realised how horrible those early zoos were. I genuinely don't think the owners meant to be cruel as such, but they, and the patrons, certainly had no idea the misery these creatures were in. So I'd seen an Elephant before. But not like this. A herd of healthy, naturally living magnificent creatures, walking majestically across the land.

We saw Zebra galore, along with Gazelles and Giraffes, and saw eagles soaring overhead. In fact, we were having our breath taken at pretty regular intervals. Then towards the end, as we had to leave by six, as all the vehicles did, we caught sight of a mother Rhino by a waterhole, with its calf. Amazing. As we were leaving, we also passed a herd of Buffalo, another of the so-called "big 5". Certainly a day to remember.

Back at camp, the Maasai guys guarding the camp offered to do a traditional dance for us, for 100 shillings each, which was quite a bit of cash. However, we agreed, and they did the traditional dance that we are all familiar with, which involved a lot of singing and jumping up and down. I pondered how the elderly Scots in the Tam O'shanter club would have felt about this. They'd found the Cossacks annoying enough. I could just imagine it.

"I hope they don't damage the ceiling with all that jumping up and doon. Have you seen the bloody height of them?"

If I'm being honest, I felt a bit cheated. Sure, it was interesting, but we knew it was just staged. For all I knew, they'd seen a video of Sid Vicious pogoing, and were doing that. Nevertheless, they were doing a fine job of looking after the camp, so fair's fair.

Next morning, we set off again and I did indeed buy a bracelet of a Maasai girl who came down by the camp. I didn't really want a bracelet, but wanted to see her clothes close up. The people in the last couple of villages we had camped near were not especially in traditional clothing, a lot of the young guys wore jeans and shirts and it wasn't deemed correct to approach the girls as such. But this girl, as she was selling stuff, was in full traditional gear. Like most of the women, she had a shaved head, and was wearing a blaze of colours, from the traditional Kanga, a kind of cape or robe, to the jewellery and various other pieces of clothing. The only thing out of place were a pair of old trainers. What also struck me were her features. She had a strong, proud look about her that I found impressive. This turned out to be quite representative of the women. They also seemed generally happy.

In fact, travelling across the continent, you are struck by how happy a lot of the people seem to be. Mention this back home and someone will always tell you that yes, this is common among the poorer nations, that they don't need as much to be happy, and in fact we have too much and it doesn't make us happy. This may or may not be true, but I learned that I would not call all these people poor. In relation to Europe in terms of money, and wealth, and stuff, sure, but I believe poor to be subjective. I don't mean poverty, that's a different and more brutal issue, but the line between rich and poor. We have money, and a huge chunk of it goes on buying a house. A couple gets married in many of these villages and the community builds them a house. I was to find that as we explored and met more and more communities that most of the people didn't consider themselves poor at all. I'm not sure they felt we were especially rich compared to them either, contrary to what a lot of people seem to think. It does begin to get you to think about how valuable money actually is, on a deeper level, though I'm not going to say it doesn't buy you happiness, as I've found that it has over the years, especially in pubs, seemingly. Happiness with a delicious frothy head on it.

Like a lot of these sorts of questions, there is no definitive right or wrong answer. Only opinions. And people will never agree on those.

Well, the next day's safari did not let us down either. Again, plenty of zebra and various bouncy deer like critters, but also hippos in a river. Hippos are actually the large animal that kills more humans in Africa than any other, for even though they are vegetarian, they are immensely territorial. Oddly with that, on various occasions we'd camp somewhere and a hippo would walk through. Emma explained that they don't really know what to make of tents. They can smell you, but don't see any danger.

Then, finally, Lion. I think everyone wants to see lion. If they don't, they should. The first pride we saw were merely basking on some rocks, and eyed us quite nonchalantly as we went slowly past. None of the wildlife see anything particularly odd about the jeeps. They have seen them all their lives, and to them are no different to the other beasts and critters they come across, except usually less threatening. Usually. We later saw another pride lazing around on the edge of a big herd of zebra. I was surprised that the zebra, and other prey animals seemed so relaxed whilst grazing near the lions. Hell, if I was a zebra I'd be nowhere near those things. Or if I must be, I'd make sure I was by some sick or older zebra so I could make a bloody good dash out of there when the buggers got hungry!

So a truly fantastic couple of days then. Which was great. Because we weren't to know it then while still wide eyed and mesmerised by what we had seen, but the longer you are out there, you can in fact become a little blasé about some of the animals. For the first couple of weeks, while we were driving along, someone would shout "zebra" or "Giraffe" and bang on the back of the lorry cab for Ron to stop, which he would, but shout back for us to 'get a fucking move on taking photos as he had a bloody schedule to keep.'

But then after a while, someone would shout "Zebra" and everyone would kind of grunt and look up from their book for a moment and mutter "cool", and that was about it. Except for a girl called Ingrid. Though she had that name, she was in fact English and a bit of a strange one. She had a way of telling a story that would have you dropping off, then she'd hit you with a remarkable ending such as,

"....And That's how my Uncle helped set up Virgin Records with Richard Branson." And you had to get her to tell the story again. And these things were not made up, she was remarkably truthful, just a shockingly bad story teller.

She also picked her nose a lot, with no shame, and would look at the contents on her finger. I guess a lot of people do it in private, or a quick sneaky poke when no-one is looking, but it should be reminded that we were on two rows at the side of an old army lorry, facing each other. And the journeys between places were usually quite long. There's only so much book you can read, or crap you can talk, and you'd at some point find yourself with nothing to do except look at the people opposite. Of course, as is the way with people, everyone had 'their' seat. Ingrid sat opposite and one down from me. So when she went into a good old nose dig and content muse, I'd generally have nowhere else to look. As the months roll by, it's this sort of thing that makes you want to actually strangle people.

However, to give her credit, she never ever lost that initial excitement and awestruck state that the rest of us seemed to lose one by one. Each and every animal we saw there, she gazed at it like it was the first she had ever seen. I really rather liked that in her.

When I say blasé, I do not mean to experiencing new sights and places. Or new animals. Not at all. There would be days on a long transit when you would see nothing at all, then suddenly a lake with crocodiles would come up, and that excitement kicked in. It was just certain animals were so plentiful, it became like seeing cows off a train.

I also found that my ability to do somewhat idiotic things did not diminish out there, in spite of some rather different dangers to being shot at, or owing thousands in a card game with the Chinese. I first discovered this before we even got out of Kenya, in a place near Lake Naivasha. There was a newlywed couple on the truck, Gary and Jane, who were a pretty fun pair and somehow whilst by this lake, myself and Gary got pretty drunk one night and decided to go looking for hippo, which is possibly one of the stupidest idea we had for a while, due to the aforementioned habit of them killing people. Probably stupid people, at that. The next day Jane told us that she'd come to get us and found us calling out,

"Here, hippo, hippo, hippo, here hippo, hippo, " like we were calling for Lassie. Luckily, the hippo's took no notice, and we clearly lived on to do other stupid things. A good job too. I did wonder afterwards that if I had been lying on the ground, semi chewed in half and my head rather flat from where a hippo stood on it, would the last thing I saw have been a large fat gay Maasai guy in a multicoloured flowery kanga saying to me, "Oooo....Uko Sawa?"

A couple of us hired a boat the next day and went fishing. There was Bob, the oldest guy on the trip, and a bit of a seasoned traveller, Baz, who was nicknamed Baz the Barman, as he had turned his locker on the truck into a veritable bar, and Toby, who had quickly earned the nickname Fuckwit. Unfortunate as this was, it was not due to him actually being a fuckwit, for he certainly wasn't. He was, however, the group's hippy, whose first port of call in each town we came to would be to go off to find his man, to top up his own supplies of happiness. The nickname came when he told us he looked like a character called Terry Fuckwit in a spoof adult comic of the time called Viz. It just kind of stuck after that.

This was actually the first time in my life I had ever been fishing. I had no idea what to do, but we took a cooler of beer, and sat out on the lake all morning. I did not catch a single fish, but found I had one of the most relaxing days of my life. We just sat, drank beer, and talked about all sorts of crap. I vowed that I must go fishing when I got home, but to this day never have. A shame. I got off the boat that morning fishless and extraordinarily happy.

Later that day we headed off to a place called Elsamere which is in fact the old home of Joy Adamson, who wrote the Born Free books after raising a lioness. It was also where she was murdered. Said to be by a servant over a wage dispute, the people at the lodge suggested that she had in fact had many run-ins with the local poachers, who strongly despised her. The area is now a conservation area, and working very much for wildlife. In fact, we got to watch a film there all about her, where I sat with my two favourite girls on the trip, Tanja and Jacinta. A pair of Australians, these were two down to earth, fun loving, much travelled crazy girls who were looking for adventures. Whatever we would do, you could guarantee these two eejits would turn it into a laugh...

Which was a skill that would come in handy for our last stop in Kenya for a while. We arrived at a place called Naiberi River Camp, in

Kaptagat. Now here was a place where shenanigans were made to happen!! There were other trucks parked outside, and a number of tents already pitched. We pulled up, as usual, and set up our tents, and wondered why a passing Swede walked past and told us, laughingly, to remember exactly where we pitched. Then Ron took us all in as a group. The place was extraordinary. It was huge, and seemed to be made of large stilts with sheets of the kind of canvas old mail sacks were made of for walls. A brook ran right through it with a wooden bridge going over it. The floor was just simply the ground, and a number of cut down trees served as tables. At one end was a bar made out of bricks, and a series of passages ran off into other little rooms.

As we arrived, there was an English-Indian guy at the door, who had a shot of vodka waiting for everyone, plus a huge spliff for the smokers amongst us to take a blast of. As this was not my thing, I got a second shot of Vodka. What a welcome. You just knew things were going to be hellish crazy.

And they were. Oh yes. During the early part of the evening, we mainly sat having a civilized drink, and even a meal. The meal was a welcome treat as essentially we took it in turns most nights to cook a huge collective meal. We'd split into little groups – I was usually with Barman Baz – and took it in turns, after lighting a campfire. It could be anything, and it was surprising the variety for 20 odd people you could come up with. This was great, and a huge kettle provided our tea and coffee needs, but nevertheless a nice meal cooked elsewhere was a pleasant change.

The place began to fill up as the night went on. As far as I could see, it was mainly backpackers, travellers and Overlanders, and not really locals. As it turned out, you didn't just go there for a night out. You camped there and drank or smoked or whatever for days at a time. There was loud dance music blasting out, and the owner or his staff encouraged people to get up on the cut down trees and dance. And boy, did we dance!

At least 3 of the girls from the group fell sick, Jane knocked her head on the tables at least 3 times, Bob passed out twice, but got straight back into it, and one by one other members of the group would drop. At this point, there were a couple of guys whose job it was to carry you back to your tent. They wouldn't stick you in your sleeping bag, of course, but at least bunged you in, so long as someone knew your tent. Hence the advice from the Swede.

Myself, Fuckwit, Tanja and Jacinta were the last four of our crowd left at some point. We were sitting on the floor when the owner came up and told us it was fine to sleep under the mats on the floor, and if we woke up, just shout to the barman and he'd bring us drinks over. Now that's service. I think, though, that we eventually staggered to our tents where I know I was woken up by more trucks pulling in. It was impossible to say if this was in the morning or afternoon. Our sister truck pulled in, with some of the others that we had met on the beach which was a great excuse for a party, and drinking competitions. I guess night rolled round again, as there seemed to be more groups of overlanders, and we were dancing on the tables again at some point, until we would drop.

Three days we were there, and the memory was just one big blur. I'm sure there were more shenanigans that happened that I have completely forgotten, or never really knew. I did however, after our final drink and going out to pack up our tents, notice a rather pretty girl from an overland truck I didn't recognise which had just arrived sitting at a table with some older blokes who had been listening in to our conversation as we tried to piece together what the hell we had been doing, which was a much mirthful and hazy bit of recalling, and she gave a big smile and a wave as we left.

"Shame she hadn't been here for the last three days," I mused.

However, it was just a passing thought. We were hitting Uganda the next day, and heading towards the Zaire border. Now, much as I had been enjoying the wildlife we had been seeing – and by that I mean the lions, Hyenas, Elephants, etc, rather than the wildlife in the River Camp – there were other animals in Africa that I was much more excited about seeing. And Zaire was where I was going to see them!!

III

To get to Zaire, we had to travel through Uganda. I knew of Uganda from when I was at school, as Idi Amin had decided to expel all the Asians of mainly Indian origin from the country. The news was full of the usual scare stories of thousands of these people arriving in Britain as they held commonwealth passports. I didn't know many Indian people as a kid ... .County Coundon was mainly white Irish, as opposed to Foleshill district, which was hugely Asian, and very few of the Asian kids went to Catholic school. The main difference that I could see was that every time a corner shop got sold, Asians – who we naively called Indians, no matter which country they were from – bought them and kept them open later. Till then, the local shops shut at 5 or 6, and that was that. If you had no milk, you drank black tea. Even if you turned up as they were closing the door, you got a stern look, and the clock being pointed at. The Indians opened till 8 or 9. Imagine!! You could get bread at 7.00pm. This was a truly radicalised concept that pensioners thought was the beginning of the end and led to the odd egg being thrown at their windows, presumably bought in a pack of six well before 5 O'clock or else they would have had to pop into an Indian shop to get them. Casual racism is always fraught with paradox's like that.

Clearly then, Idi Amin had no real desire to purchase milk late so expelled a huge community of people who had worked hard, set up businesses and contributed to the society, then as these kind of Despots do, handed the business's over to the sort of people who didn't work hard and had no idea how to set up businesses and promptly watched the country get poorer and poorer till it was struggling so much, he had no choice but to blame Uganda's woes all on Britain's Colonial and invasive past, before going on to unsuccessfully invading Tanzania with the help of the Palestine Liberation Organisation, which was oddly enough a group of people upset over their country being invaded.

Apart from the fact we were worried that we couldn't get milk late, all of this was long gone by the time we arrived. You could start to see the difference in the scenery fairly soon over the border. It's sometimes hard to pinpoint why exactly, but all countries have a unique look about them, to the point that if you see a picture of a country you have been in come up on TV say, you recognise it, even if you weren't at that exact place. I did see my first – and only – Chimp casually crossing the road at one point, which I truly enjoyed seeing, and also my first glimpse of Baboons. I have had a love of primates since I was a child, and these got my attention more than the big 5 to be honest. However, by the end of the expedition, I'd had a lot of run-ins with these monkeys.

I had a stand-off much later on towards the end of the trip when I heard a girl scream and run out of her tent. I ran in, and a baboon had her backpack, something they are notorious for. She had gone to grab it but it lunged at her and she ran. I went to grab the bag, shooing the baboon, but this was a huge male. We both weren't letting go. They would usually scram, but this one stood its ground, and we faced each other off. I could feel its strength pulling the bag. I knew those teeth could slice me up, but I just stared straight at it, till it let go, hissed and left the tent. I must have looked a lot braver than I felt, because once I saw it wasn't going to scram easily, I'd be lying if I said I wasn't very aware that it could probably rip me open.

We did the usual stuff of canoe trips round islands on Lake Albert and such; One island had a deserted village on it that had literally been wiped out by AIDS. Back home, AIDS was still being seen as primarily a gay issue, though awareness was growing. Here it was sweeping through whole communities. A village community needs so many people to survive, and below that it can fail. Here we were looking at the result of that.

At one point whilst camped by the river, Me and Bob went for a wander till we came across a large village, and entered. We were told it was polite to ask the village chief to enter, so we went to see him. The village was as we imagine Africa to be, with streets of mud brick houses and poled, thatched roofs. A lot of the villagers were in traditional attire, though not as immaculate or ornate as the 'professionals'. So it was a slight disappointment when the chief came out and was wearing an expensive shirt and Ray ban sunglasses. Damned progress. Permission granted, we went to the one shop we could find in the centre, where we got some warm coke. It was becoming apparent that there is no place on earth where you cannot get Coca cola. Though as we found out along our route, a lot of the time you buy the liquid, not the bottle. Often sold by young kids, they waited while you drank it, then took the bottle back. There is, I noticed, a particularly obnoxious type of tourist, which included some on our truck, who would drive off with the bottle, laughing that they'd bought it so it was theirs. They'd probably throw that bottle away. Meanwhile, that kid was going to get beaten, or make no money till he could save up for another bottle. You could see the distress in their eyes. Maybe travelling so much had made me more observant towards looking out for local ways, but I never failed to be angry and disappointed in such ignorant behaviour. I had many a row about this kind of thing before we finished.

The woman in the shop, a lovely lady in a tall headscarf and well-worn dress, had a lot to tell us. In fact, she shut the shop and we sat down while she told us about the local poll tax, village problems and how kids were spending money on records instead of school fees. Anyone who came to the shop also sat down and talked instead, which was to prove quite typical of village life as we passed through. They also knew where we were camped, and exactly how many of us were there, but kindly invited us to the village that night with everyone, as they were having a party, as a nearby village contingent was there talking trade, which could take days.

So that night we all went to the party, apart from Ron and Emma, who stayed behind to look after the truck. We arrived way too early, of course, and sat around drinking beers from the shop. After a while , some of the men got out their drums, and a group of girls decided to show us a traditional local dance. It really wasn't like the movies. The girls were tripping up, and the guys were out of time. Everything ended up in laughter. It was fun.

But as the night went on, this changed. As it got darker, fires lit up around the village. More and more people came to the square in the centre where we were, and the drums began to beat out a more steady, hypnotic rhythm. The dancing and singing also began to get more intense. There was no more clumsiness and tomfoolery. The other traders also performed their local dance, and then the night carried on like this. I talked to many people over that night, most drinking a local brewed beer rather than the shop. No one told us about that till we had bought most of their supplies. I had some. No idea what it was made from, but it was strong and done the job.

I was sitting on my own, watching all this unfold at one point when something blatantly obvious struck me. The dancing lights from the fires, the steady, base beats from the drums, the village all dancing and singing as one. This was a rave. Or more correctly, a rave is this. And this is what people have done since they first built villages in the Rift Valley. For all our wizardry, our progress, our civilization, there are still masses of people who go out at the weekends and electronically recreate what we instinctively do naturally. And there is a moment when you do this, as there is in the mass such as I saw in Bethlehem, where you all become one. You are in communion. I realised this and I laughed. I laughed a lot. Then I got up and danced.

As I became more familiar with the place, and the initial WOW factor of the wild animals and the scenery was wearing off as sometimes there were days of just road, it was occasionally easy to forget that this was actually a dangerous place. Stumbling across a peaceful, hippo free lake one day, we decided on a swim, and maybe a few beers. We had picked up a trick of putting a few cans in a wet canvas bag, and hanging them on the side of the truck so as to chill them a bit. Lost half the beer opening them, though. But this lake was very picturesque, with a nice forest background. We'd been splashing and swimming for about half an hour when two German guys drove up, who were apparently Water disease experts. You got used to the fact that most white people you met appeared to be an expert in something or other. Usually warning you about something you wanted to do. That was the case here too, as it seems the water was pretty dismal and a bubbling pool of various diseases. Sure as heck, though nothing too bad, we were all a bit ill for the next couple of days.

Another occasion on the road, we had begun to run short of good drinking water, and were boiling up water from similar waterholes to the one where we got sick. We got round this by adding iodine, which sure did nothing to improve the taste, but we didn't get sick.

Also, night time was a war with the mozzies. Many of us, including myself, left the tent covered in bites where we'd missed a hole in the mozzie net that night. I wondered what made the holes, until the night we heard yelling, and two of the lads were scrambling out of their tent as they had been invaded by rats.

"Of all the animals here, it's pretty piss poor if you got bit by a rat," one of them mused later. Yes, I thought. You wouldn't want one of them hanging off your penis in a squat in Amsterdam either.

We also parked up for a couple of days outside of a YMCA in Kampala, the capital. I must admit, I was tempted to get a bed in there. I was regretting that I bought the cheapest roll mat available when I came out here, and hadn't found any ground without rocks in it yet, it felt like. I was particularly annoyed that one of the student lads had brought a blow up one, that seemed mighty comfy. He liked to brag about it. So I was particularly happy when I found out it had mysteriously punctured, and he had no patches. Finally in Kampala he bought a packet of cycle patches, none of which stuck. That made me even happier. No one knows how it punctured, but I'd put good money on Tanja and Jacinta.

Exploring the city was interesting. Clearly it had been much more prosperous at one point, but many of the buildings looked like run-down versions of what would have been quite stylish colonial structures. I noticed that things were a lot more expensive here too, but we did get to stock up on fresh water. We also went out for a Chinese 22 course meal for Ron's birthday. Never did get a late pint of milk though.

Last stop before the border was a village called Bunagana. Here, Ron was securing the bookings for the next port of call, in Zaire as it was called then. We were also aware that we did not have visas for Zaire, but Ron assured us that this shouldn't really be a problem. It took a couple of days to get the booking we wanted for what was to be one of my best adventures in Africa. It was also a pretty dull camp site, possibly because by now people in the group were getting a little tense with each other. It was a large group of people with very little in common, and stuck with each other 24/7 could bring that out.

But finally we got the nod that all was well and it was time to head over the border. Though the Baboons and other monkeys had been great to see, what with my love of primates, I was about to top all of that.

We were heading off to sit with wild Gorillas.

IV

I was accidentally chased by a pissed off mountain gorilla.

So, it seemed that neither Ron nor Emma would be coming with us over the border, as they were to stay with the truck. We were to take the minimum amount of gear possible too, in fact we were to sleep three to a tent. I arranged to crash in with Tanja and Jacinta, and we packed accordingly, and hired some local kids for a dollar to porter the bags, and show us the way to the border, which they happily did as far as the crossing post. And this is where we found ourselves about to learn about African negotiating, or as some might call it, bribing our way over the border. Though I'd recently had a bit of an argument with some of the group about getting up early and being loud – which was true, being a postman and everything – strangely the same people seemed happy enough to let me do the negotiating.

210

"You can't all go over." I was told at first, by a border guard. "Only the men."

"And how much for the men?"

"$200 each. Hard currency."

And so on. They said we couldn't all go, we said that we didn't carry that much hard currency. They claimed they could give us a discount if we promised to be back by a certain time, we said we were not going to go as the women needed to come too. This took about 2 hours, till we finally agreed on the whole party going over for about 50 quid each, paid in US dollars. And there were more kids waiting to porter for us, plus a guide. We had about a 7km trek to take us to where we were going, and that was a small campsite situated in Virunga National Park.

"Bit of a problem, guys," Jacinta announced.

"What's that?"

"I've kinda forgotten to put the tent poles in the bag."

So, here we were. This was literally the middle of nowhere, and we had no tent. Everyone else was also three in a tent which gave no room for sharing. However, there was a log cabin place where we had booked in, and I had noticed a room there with some beds, of which I had no idea what they were for, so asked the warden who had taken our fee when we arrived.

"Could we rent the room for a couple of nights? Here, I have Dollars."

The warden, an old African guy, firstly said no, but seemed to consider the dollars. Judging by his pondering expression, these beds really weren't to be let out at this time for whatever reason, but the dollars could clearly open doors. He finally put the money in his pocket, said nothing, and let us into the room.

It was bliss. Finally, a bed. And in a warm, heated cabin too, as the nights in Africa can be surprisingly cold. Unwittingly a good call on Jacinta's part, forgetting those poles. Bit by bit, the others began popping into the room to say hallo, apparently, and not popping back out. I couldn't help but notice that they seemed to need to bring their sleeping bags in whilst saying hallo too, clearly for safe keeping. It ended up like one big sleepover in the end. And who knows, maybe at least one of them offered to throw in some money as me and the girls had paid for it on top of our camp fee, but I probably missed it, what with being so loud and everything. But it was warm, cosy and snug, I had a real bed, and I was about to see actual gorillas so to hell with it, have a great sleep everybody. They did. Till I woke up early and decided to be extra noisy.

Virunga is one of, if not the oldest of the National parks in Africa. The idea of a protected area for many of the species that live here for both scientific and ecological reasons was actually championed in the 1920's when the area was part of what was then called the Belgian Congo. This made a lot of sense, other than to do this they also went about displacing about 85,000 of the local indigenous peoples, who lost all their land rights and were moved to the Masisi region of the same province. Not, however, the pygmy people. The protection apparently included them, making you wonder how the champions of this cause saw them. This might sound derogatory, but until the 1890's- only 30 odd years earlier – the pygmy people were regarded as a myth by Europeans, even though various groups of explorers over the last 100 years had claimed to "find" them.

The Pygmies themselves do not care much for the term, instead using their own tribal group names. In fact, there is not a direct translation of the term as an umbrella expression for themselves. We were to meet some on the way back. Or rather, witness the porters mocking them as we walked past a man and his wife in tribal attire on the edge of a path. The porters pointed and laughed, and said something to them that clearly wasn't a cheerful Good Morning. These would have been from the Batwa people, originally Hunter Gatherers but now partial forager and traders from this region. The man was holding a large club – Well, it looked large – and waved it at their antagonists. This interaction took the rest of us somewhat by surprise, and we didn't really intercede, something I felt a bit bad about after. I guess we were just witnessing local sizeism, if that is a thing, and certainly local prejudice.

It is a large enough area that there are two active and two inactive volcanoes in the park. Starting at 1127sq miles, or 2921sq km, today it stands at about 3,000sq miles, or 776sq km, meaning that my own county of Warwickshire would fit into it 3 times with a bit left over. There are rivers, forest, mountains and over 3,000 fauna and flora species, 300 of which are endemic to the Albertine Rift, of which it is a part. One of these species is the Eastern Gorilla, of whom we were going to see.

I saw them quicker than I expected, if seeing them is the right expression.

"Fancy exploring this trail?" Tanja had asked on the second night there Leading away from the camp was an interesting path through the trees which was also one of these 'Go past the bloke with the gun and you are on your own' kind of places. So we went past the bloke with the gun and wandered down for about a mile or so, without really seeing anything of note, till we walked past a bunch of bushes where we saw a small tree just behind them moving. So with the kind of logic that gets you calling for hippos, we tried to see what it was, but nothing seemed to be there and we carried on.

Seeing it might be getting dark soon, we turned back at some point, and Tanja pointed out the spot.

"Isn't this where the tree was moving?"

"Yep, I think so. Shall we have another look?"

We didn't get time. First we heard a loud, animal noise we did not recognise, then caught the sight of something black and furry moving at speed towards us. We had a split second to think. We knew from what we had been told that if a gorilla attacks you, you squat down with your hands over your head, a sign of submission, and hope for the best. But if it was a chimp, we were in definite danger. I thought about the squatting thing, then thought fuck that, and turned and shouted "Run" to Tanja.

No need to worry about that. She was already way up the path, running at some speed. I bolted off too, and heard the Ape come out of the bush and partially run up the path, though not for long. It had seen us off. Boy, had it. I didn't look back just in case, so I was still a little unsure of what exactly was chasing us. We got back to camp, adrenalin up and pretty excited and told some of the guys working there who assured us it was most likely a Buffalo. Well, I'm no anthropologist, but I'm pretty sure Buffalo aren't black and furry and move anything like the shape we saw coming. Not that buffalo was a safe option had it been one, but that was no buffalo.

It was the next day that the first of our group went out with guides to track the gorillas. And it seemed there were two routes. One party apparently had to track for some considerable way, though felt it absolutely worth-while. The other group Didn't have to go so far.

"Yes," said one of the student lads, "We went down that trail that leads from the path. The one you and Tanja tried to wisely look and see what could shake a whole tree down."

"A-ha. And by any chance did you go a mile or so that way?"

"Yep. About that, give or take."

It cost $125 each to go out with the guides to see these wonderful creatures. Apparently we got a bit of a freebie, though it would be fair to

213

say that we really just caught glimpses. Some of black fur, some of an unknown beast over our shoulders, and some of my life flashing in front of me momentarily.

The next day was our turn. There are things you are told before heading off. Tall males, for example, are advised to keep as low as possible and long haired men are advised to wear a hat and keep it on. No food. Don't wear leather. No taking a dump nearby. This last one isn't as disgusting as it sounds. A lot of the places we camped either had a basic latrine, with a small hut covering a pit with a few planks or thin logs covering the pit, or they didn't have one at all, meaning you shit in the trees. So we mostly all had a small trowel, a bit of toilet paper and a lighter. And with some of the water, this essential kit came in pretty handy.

We got the long trek which turned out to be a bit of a groan moment at first, but I found I enjoyed the journey. We went about 2 ½ miles. Gorilla families move around, and set up a new camp every night. The guide would start from the old camp and track the family. I wondered at first what these families thought of humans coming in and sitting amongst them, and if they felt intruded upon. Apparently not, it seems, as they are used to it and see it as something that just happens, in much the same way as Zebra and gazelle graze together with a family of lions on the edge of the herds, and jeeps drive around. They have no concept that this is in any way unnatural.

I was excited for the whole trek. My love of primates as a kid had enabled me to achieve a top prize in my year for a project I had done on them in my last year at junior school. Not used to winning anything, this had me bustling with pride. This was a huge deal, mainly as the projects were, we were told, judged by David Duckham, who at the time was a Rugby Union international player, capped 36 times. He had been a pupil at Coundon Junior, my school, himself, and the reason he judged it was that his father was our class teacher. Now, whether or not the esteemed Mr. Duckham junior did actually read all the projects, and found my scrawly written ink blotted pages – I am left handed, and when we wrote in ink my arm followed my hand and smudged everything – on Monkeys and Apes to be the best one is a matter of debate, I suppose, but at the time we thought he had, so I was honoured. Surprisingly, my parents also thought this was quite grand, and my father even went on to see it as a great sporting achievement of mine, even though I'm sure writing about lemurs and, mistakenly, sloths, is not any sport I am aware of, but hey, it was David Duckham, so it was a sporting achievement.

Finally we found the family, belonging to a great Silverback known as Oscar. He wasn't visible as we tentatively squatted down amongst the family. They honestly took very little notice of us at first, and saw us as completely non-threatening. Then curiosity got the better of them, and a young male came over and pulled gently at my shoulder. What immediately struck me was the eyes. They had intelligence in them. You could see that this wonderful creature was capable of abstract thought. He wandered around the group. A couple of the very young gambolled about, but you could see the mothers looking to make sure they didn't come too near us. After 10 minutes or so Oscar appeared. Now, I'd seen gorillas on the TV and in pictures, but nothing prepared me for the size of this thing. It came and stood on all fours right by us. He was huge. His head must have been twice the size of mine. And he looked right at me.

Here it was, the moment I hadn't realised I'd been waiting for most of my life. For maybe just a few brief seconds, I looked into the eyes of this most dignified being, and he looked back. A living, breathing human cousin, with whom by historical timescales, we shared a recently common ancestor. It was one of those moments. Those moments why I live for travelling, when an event becomes so much imprinted on your brain that even to think about it at any point later on brings up an image as clear as a high definition movie right in front of your eyes. No matter what happened next, my African safari had just paid for itself.

He stood there a while and wandered off to one of the females. The other gorillas carried on doing gorilla things, and fascinating us. Finally, our hour was up. It seemed like 5 minutes. We took a walk back down the side of the mountain we had been trekking up, sharing how we felt. And then, crossing a farm, we remembered that there were huge Marijuana bushes growing quite openly, and naturally took pictures of each other standing by them. This time, the guide told us we were walking round them, and pointed to two young male gorillas playing about by one of the bushes. I'm not sure, but it looked like one of them was eating some.

This of course opened up the question of do the local gorilla populations have a drug problem? Is it linked to unemployment, and would youth centres with ping pong tables help?

It was later that it struck me that we had been advised that tall or hairy males could be seen as a threat, and what this actually meant. To me, it meant that they see us as we are, a close relative, something so similar that we were probably harmless, but we weren't getting near the females. That's creative thought. Many humans, on the other hand, were horrified and had for centuries been in complete denial that we could be related to such beasts, that evolution was just so much hooey, and would argue that point to the death. It's a shame that those people had never looked into a gorilla's eyes.

There was only time for a quick lunch when we got back, and hired what turned out to be the pygmy mocking teenagers to porter for us. We were heading downhill now, and got back to the camp in Uganda in a couple of hours, with just a small debate with the border guards, but hell, we had Ugandan visas so it wasn't an issue. We thanked them and tipped them a small amount. No respite by the truck either, we were the last group back and the truck was ready to go. We would be heading back through Uganda and towards Tanzania, where we would be crossing the Serengeti.

So just a short visit to Zaire really. Short, but packed. Coming across pygmies, adventures with Gorillas and exploring the Congo. I've had less exciting weeks.

"*It is the fate of the white man, with his shackles of civilization and acceptance of his economical bondage, to never understand that there are things in the Earth from a far older race. The older people of the world saw these as Gods or spirits. But even they never understood, they simply avoided crossing their paths. The white men from the new lands ridicule their elders as superstitious fools. But as a child discovers his parents advice to be right as he grows old and mature, the new people should not always ignore the old wisdom.*"

Frederick Douglass.

And so it was that we managed to completely piss off a River God.

After a few minor adventures travelling through Uganda, we eventually reached the town of Bukoba, about 60 KM into Tanzania. A grimy place, on first impressions, but never-the-less we camped in the grounds of a rundown hotel, and our sister truck had turned up so we had a bit of a party, as both trucks had someone on board whose birthday it was. For some reason this seemed to really annoy a small group of rough looking men sitting in the same bar as us out in the grounds. It was to turn out that these were miners from South Africa, who'd been drinking all evening. One in particular seemed ready to kick off, and rather than worry about that, I found myself pondering that the glasses I was wearing were already pretty battered, and I didn't fancy having just my contact lenses for the rest of the trip. Convinced a fight was going to happen, I went back to my tent and put my lenses in to spare my spectacles, then headed back to the bar. My instincts were right, but my timing was a bit off, and it already had started up. One of the miners, who had been particularly vocal about us in the bar, had challenged anyone to a fight, and went outside. Ron the driver, though a spawny little feller, had gone out too and as I arrived they got to it. It didn't take long. Ron, it seemed, was quite the fighter. He absolutely trashed the idiot, till another of his friends, a huge blonde guy stepped in to pull his mate away. It was just then that the police arrived. I guess the hotel people called them earlier.

The police didn't mess about. They seemed to go straight to the mouthy South African, even though he was clearly hurt, and threw him in the back of their car. They then walked over to the big blonde guy. I felt obliged to tell them that this feller had in fact tried to break the fight up.

"Hey" I called out, walking over to them, "It wasn't this guy's fault….."

I got no further. One of the policemen pushed his rifle right onto my forehead.

"What did you say?"

"Nothing. Not a word."

I figured that the blonde guy could speak for himself. The policeman lowered his gun, they spoke to the other miner, then Ron, then drove off. The miners left, and we held a bit of a war council as we figured that depending on if they were camped close by, we may get a visit off a bunch of them in the night. Ron did remind us that he actually carried a few weapons, including machetes on the truck for just such incidents. The party was pretty much over, so we bedded down, weapons handy.

Nothing happened. In fact, in the morning while we were cooking breakfast, the blonde guy came back to the campsite and apologised for his friend. Apparently it wasn't his first time, which is probably why the police went straight to him.

By itself, this would have just been another bit of shenanigans, but it was yet another odd bit of bad luck that had beseeched us since we made a stop off somewhere just before we left Uganda. We had pulled up near a waterfall to camp, and some of the group decided to indulge in a bit of splashy larks. I missed out on this, as we had a rota on who should clean the truck. Whoever cleaned it got to sleep on it that night, which was marginally more comfortable than the tents. So a little annoyed, I dutifully cleaned the truck whilst most of the others headed off with their bathing costumes to the waterfall.

On arriving, they met some locals washing in the river who quite seriously advised them not to go under the waterfall. It was a fairly small waterfall, but enough to have fun under, so the group thanked them but said they would be OK.

"Not OK" they were told. "The spirit of the river lives under the waterfall. You may use his river to wash, but not his home."

218

"We'll be alright" The group replied, which must have sounded a little condescending, but a few of them were pretty good at sounding like that anyway.

They were not alright. In fact, amongst the group, the next couple of weeks became known as the Curse of the River God. Apart from the incident with the miners, all sorts of little, and not so little things went wrong. But, and this was the thing, only to the people who swam in the waterfall.

The only contact with home was having mail sent to a forthcoming post office in a town or city, which Ron would advise would be the next one when you sent your mail. We only got mail about once a month as a result. Before getting to the next one my little tent mate, Rhonda, had a bag of her gear stolen from the very next camp, which included her money. We all chipped in till she could get some more sent. Later, one of the quieter guys, Kev, managed to cut his arm pretty badly in a freak accident. One of the girls had her boots stolen from her tent as she slept. Another one of the lads, Andy, had been getting close to one of the girls, and was gobsmacked when suddenly she got off with one of the non-swimming group. This also happened to one of the student lads, who had hit it off with one of the girls, who also very suddenly went off with a lad from another truck. Then at the post office, The kiwi girl got some tragic news about a close relative, and another of the student lads got no mail whatsoever from his girlfriend back home, who had told him if he went out here for that long she would end things with him. Looked like she was honest. Things carried on like this until we finally got a ferry across Lake Victoria. It seems crossing more water would do the trick. I escaped completely from any of it. Mind you, I thought, if that whopping big rock god in Australia didn't get me for climbing all over it, then I'd take my chances on some wet feller.

If I'm being honest, I didn't really care for Tanzania much. Walking through the towns, or even villages, people had a habit of pointing and whistling at you. Or pointing and laughing. Certainly a lot of pointing.

"It's because of the aid workers" I was told. "They have no respect for them, and assume every white stranger is here "to help".

Well, that's gratitude for you.

However, there were sights to be seen. We were on the road, about 15 miles from the nearest town one day when we spotted a bloke painting lines in the middle of the road with a paintbrush and a pot of paint. The paint pot was hanging off the handlebars of a push bike, which he had propped against a tree.

"What?" we all thought. How long has he been doing this job? This man must cycle out a little further every day, paint lines till his tin runs out, then cycle back. We waved at him as we went past and he whistled.

Another day, we saw a flat back lorry carrying bales of hay, and 3 African guys singing and dancing on the back. These guys waved. Some of us started dancing too, and for the next couple of miles the trucks went alongside, and we danced together. Probably to different music. They turned off and we all waved at each other and laughed. I liked these kinds of Tanzanians.

We caught the overnight ferry across the lake which took us straight to the Serengeti. To say the ferry was overcrowded was an understatement but a couple of us sat on the deck most of the night amongst the sleeping bodies. You slept anywhere you could. This was to be a great safari. It would take us a couple of days to cross, then we would enter the Ngorongoro crater, also a national park.

For context, the combined areas of the two regions make them slightly larger than Wales. We were also back into Maasai territory. In fact, the Serengeti – which roughly translates as Endless plains from the Maa word – runs into Maasai Mara in Kenya at the border.

We could take the lorry to campsites, but we would then embark onto the familiar white open topped jeeps. The first day was pretty fantastic, as though we had started to become used to seeing zebra, giraffe and such from the truck, it is all the better seeing them here in the remains of their natural environment. We did see these, plus Wildebeest, amazingly coloured birds, and lion. Not many Elephant, we noted, which was due to the numbers being badly poached in the 70's and 80's, though numbers were building back up. And yes, a couple of lions. Myself, I was pleased to see a large troop of baboons, along with other small monkeys that I did not recognise. It would seem the esteemed Mr Duckham overestimated my knowledge. Not to worry, I could watch the baboons all day.

In fact, the more I saw of baboons, combined with the gorillas and what I have seen of chimps, the more I realised as I observed human behaviour that the answers to all questions along the lines of "Why is he/she like that?" "How can they behave like that?" and such are right there. Right there in our cousins' behaviour. For all we have educated ourselves, civilized ourselves and moralised ourselves, we are, at heart, just slightly cleverer Chimps. Every bit of interaction within their societies we can see on a daily basis in ours. And Baboons, though monkeys, so technically a bit further down the primate ladder, are also remarkably reflective of ourselves. Especially, it would seem, in regards to stealing stuff. They do, it has to be noted, know it's wrong. So they are crafty. And it's exactly the same craftiness I have often seen in the type of thieving bastards that are so quick to take offence when you call them out on it. Oddly, I found that remembering baboon behaviour made it a lot easier to tolerate some of the more idiotic things that came along in life. Especially the idiots that cause them.

It had been a great day, but I'd got one of those recurring problems that my stomach had begun playing up a little bit. Like everyone, I'd gotten used to it every so often, and even though it was my turn to sleep on the truck I'd still give it a decent cleaning. We were in one of the designated camp areas, which was good as we had heard so many horror stories about people who parked off them. Always last week, of course. There were Maasai guys there who seemed to act as watchmen, though I'm not sure who was paying them. As we'd sat round the campfire for dinner that evening, one of them had pointed out a pair of bright amber eyes on the edge of the camp, where some large rocks met the trees.

"Probably an old lioness," one of them told us. "They don't normally come near humans too often. They know we are dangerous. But when they get old, and can't run so fast, they take more chances, and try new prey. It will go away."

I was struck by how vivid the eyes had looked in the firelight. We all joked about the lion running off with Barman Baz, and how drunk it would be after eating him. Though I must admit, I was a little relieved I was on the truck. However, into the night I woke up with my stomach churning a bit and the strong desire to use the toilet. I was getting off the truck with my torch when I remembered the lion. I shone the torch all around but there was no sign of those amazing eyes. Neither could I see any Maasai, but they tended to blend in by sitting or sleeping under long dark blankets. It was only a short walk to the latrine, but it was concrete nd had a bent nail for a lock of sorts.

I squatted down and let nature take its course. When you gotta go, you otta go. I was sat a while, as I knew there was no point walking back nd forth all night. We'd learnt how this works, as in the follow through lub in the earlier days of the expedition. And it was there, sat squatting ver a latrine full of shit that the bloody lion appeared outside the door.

221

The first I was aware was a loud thump on the door, like something very heavy falling against it. For a split second I thought it was someone else in the same predicament till I heard a deep growl, from roundabout where my head was.

"Shit!!" I thought, realising then what it was.

"Shit, shit, shit."

I could hear a heavy breathing, then another low growl, then another thump. And that is when I discovered that I had nowhere finished shitting myself. My bowels completely evacuated and I experienced the most terrifying moment I had ever had, and would ever have, in my life. I just remember praying. Not a well-chosen Catholic prayer. Heck, we'd probably be in more trouble if we met our-maker and had only got half way through the Hail Mary before our throat got bit out, but instead I actually prayed to please not let me die in this position. The idea of being found half eaten in a filthy latrine covered in shit struck me as a shocking way to go, more so than the actual dying part of it, which I also didn't fancy.

Then it went quiet. I cleaned up, stood up, and stayed still for what seemed like forever. First of all I thought that I couldn't stay in here all night, then I thought why the hell not? The nail seemed to have held. I should have made a note of where the Maasai get their ironmongery. I'm also not proud to admit that I kind of hoped someone else would get up and to go to the toilet and become a more likely ready meal than myself. No one did.

Eventually, I figured it had gone, and I could leg it to the truck. So I tentatively opened the door and stuck my head and torch out. I was later to think that this was a pretty stupid thing to do, but my etiquette in avoiding lions had been somewhat neglected back in County Coundon. I could see nothing and hastily got to the truck. I could see nothing. I also probably didn't need to go to the toilet for another week. I can only guess that the Maasai watchmen shooed it off maybe, but no one said anything the next day. In fact, I suspect that like my companions, they slept through it, and maybe the lion just didn't like the smell. I certainly didn't.

Interestingly, this incident was to become my infamous lion story for ever afterwards. It became, and still is, a running joke. If the slightest thing about big cats ever comes up, or anything loosely connected, shake my head and say 'Don't talk to me about lions.' This draws many groans from my friends who mutter 'Not again, for fucks sake' or something similar. The real joke is that I never actually tell the story. Except on the odd occasion when someone I don't know replies,

"Why, what happened?" which will have my friends moaning all the more, much to my glee.

"Well,", I begin, "There I was, out on the Serengeti….." and then tell the story not so much to impress the unsuspecting newbie, but to enjoy pissing off my friends.

Every traveller needs a signature story. Because it's always about the story.

The Serengeti did not let us down the next day either. There were more lions, Hippo, a good few crocodiles, and even a leopard later that day. One of the highlights was passing a herd of Wildebeest that must have numbered thousands. But special mention must go to the sharp eyes of the guide who stopped at one point, and signalled us to be quiet. It was a pair of African Wild Dogs. Sightings of these are so rare, that he had to report and log it when he got back. We were, apparently, some of the lucky ones to see them.

The Ngorongoro crater wasn't to let us down when we arrived there a couple of days later. Though the reserve area is much bigger than just the crater, it was only the crater we explored. Over the centuries, many animals have got in, but not been able to get back out, so it was a very condensed version of the other areas we had explored. We saw everything that we had seen already, plus both white and black Rhino. And there on the lake was the famous Pink Flamingos. After years of DJ work in nightclubs, it was good to see the origin of so many of their names.

So far, we had done a fair bit of zig-zagging around East Africa. This was down to the fact that we were on a jumble of shorter trips and safaris to compensate for not being able to do the long trans due to the warzone up North. So now we were about to travel back through Kenya again, to the beach where we started, via Nairobi to drop some of the group off who'd only booked on for a couple of months. This unfortunately included all the people I got on best with, including Tanja and Jacinta.

Now this should have been party time, and indeed it was for some of the group. At every camp near a bar we had managed to have some kind of partying. However, on the journey towards Nairobi, I began to feel really ill. The first night I dosed up on paracetamol and hoped it would shake off. It did not. I woke up feeling much worse. It was, I began to realise, very likely Malaria. This was always a real risk out there and once you got it you had it for life. I tried to convince myself otherwise, but we went out later to Carnivore again, though just the club part to celebrate and I simply couldn't. I went back to the tent early, which is most unlike me, and slept right through. Apparently the girls came back and caused chaos in the camp, playing tricks on the tents and all sorts before leaving early in the morning. I was so out of it I missed them leaving, which I was pretty pissed off about. Later that day, Emma took me out to a doctor somewhere and I really don't remember how we got there.

But it turned out that I didn't have Malaria, or any of the other various horrible diseases that you can catch, most of which have the same symptoms. It seemed that I had actually dehydrated. This was down to the fact that I have never really drank a lot of water and certainly should have been drinking more out there, but also due to the fact that it was a very dry heat, meaning you didn't realise just how much you were sweating, as it evaporated straight away. Hence, I had no idea I'd been getting rid of fluids at a far greater rate than drinking them. It was an absolutely horrendous feeling which took me a couple of days to recover by taking some sachets of some stuff or other the doctor gave me. It tasted disgusting, but eventually did the trick. From that moment on my water bottle became my best friend. And the irony that I missed the last night of drinking with my two favourite Australians due to, well, not drinking, was not lost on me.

We got to the beach, where some of the others departed, some of whom I would miss, others I was glad to see the back off. It was then Ron announced that we should get comfy as we were going to be camped on the beach for about 10 days, whilst we waited for new arrivals before setting off on the next stage of the expedition, where we would be travelling West, with the eventual aim of hitting the skeleton coast. Now that was a name to get the old excitement levels up!

V

Seeing a dinosaur coming at you can be a hell of a surprise!

Well, the beach turned out to be a pretty good call. We were only there for 8 days in the end, during which time I got to know some of the people from our sister truck better, plus people from the other trucks which were also parked up. The new people also were making themselves known, so after much swimming, exploring the beaches and some nights heading into Nairobi with Terry Fuckwit and Barman Baz, it was time to go.

Actually, the nights in Nairobi had been worth the visit. One day, a couple of us went to the cinema to see whatever was on. About 2 thirds of the way through, it started showing the middle bit of the film again and no one seemed to think this was unusual. No calling out or booing. And then the film finished bang on time, meaning it didn't get to the end. Even then, everyone just seemed to get up and go. We decided to follow the flow, and not bother trying to get our money back.

We'd also tried out a place called the Green Bar, which apparently had been open for 32 years, 24 hours & 7 days a week. It never closed. We had been warned it was dangerous, but an experience. The bar itself had thick iron poles all round it, with a small hole big enough to hand your money through, and they handed you a reasonably cold can of beer back out. We were to see this in quite a few other places too. It was pretty quiet really, which surprised us.

Fuckwit unfortunately, had made friends with his new dealer, and had been letting him listen to some of his tapes on a personal stereo tape player. This lasted till the guy went to the toilet still wearing it, and we never saw him again.

The last night we were in there, we remarked how it didn't seem to be the God forsaken place that its reputation suggested and carried on enjoying our beers. That's when someone then came in and shot someone at a nearby table. The guy wasn't dead, but fell to the floor twitching. A couple of the staff strolled nonchalantly out from the back, and dragged him out there, before running a quick mop over the blood he left behind. We had no idea what happened to him and the barman just shrugged when we asked him. A policeman wandered in about an hour later, and had a chat with the barman, they laughed a bit, and off he went. We carried on drinking.

"You know what," Terry remarked. " I wish that had been that twat who nicked my stereo."

We nodded and got another drink. You get a bit like that out there.

So, the pack of travellers on the truck was shuffled up a bit now, some gone, some new. This couldn't have come at a better time, as those little frictions and annoyances at people you're cooped up with can only get worse. But the new people reminded us of that spark of the wow factor we had all begun with before you started to get annoyed at wild animals crossing the road. Once the crew had finally all arrived, we headed off to Zanzibar, via Dar-es-Salaam, business capital and with 6 million people, the largest city in Africa.

Zanzibar is a couple of islands, with Unguja generally being known just as Zanzibar. It is an autonomous region within Tanzania with quite a history. In the 1500's, it had become part of the Portuguese Empire, but before that and at least from the 9th century it had been a base for Swahili Traders who dealt with many Arab and Persian traders, with many goods from India and Asia arriving. By the 17th century, it became a Sultanate, until eventually becoming a British Protectorate when it was decided to end slave trading from there. After the couple of months in East Africa, with its towns, small villages, massive reserve areas and forests, I found stepping off the mere 3 hour ferry and finding a place with its stone buildings, medinas, and the sound of calling to prayers from the mosques was like a feeling of walking into a different kind of Africa. As indeed it was, as all the various influences made it a quite unique place. After self-government was established in 1963, the sultan was deposed as soon as 1964, followed soon by the region merging with the then Tanganyika to form the Republic of Tanzania. Many Indians and Arabs had left due to the killings in the take-over, but enough remained to be a sizable population.

We actually stayed in a guest house, so it was the welcome feel of a bed again. Whilst the town we were in was fascinating to explore, it was a town of contrasts. Walking down a street on the first day I saw a young Arab boy sitting in the doorway of an arched doorway to a fine old house, a scene that could have looked the same two hundred years ago, except that he was playing with a Gameboy. It was little things like that which just stopped you feeling you had walked back in time.

We also took a visit out to Prisoner Island, or Changuu island to give it its proper name. It was about 30 minutes from Stone Town by motor

226

boat. It had seen part of its history as a prison island for rebellious slaves, but the name didn't come from that, but in fact came after a purchase by the first British Governor there who built a prison complex on it. This was never used as a prison, but instead became a quarantine station for sufferers from yellow fever. I'm guessing that the poor souls with yellow fever were not especially happy about this, having first the misfortune of contracting the disease, then being put on an island built as a prison – And we complain about the National Health System – but they were soon joined by some Giant tortoises gifted by the Governor of the Seychelles, which turned out a good move as they are now endangered, but here there is a thriving population.

I had a tortoise once, as a kid back in County Coundon when you could still buy such things in pet shops, though I believe my Dad got it from a bloke in the pub, where most things outside of groceries came from. With that kind of general way of naming pets with the same letter as its species he was called Tommy. Like Hammy the Hamster or Roger the Rabbit. Good job the Africans didn't keep the zebras as pets really, that would have been difficult. Anyway, it wandered off somehow one day and we never saw it again. Though oddly, in much later years, I dated a girl for a while who had lived just round the corner from me when we were kids. Turned out she had been given a tortoise the same year, by a neighbour who faced us, and whose back garden met the girl's back garden. Clearly it had to be the same critter, and yet though it was highly unlikely to be any other tortoise wandering around our street that year, she insisted I look at it to see if it was the same one, as it was still alive. How the hell, after 40 years, she thought I would recognise it I don't know, or maybe she thought it would come running towards me, slowly. To save debate, I told her I recognised it and she decided that I must have been horrible to it or it wouldn't have run away. That relationship didn't last very long.

So the few weeks I had a tortoise was about my only experience of them. So it came as quite a shock, wandering down a path on the island when out of some trees came one of the giants, which stopped, kind of looked at us, then took its 500pounds plus across the road and into the trees.

"Fuck." The guy with me said. "That looked like a dinosaur."

"Nah," I answered, "Big though." I only disagreed as it was one of the students that were bugging me at the time. Because that bloody huge thing looked like a dinosaur up close.

It was Ramadan, and as Zanzibar is 99% Muslim it was being observed. So not much in the line of food in the day. We had gone along the East and south coasts, which were beautiful. I swam in the Sea one day, and it was actually hot. Not quite bath hot, but hot rather than warm. Crystal clear water too. The unique plants and fruit we came across were amazing as well. Then at night, there would be night markets, where we could eat our fill of local and standard food from the different stalls, and enjoy a couple of beers in the cooler night air. All in all, I enjoyed Zanzibar, which in my mind I still cannot marry to the rest of Tanzania. In fact, It has its own embroidered patch in my box of many patches.

Malawi was next. We did however stop for a couple of nights bush camping on the way at the Mikumi National Park. It was another opportunity to see the big animals again, including jackals this time. Looking at the expressions on the newbie's faces, I guessed that must have been how all of us were at first. It was nice to see them like that, and realise just how awestruck we can be at nature just being itself.

Heading across towards the Malawi border, someone shouted out "Elephant" one afternoon and most of the group went to the side of the truck with cameras to take the usual photo. I really wasn't that excited and looked out of the other side of the truck to see where we were. There was a ditch. And there lying in it was a dead giraffe Calf. Creeping up to it was a large young lion. I'm not sure if he was returning to a kill or had just spotted it, as he seemed to be stalking. This was just a few feet under where I was leaning on the side of the truck, which he was ignoring. He pounced on it, and seemed almost surprised it didn't move. Then the truck started up, and he backed off as it heard the noise as we drove off. I didn't tell the others. I just thought I'd have that little memory of a hunt all to myself. Or at least to two of us, as one of the new girls must have done the same and whispered,

"Yeah, I saw that too," as the others were comparing notes on Elly the elephant.

VII

I really rather liked Malawi.

I was a little apprehensive coming up to the border. We had heard that till recently they had not let men with long hair over the border unless they cut it. I didn't have long hair, in fact most of my head was shaved, but I was sporting a long bunch of what had started as plaits, but were by now pretty much dreads. This was, to coin a phrase, the last of my Mohican. I'd like to say it was purely for style, but the real story is nature was putting a stop to my crazy punk hairstyles from earlier years. However, I had my plaits left, and didn't want to lose them.

It was OK, it turned out. That rule had recently ceased. This also was a relief to Fuckwit, who had a variation of dreads himself. First things first, we made camp near a town, where a couple of us headed off to exchange some money on the black market. We didn't need much, Malawi was ridiculously cheap. A bottle of beer was about 25p, so we bought lots to celebrate one of the student lads birthdays.

Though there was never a shortage of beer, we hadn't particularly been drinking much for a couple of weeks at this point, so it was time to let the hair down. Especially as we were allowed to have it to let down! So party into the night we did. There were another couple of trucks there, and by the end we had all been mingling merrily, sharing our various shenanigans. At some point around 5am, me and Barman Baz were debating that it must be time to get some kip, when we saw a stirring from one of the tents belonging to another group. Assuming it was someone going out for a pee, we took no notice till we saw who it was.

It was in fact Ingrid, she of the strange appearance and the perpetual nose picking. I was still sitting opposite her, and her various habits had really managed to infuriate me. I really bit my tongue on this though, as she was actually a nice person at heart, just hard to interact with. She also fell asleep a lot. But in any case, out of the tent she crawled, gave us quite a big smile, and went back to her own tent.

"I think we've all definitely had enough," Baz said.

Yes. Yes we had.

Most of the journey took us along Lake Malawi, which more or less ran down one side of the whole country, where we stopped off at various camps. One of these was Nkhata Bay, which was a great place to go exploring. We had spotted a waterfall, and a few of us decided to climb up to it. It was deceptively further than it looked. But standing on a ledge under the freezing water made it all the worth-while, even if I did nearly meet my maker on the way down. Climbing over a log amongst a pretty dense patch of trees, I suddenly felt it move. In fact, for a little bit I found my old skateboarding skills kicked in as it began to slide down a hill. An overhead branch caught my head slightly, which was probably a good thing as it made me aware of branches and I grabbed one as I passed. It was strong enough and I was swinging on it watching the log head to the edge of a huge drop not much further ahead and nearly go over. I'm guessing my weight would have made that difference. Luckily, one of the guys with me was the lad with the basketball player height who had managed to crap over my tentmate, and was able to help me off the branch without breaking an ankle. Well, those baboons may well be a bit light fingered, and chimps could snap your arm, but I for one was grateful for our monkey ancestors and their tree swinging hand genes still kicking about in my DNA, and decided there and then I would never throw poop at them. Well, not first, anyway.

At one of the stops, we hit a town and did a bit of trading. Disappointed as I am sure we all were that we could not get any snow-globes, nevertheless there were plenty of things to buy at a great little market we found. I had my eye on a carving of a witch doctor, and put all my recently acquired bartering skills to use and managed to trade a pair of old trainers I had brought that were by now falling apart. I also picked up some little statues of people that came with a story. The feller selling them told a little story about each one, for example how an old smiley guy didn't want to go to work that day, and had gone fishing instead. I really enjoyed the way the guy told them, and paid a bit more than I maybe could have gotten away with, but heck, it was stories, and it's always about the stories. That was my presents for the parents taken care of.

Wandering back to the truck with an armful of little people, a drum, a really heavy witchdoctor and a set of small carved elephants, I passed by a white girl who looked oddly familiar, but I couldn't place where from. This familiarity was compounded when she smiled at me and said,

"Hi again", before wandering off with the two older blokes she was with. She kinda had a Bjork-like look about her, but I was pretty sure

Bjork wasn't likely to be wandering through a Malawian Market, recognising a bald overlander with no trainers on.

There was no bad place we stopped over at. We had been warned that due to some extreme poverty there that we had to be extra vigilant, but luckily nothing untoward happened. At the last camp we stayed in, our sister truck had arrived too and most of the others combined into one truck to head over to another national park, but I decided to stay behind. All from my truck had gone, and a lot from the other truck. I'd been getting on well with the folk from the other truck as we pulled into more places at the same time, mainly due to the desire to see new faces. This time though, I had the truck to myself, waived the invite to join the others, and got stuck into a book on my own. It was absolute bliss! I made tea, read, listened to some loud punk which hadn't been going well with some of the others, made more tea and read again. I don't think you can ever appreciate solitude as much as when you have been forced to abstain from it. The others were camping elsewhere overnight, so the next morning I wandered over to the other truck to see how they were doing. They had a fire going, and were sitting with two big lads in motorbike leathers, drinking coffee.

The two lads were kiwis, and were going round the world on their bikes which were parked by the truck. I've no idea about bikes, but these were two pretty powerful looking bits of kit. Boy, these guys had some tales to tell. We drank coffee, shared stories and eventually the two guys powered up those cool looking bikes and headed off in a roar of thunder. I watched them go and realised I felt quite jealous. Now that was the way to see the world.

There was a little shop on the edge of the site, and I wandered over to browse at nothing in particular. There were a few overland trucks parked around as it seemed that this bit of the beach had been bought by a kind of collective of overland drivers, so people came through all the time. Nice.

I bought a bottle of coke, with a hefty deposit on the bottle, and sat on a bench just outside. I was thinking how great the time alone had been, then meeting new people travelling differently and decided that I had really enjoyed Malawi and it couldn't get much better than this.

And yet then it got much better than that.

231

A small group of people were heading into the shop when one broke off and sat beside me on the bench. It was the Bjork looking girl.

"Ha-ha, coke? Where's your beer?"

"I'm not really a drinking man," I answered, smiling as I explained my usual fib that I liked the odd snifter of port, or maybe a small sherry at Christmas.

"Of course. You look like a sherry man. Do you drink it from a bucket?"

We laughed. I liked this girl

Her name, she told me, was Gudrun and she was from Iceland where, yes Bjork came from, and everyone mentioned that she looked like her. It was then I suddenly remembered why she had looked so familiar, aside from a strong resemblance to the Icelandic indie sensation.

"You were at the real party bar near Nairobi?" I asked.

"Yep, I saw you and your friends all dancing and partying. I've seen you guys at some other stops too. I was going to talk to you in a club at another place as you always seem to be laughing, but you were with two crazy looking girls, and you were all having so much fun, I felt I'd be invasive. Hey, the people on my truck are great, but all a lot older. I'm the youngest and just want to get a bit smashed sometimes. You guys must have the coolest truck on the road."

Boy, was she wrong. I guessed she'd meant Tanja and Jacinta in the club, and when they had still been on the truck with some of the others that had left at the same time as them, it had indeed been a bit of a party truck. Since then, however, the partying had died off a bit. Sure, there were a few good folk on there, but very straight-laced compared to the others. If Gudrun had saw us sitting in the back, watching Fuckwit being permanently stoned, or Ingrid picking her nose, or scratching her arse, or the students repeating the only two life stories they actually had over and over again she would probably have tiptoed past me and hoped I hadn't seen her.

But she did not tiptoe past. In fact, we bought a couple of cans of beer, and sat and compared stories. The trucks had taken pretty similar routes, probably down to the same problems with the warzone up north, and the situation in South Africa.

This was 1994, and literally a couple of weeks away from the forthcoming election in South Africa. Not just any election, but this was to be the first one where people of all races could vote. It was to go down in history as the culmination of a four year process that was to end apartheid. Nelson Mandela was going to be elected the first black president and the African National congress party was to gain power. And it scared the crap out of a lot of people. Analysing the results of the election would be pretty complicated, and naturally there were accusations of cheating and fraud, but the nature of the results gave KwaZulu-Natal to the IFP, and gave deputy presidency to the white national party which went towards preventing a civil war.

It was the threat of a civil war and mass violence that people outside of South Africa were scared of, as it was a powerful country in Africa and held much sway, trade embargoes or not. It was also the reason why the Overland trucks had decided not to go into the country, in case they got caught up in any subsequent violence either before or after the election. In fact, hindsight showed it would have been OK, but after the Algeria problems, no one was taking the chance.

It was due to this smoking cauldron of political upheaval, a moment that would make history and the change of a complete way of life that I came to be having a couple of beers with a pretty Icelandic girl. In fact, to this day I will raise a glass to either Mandela, (well, the good one), or F.W. de Klerk if their names crop up, not because of any particular political views, but purely because I love drinking beer with attractive women. There are those that would say that this was very self-centred of me, and they would be quite right. I'll raise a glass to people who criticise me as well, for they are usually right, though with not much chance of seeing any change forthcoming. Growing up in my house left me pretty oblivious to criticism. Mind you, sticks and stones may break my bones, but keep on at me enough and there's a good chance I'd pick up either if they were nearby and shut some moaning eejit up.

So we drank some nice early beers, and had a hell of a good laugh. This girl was like a personality rocket firing out jokes and funny stories by the bucketload. And this was to carry on for the rest of my trip. I found myself looking out for their Encounter Africa truck at camps and rest stops and if I saw it, I'd look out for her, and vice versa. And for a good few times to come, whenever we met up, we'd end up partying. We would go for many days without meeting up, but every time we did it really was the best of times.

This first encounter, however, ended with a slightly tipsy Gudrun getting back to her truck and then heading off about an hour before our people arrived back with their enthusing about the wildlife in the place they had been, and how I really should have gone. I just smiled. I really couldn't have had a better couple of days. So after packing up and a bit of lunch, off we headed towards the Zambian border, and I got to watch Ingrid picking at some scabs on her knee, and listen to the students telling their two stories again.

We were literally just passing through Zambia, with the Zambia-Zimbabwe border being the real destination. Why? Because of Victoria Falls. And not just because we wanted to marvel at this natural wonder of the world either, though that was important too. No, we had heard they ran a bungee jump there, and it was the world's highest, no less. There was absolutely no way I was going to miss out on this. One thing that was quite obvious as we drove along was the amount of huge trucks laden with belongings driving through the country that we passed. This was the Afrikaners. In the run up to the elections, concerned with the inevitable voting in Mandela, many Afrikaners were packing up lock stock and barrel, and heading into Zambia. Ron reckoned it was that they were intending to make it the new South Africa. We didn't get to meet any on the road which was a shame, it would have been interesting to hear how they intended to do that. At this point in time, Zambia was suffering an economic depression, mainly brought on by the low price of copper, one of its principal exports.

I chatted to a couple of Zambian guys on a campsite, one of whom told us that the South Africans had been coming for a while. 14 years earlier, the neighbouring Zimbabwe had ceased being Southern Rhodesia after the elections ousted the white government, and led to the rise of Robert Mugabi, first as Prime minister, later as President. Very slowly at first, people were seeing the deterioration of a country once known as the breadbasket of Africa and began to see some rather nasty situations potentially arising. This guy himself had left after some of his family had been caught up in one of the massacres attributed to the then newly established Fifth Brigade, formed and trained with Mugabi's alliance with North Korea. Zambia had once been Northern Rhodesia, but been independent from its ties with the British since 1964. There had been about 70,000 Europeans in the country at the time, who had a disproportionate amount of the economic wealth of the country, but these mainly stayed on, and Zambia flourished at first, even working with the Americans to look at solutions to the problems in Southern Rhodesia. A it would flourish again, when the copper situation resolved itself by the late 90's. Meanwhile the South Africans were shit scared, basically, and some were bailing out.

Much as this all fascinating to find out, and part of a huge web of world changing history in the making, I couldn't help but consider that as long as it did not interfere with me doing the world's highest Bungee jump, there was very little I could do about it, other than potentially buying a snow globe with a statue of Nelson Mandela in it.

VIII

Yes, I did the world's highest Bungee Jump.

Well, eventually. After travelling with not much happening for quite a while, Victoria Falls was a revelation. We pulled up, and a mere 5 minutes' walk from the camp was a bar/restaurant called Explorers, that was a buzzing hive of adrenalin. Because here at the falls was every activity you could possibly fit in. White water rafting, Bungee, microlighting, parachuting and more. And at any given point, groups of people would be arriving after completing some amazing adventure, and the shenanigans would begin. It became my regular haunt for the whole time we stopped there.

Well, The Afrikaans migration may not have interfered with the bungee jump, but death in a family did. It seems that the lads who organised it had closed it for a while to attend a funeral. Well, I assumed it was family. It was better to assume that than find out it was one of their customers. I was bitterly disappointed, but there were other things to do.

I had also got friendly with a girl off our sister truck that also had arrived, a German girl called Claudia. She'd told me she was feeling quite isolated, being the only German on board since she'd joined back at the beach with the second wave of travellers. I actually don't think it was that, I'd travelled enough with, and drank with enough Germans over the years to know that being on the road sure breaks down those sorts of boundaries. Though she didn't say it, I suspect the real issue was that she was the only gay girl, and like our own truck, people had been pairing off bit by bit. When I mentioned how my little tentmate did not seem interested in any of the guys, she perked up and asked if she was a lesbian girl, as she put it. The look of disappointment when I told her I didn't think so, she was just a kind of adult child pretty much told the story. In fairness, I hadn't paired off, or was likely to, with anyone off the truck either, so I kind of felt her pain. Kind of. I was looking out for a certain other truck that didn't arrive at the Falls while we were there. A pity, I'd have loved to have partied in Explorers with Gudrun.

The whole time at the Falls was the perfect mix of adventures and shenanigans, the perfect place to share stories and party. There is a National park on each side of the border, and I made sure to do both. Back in Canada, myself, Brody and Ferret had taken the boat out under Niagara Falls and been incredibly impressed so I'd expected something similar. Though similar in as much as it was a whopping big waterfall, this was a completely different league. Like most of the mighty waterfalls, it is not just one cascade of water, but a series of drops. In fact, it was so wide, I could not see it all in one panoramic view. It takes a fair bit of walking. Which is fine, as there is plenty to see and feel. Due to the constant spray of water, the area for about a mile each way has its own little ecosystem going on which is intriguing to see.

On one of the days, a couple of us headed off to climb down to an area known as the Boiling Pot. Unlike the dry heat we were used to, this was a more humid kind of heat, again due to the unique circumstances. The flora was different, and there was the permanent noise of the nearby falls. It was here I caught a break with some monkeys, though I wasn't sure what type they were. A small group of them were sitting on a rocky area I was walking past, so I stopped to look. Clearly used to people they seemed to take not much notice. The others I was with walked on but I edged nearer and slowly towards the little scamps. I had no idea if this was wise or not, but decided to take the chance. It worked. I got pretty close and sat down, and it wasn't long before a couple of them tentatively came near me. One came up and poked my pocket, then scampered off. It was clear that to them I may have been a source of a tasty snack, but they were out of luck today. I sat still and let them be, and though only there for a couple of minutes, it felt like I'd been watching them for hours. I carefully got up and left, aware that no matter what I saw next, this hit the button for me.

Over the next few days, our adventures were many. In one of my "Why am I not dead yet" moments, I wandered into the water at a quieter spo

236

and got as near to the edge as I could. A couple of us microlighted and saw elephants, hippos etc from the sky, which gave them a whole new context. We hired a kind of floating platform for a booze cruise one evening, and got to see hippo at night pretty close up. Then there was the kayak safari down the Zambezi. A couple of African guys drove ahead for two days, and rigged up the tents and had food ready as we bravely paddled our way down the river. So we basically paid to half kill ourselves paddling, whilst our luggage and the people with our money drove on ahead in comfort. We had a health and safety talk before we left.

"So….You might fall out of the kayak, in which case you need to know what to do. Mainly, swim to the shore. Except if there are hippos there. If there are Hippos swim out to the middle. If the waters are deep enough they won't follow you out. If they do, you're probably fucked."

"What if there are crocodiles?"

" Then definitely swim to shore, and run. To be honest, they are quicker than you, so if they are close enough you're probably fucked too."

"What if you see both?"

"It's not likely, but if you do, it probably doesn't matter which way you go because you're totally fucked. Now has anyone got any more questions?"

Most of us didn't, as the news we could be croc lunch seemed to make stuff like 'what time is dinner' take on a whole new meaning. Till fuckwit spoke up

"So…Is it OK to smoke on the kayaks?"

"Sure. But don't get your cigarettes wet."

"Cigarettes. Yeah. Let's call it that."

We managed to all survive the safari, though there were a couple of us I was kind of hoping might have fallen out in the croc and hippo scenario. Each and every adventure meant another night in Explorers, which included snogging the odd pissed up backpacker and a pretty good punch up with some white water rafting guys who felt they owned the place. In fact, one of them might have. No problem, we drank with the same guys the next night. It was the day before we were due to pull out that Ron made a bit of a surprise announcement.

"The Bungee guys are back. They can get us in tomorrow afternoon. So fuck it, I'm going to stay on for the extra day, and try to make up the time on the way across Botswana."

Hell ,I could have kissed the guy. Except, after I saw the pounding he gave the Miner in Tanzania, it probably wasn't wise.

And so it was, that at some point the next afternoon, I was standing on a platform that is on the side of the bridge between Zimbabwe and Zambia, 111 metres above the Zambezi River, with a bungee rope tied round my ankles, and possibly the most perfect mix of fear and excitement I had ever experienced.

I was very aware all my life of my limitations when it came to sports and the like, much, as I have mentioned, to the annoyance of my parents and a kind of shame that seemed to go with it for no reason that makes any sense. This may have been because I was a bit of a cowardly wee child when I was little, scared to say boo to a goose. Not that I'd have gone near a goose. Oddly, no matter what I achieved, how many fights I got in, how many adventures I had, that little nervous Mulligan never seemed to completely leave me. I beat all my fears, but they are still there, causing daft little things like not liking to initiate phone calls with tradesmen and the like.

Yet here I was, about to plummet headfirst into a river, and had given some guys $90 for the privilege. I looked down. Everything around me was locked out, I couldn't hear the falls, or my comrades, or even the bloke count down. I was vaguely aware of him reaching '1-bungeeeeeeee' but was oblivious to it as I focused myself, then plunged off a couple of seconds later.

There are certain moments in your life, such as when I'd looked into the eyes of a gorilla, that the memory is so strong that the image literally burns itself into your brain. Not just your memory, but all your brain, including the bit that puts what you see together. Which is why to this day, even if I'm walking down a wet, cold Coventry street, or sitting typing my shenanigans up on a laptop, the moment I think of the next 30 or 40 seconds then the image is as clear in front of me as the day I jumped.

The first thought in my head as I left the platform was not a kind of euphoric yay, or a terrified Nooooo. It was a massive rush in my head and I thought, I've done it! I've fucking done it!" It may have been that moment that the scared wee Mulligan realised that there were no monsters in the wardrobe in his room at his Granny Strong's house, if you punched someone hard enough in a fight you were in with a chance, and that if you keep putting off asking a girl out till someone else gets her, it's your own fault, because being said no to isn't the end of the world. He finally realised he was no longer wee, and no longer scared. And aside from popping back to say hallo when I have to phone a plumber or something, he left pretty much for good.

So I can still see in front of me, the water getting closer fast, the beautiful scenery of the rocks to the side and the trees, and the noise of the falls suddenly kicking in, then finally the euphoric Yay burst through and suddenly I was going back up. Then down. Then back up. And so on for a couple of bounces and swings till it stopped, and I was dangling above the river.

Usually they would unload you into a little boat, but due to the choppiness of the river today, I was winched back up instead, and unstrapped in a kind of underpart of the bridge. Back to the comrades who were all waiting their turn, and watched one by one as the small number of us who had dared do this took their turn. And boy, did we sink some beers and laugh some laughs in the bar that night, before pulling out back onto the road the first thing next morning.

No snow globe, but I did buy the tee-shirt. World's highest Bungee Jump, it says on it. This tee-shirt has not fit me for a long time, and odds are, never will. Which is not so bad as it was only a couple of years later that I heard that Angel Falls in South America had officially become the highest jump. This was kind of gutting. I was no longer a Jake Armstrong amongst jumpers. I was relegated to a Buzz Aldrin, doing the second highest jump in the world. My Tee-shirt not only ceased to fit as I continued my love of food and beer throughout my life, but it sat in my drawer developing strange little holes, fading, and lying to me. For years, boring the arse off my friends with my bungee story, I would complain in a humorous way about only being a Buzz Aldrin now, until many years later when a girl I knew messaged me and asked what the highest jump was, and would I fancy going out there and doing it? I mentioned Angel Falls and said I'd look it up. I wish I hadn't. It seems both those jumps had long been beaten and were not even in the top 10 anymore. The highest is in China somewhere, I gather. I'm not even sure if Victoria Falls is in the top 20 now. So I suddenly and belatedly found out that I had not even been Buzz Aldrin for the longest of times. Do you remember the last astronaut who walked on the moon? No, I don't either. And I am not even troubled enough to look him up, though that's who I am now. Some bloke who jumped off a bridge in Africa.

239

But you know what? Just for a little while, I could brag I'd done the highest Bungee jump in the world. So I'll still have the odd brag, just not to intrepid looking young backpackers who have been out in China. And much as I might think in my head that I will get out there and do the current highest one day, I won't. Not because of fear: I know that that will turn to bliss on the way down. No, it's the fact that I have a couple of blurry photos Fuckwit took of me jumping on my cheap camera, whereas now there are amazing digital photos of these fit young backpackers and adventurers, without an ounce of body fat between them. No, it's not that, it's like hell I'm going to stand in a pair of shorts amongst them all.

"Hey, who was that old guy you were talking to in the queue?"

"Dunno. Some Fat Bastard who says he jumped off a little bridge in Africa once."

Yes, I'll pass on that.

IX

We pretty much drove for the next couple of days through some not so good roads starting with the Caprivi Strip over the Namibian Border, bush camping. That is, until we reached Etosha National Park. To be honest, I had never heard of it, and wasn't even aware we were going to another such area, but boy was I in for a treat. All of us were.

It would be fair to say that as amazing as the Serengeti and Masai Mara were, this park of around 22,000sq Km took the prize. The animal life was teeming. I noticed that the elephants seemed to be much longer legged, though not necessarily taller than those back east. This turned out to be true, as they were in the main Desert Elephant, adapted to the different terrain that their Bush cousins lived on. One of these came up to the truck once, ready to charge. Clearly a huge solitary bull. The size of the thing was frightening. It changed its mind as we sat pretty still. I'm half convinced it could have knocked the truck over. We saw a lot of these.

Also Kudu, Oryx, Springbuck, lion galore, Bat eared Fox, Mongoose, Giraffe, Zebra, Wildebeest, Jackal, Hyena and flamingo. I decided that my blasé attitude to the wildlife could take a hike, and was pretty enthralled. The next night we stayed at a lodge at a place known as the Okaukeujo Waterhole. This was amazing, a floodlit manmade waterhole with the lodge behind a safe fence. There was, of course no guarantee of what you would see, but on the first night there we were behind the fence when no less than a line of 8 Rhino came right past us. I watched one of the student lads freeze, which was hardly surprising until they wandered off to the hole to drink. They were waiting for an elephant to move off. It did, and the rhino took their turn, till satiated they too wandered off. This was more Rhino than we had seen on the whole of the trip so far. Numerous critters came and went, then finally a large male lion. It had not long been there when another huge bull elephant arrived and walked towards it. The lion didn't even wait, it turned and ran off, then sat a little further away till the elephant was long gone.

The next night was better. The Encounter Africa truck had pulled in during the day, and I found Gudrun in the bar in the lodge. We arranged to meet up at the waterhole later, and took a healthy supply of cans of beer along. It was quieter than the night before, but still caught a fair few sights, the top one being a stand-off between a rhino walking towards the hole, and an elephant walking away. Neither seemed prepared to give way. It was like two stubborn drunks on a city centre street on a Saturday night. Finally, the rhino turned and walked off, till the elephant had gone, then stayed by the hole like it had won something.

We headed off the next day in the truck aiming at a seal colony at Cape Cross. We did eventually get there, and the smell of the place was something else. I'd never considered how big seals were before. We were looking at a colony that could number between 80,000 to 100, 000, so the noise as well as the smell of rotten fish was pretty memorable. However, before getting there, Ron had for the first time on the trip taken a wrong turn somewhere. We eventually got to the coast, but too late to head to the colony so we camped offsite, a bit further south down the skeleton coast.

We were alone here. Really alone. Not all of us had come along, just about 5 of us who wanted to see the seals and the coast. The rest stayed at the lodge. This place was completely different. The name originally came from the bones of whales and fish washed up as a result of the whaling industry, but also in later years to do with the skeletons of boats wrecked by the rocks and the fog. And this was the eerie thing about the place. The cold gives rise to the Benguela current which causes dense coastal fogs. The climate is generally inhospitable, and a constant heavy surf is the only thing that breaks up the weighty silence that hangs over the place. I left the others and walked along the beach, almost hypnotised by the strange balance of this silence and surf. The Namib bushmen call this place "The Land God made angry" and the Portuguese sailors called it The Gates of Hell. There seemed to be no colour. Along my walk I did indeed see small skeletons of birds and an animal unknown to me.

With all my travels and shenanigans, I had never felt a place like this. It was cold, but I still wore a tee-shirt, and didn't really notice it. It had been a long journey so far, around the planet and across Africa. Standing looking over the slow heavy water, time itself stopped. There was nothing. And to all extent and purposes, I felt as if I had come to the end of the world. Against what I knew to be true, I felt that once you reached this place there was nothing beyond, and as I peered out over the dead looking sea, I felt not only how insignificant and irrelevant I was to this ocean to nowhere, but also a feeling of uniqueness in that even though my companions were probably not too far away, I didn't need or want them, I was here, at the end of the world, on my own and content.

It is possibly the most beautiful place that my mind has ever been to.

Seals done, others picked up, we headed to Swakopmund, where we stayed for a good few days, and found a particularly great pub called Fagin's. This town was like walking into Germany, as it had been one of their few African colonies, coming under the rule of the German empire in 1884, mainly to knock back British expansion. It remained as such till World War 1, when it was taken by South African troops, and mandated to their control by the UN till 1990 when it gained independence. The 6% white population are the predominant business force, and this could be seen in the towns. We'd been round a few bars, which were surprisingly European compared to anywhere else we had been, even eating hamburgers. This was to remind me that I had not had Fried egg and chips for a long time. I was determined to find such a meal, I decided, and it began to nag at me.

Second night there I was pleasantly surprised by Gudrun coming into Fagin's. She had seen our truck parked, and been round a few bars to find me. We actually found a nightclub called Scandals where we pretty much danced to music we hadn't heard for quite some time. In my head, I guess I knew once we left the skeleton coast, we were on the return part of our loop back. A couple of us had decided to stop off in Egypt on the way back to London, and would pick up tickets in the capital, Windhoek, which we stopped at next. We had a couple of days left in Swakopmund, which I was glad about. I had made pretty good friends with some people from there, including the owner of Fagin's, a young Scottish lad who told me if I fancied staying on, he could give me a job in the bar. I didn't take him up on it, though I must admit, I was quite tempted.

I spent the rest of the night down near Gudrun's camp and arranged to meet her the next day. However, I slept later than I thought and got a message from her via the guy in Fagin's that their truck had decided to leave early, so she'd catch me soon. But it was a great few days here, and I was a little sad to leave it behind.

We were making great time travelling through Namibia, stopping off and staying at Walvis Bay, Sossusvlei, exploring Sesriem Canyon, then Hot Water Springs where we actually got to bathe in the springs. Bliss. Most of the time we either had a cold wash, or a dodgy shower if the campsite had one, which wasn't too often. It was interesting having a bath, so to speak, while a number of villagers from nearby washed their clothes in the same water.

Here, Dave and Ingrid left us, and decided they were going to hitch from there onwards. Bit by bit we were to lose people from here on. By this time, everyone was finding the situation of being stuck together a bit much. Myself, I had little to do with the others on our truck at rest stops. Over the course of time I'd struck up friendships with people from our sister truck, and other overland vehicles. It was easier. You didn't have to see them all the time. Our crew were no better or worse than any other group cast together on such journeys, there were some great people and some complete wankers, and a whole bunch somewhere between. But I totally got the people leaving. I was aware that my ticket to Egypt was pretty much eating my last chunk of money. As usual, I had spent way more than I had budgeted for, mainly on enjoying myself in bars and such. So knowing I had paid for all my food for the rest of the trip, I decided to see it through.

I saw Gudrun at the springs as they were about to leave, and as we arrived. As our trucks only briefly passed there, we decided we'd find a bar to meet up in once in Windhoek. It was, she told me, her group's last couple of days in Africa, and they would be departing, so we needed to really party on what was effectively their last night.

Which would have been easier if we hadn't broken down on the road not far from Windhoek. Something to do with the shaft and the four wheel drive. Ron was pretty good with mechanics, but found himself at a loss. Another truck passed us eventually, and the driver dropped his people off in the city, and came back with some replacement parts. So it was late when we arrived, and I wandered around till I spotted the Encounter truck. There was a bar nearby, and myself and Barman Baz headed to go in, but the security told us that it was full, and we weren't coming in. I came back to where the truck was parked quite early the next day to say Goodbye, but it was already gone. We had not, of course, gotten round to writing our addresses and numbers down on some scraps of paper, the type that goes in the back of your journal to be never used again, which I had intended to do whenever we had met up.

I never saw Gudrun again.

At some point the next day we crossed the border into Botswana, on our way to the Okavango Delta. We camped at a bar-come-camp, where everyone except me, Rhonda and Fuckwit stayed behind. All 3 of us were feeling the pinch on money now, and the trip into the Delta was apparently amazing, but not cheap, and involved helicopter fees and being canoed around by guides.

However, it was again nice to get away from the crowd as a whole, and it wasn't too far from a nearby town. Fuckwit found a couple of guys to get stoned with, whereas Rhonda and myself hitched into the town. It was quite quiet really, we looked around then headed back.

We were picked up by a white guy called Brahms, who decided to show us around. I'm not sure what his full job was, but in his spare time he drove big containers of fresh water to small villages. He took us to one such place that he was heading to. It was a friendly, traditional village, and the villagers shared their beer with us. They had one huge vat that they brewed some kind of coconut beer in, that was pretty unique to me and mighty strong. It was a nice place to visit.

We did have a couple of the little kids come up and ask for pens. This is something I had observed all the way along the trip in the small villages. We never encountered beggars asking for money, which we had been warned about at the start. And we never encountered poverty in the way the appeals on TV would show it. Most village life was pretty good, it seemed. However, the kids would come up and put out their hands and say "Give me Pen."

This was kind of heart breaking. These were young children at school, whose parents had to buy them books, pens, etc and everything in fact that we take for granted in schools. Though not in poverty, a lot of people were poor, money wise. Imagine when you were young, learning to write or draw, and not being able to do it. It occurred to me that if I had the know-how, I'd organise a Pens for Africa campaign, as how many half used pens and pencils did we have around our houses back then? Hell, a look down the back of any couch would find a couple. Oh, and combs too. And oddly, sweets. To this day I've often wondered exactly how old sweets get down the back of sofas. Or maybe they come as a free gift from large department stores with perpetual sales, their equivalent of mints on a pillow. Actually, that would be quite a nice gesture, though I'm not sure in the history of sofa mining has anyone ever ate a sweet they found down there, apart from possibly really fat people. You wouldn't have to, there is usually enough fluffy coins to buy some new sweets. The pens however would be great for the kids in Africa.

Had a bit of a surprise on the way back. Brahms suddenly pulled his truck up and reached down and pulled a shotgun out from somewhere.

"Shit", I thought, momentarily.

However, he jumped out of the vehicle and took two shots then walked into some trees by the road.

"Has he just shot someone?" Rhonda asked.

"I don't think so, he was aiming sort of up," I answered, only half convinced.

But in fact, Brahms came back with two huge fat dead birds.

"Here," He said," Have these for your dinner. They are delicious."

I have no idea what they were, but he was right and they were in fact delicious. Not knowing much about freshly shot birds – I mainly had chicken at home, and it came with string round its feet. So we plucked them, and I knew that you had got to stick your hand into them and pull stuff out. I remembered this from the first time I ever bought a chicken when I had moved from my parents' house into our punk flat. There were of us, totally naïve, and I volunteered to do the tugging job. I put a marigold rubber glove on, and as the others watched, stuck my hand up the chicken's backside......And pulled out a little plastic bag full of the giblets! However, I knew that wasn't going to work here, so tried it again, and didn't really get anything out. So we stuck a stick through them and cooked them on a fire we lit. To be fair, they were really nice, though I found myself eating both sticks and a couple of bits of shot too.

It did teach me a valuable lesson however. The magic of HP Sauce. Back in Windhoek, I'd stumbled across a shop that sold the British favourite, good old HP Sauce. It was a mighty big price, but though I hadn't thought about it, seeing it made me drool a bit. Especially with my ever growing longing for egg and chips. So on a whim, I bought a bottle, and this was the first chance to use it. We'd asked another truck driver if he'd sell us some beans too, but he gave us them anyway, and we cooked them with the birds. I was sitting at a little outdoor table, picking shot and stick out of my teeth, when some guy, also English, came over to the table.

"Hi….Er, is that HP sauce?"

"Yes. Yes it is."

"Wow. I couldn't have a bit, could I?"

Naturally I agreed, and he went and ordered some chips from the bar on the camp, came back with them, used a healthy dollop of sauce and took on a look of a man having sex for the first time in a while. The same look I had when I tasted it on my stick flavoured bird.

And so it was that I learned a new currency. All the way on the way back, every time we pulled into a camp to eat, at least one Brit would come up and say,

"Hi…Er, is that HP sauce? I'll get you a drink if I could have a splash?"

Indeed, I wish I'd bought a load of bottles. I had so many bottles of beer bought for me until the last drop of sauce was gone that it more than paid for itself. It was interesting to see the look of bewilderment on the kiwis and Aussies faces as to why these wide eyed Brits ambled over to me every time we had lunch.

Eventually the others finished their Delta Shenanigans, and it was off to Harare, back over the Zimbabwe border as we continued our way back. We arrived at the camp we were staying at on the night before Anzac day, when all the Kiwis, Aussies and South Africans on the camp were planning a huge barbie. We would be losing a few more folk here, as our numbers were continuing to drop off.

I took a wander into town with Barman Baz to find a bar the second day there, but instead took a bit of a shock. We had a couple of drinks in a

246

unwelcoming kind of place, and came back to the camp where I saw, next to a tent, a pair of familiar looking motorbikes. It was the two lads from the camp in Malawi where I first met Gudrun. Except I could not help but notice that one of the bikes was marked up as for sale. There was no one in the tent, so I looked around the camp, and found one of the lads sitting in a little bar area.

"Hey. How's it going?"

"Oh, hi, man. Not too good, to be honest."

"Where's your mate? I asked, but had kind of guessed the answer.

"Dead. Just about getting here, he caught Cerebral Malaria. Took him out in no time. I can't sell the bike. The places in town know I'm fucked, and want to offer me next to nothing. Looks like I'm going to have to give in to that. Then I'm going to Joburg where I have a buyer for mine, and I'm going home.

There isn't really much you can say to that. I was gutted for the guy. We had a couple of beers, then he went back to his tent. He was still there with the bikes when we left a couple of days later.

Next stop was Kariba Gorge, which was to be our last fling before we took the long haul drive back to Mombasa. Ron warned us that this journey back would just be a drive all day, camp, eat, sleep, drive. So make the most.

We did. The sister truck was there, also with depleted numbers. So the drivers decided to combine both groups on our truck, and the other guy would get that one back to Mombasa for repairs and maintenance. The new people freshened the pot, and we set about our last shenanigans. We hired a houseboat between us to stay on, and actually had a mattress again.

I took a crack at water skiing on the lake and failed abysmally. However, I was the only one to actually catch something when we went out Tiger Fish hunting with a speargun. I cooked that later, and picked bits of scales out of my teeth. I hadn't cleaned it either, but it didn't seem to do me any harm. It occurred to me I was never going to present any kind of bush survival show that didn't involve picking bits of something horrible out of my teeth later. Hell, I thought, you wouldn't get this with egg and chips!

Actually, catching the fish was an interesting experience. A bunch of guys on a little boat in a river with crocs and hippos nearby, and us with the speargun. Every so often the outboard would clog up with plants, and this short South African guy who had teamed up with us, known as little man, would jump in the water and unclog, seemingly oblivious to the fact that, as I say, there were bloody crocs in there. We took it in turns with the spear gun, 3 shots each. Everyone failed. I missed with my first two shots, then concentrated on my third attempt, blocking out the guys shouting "Left " "right" "Now" and other unhelpful advice. I took the shot and the spear went right through the tiger fish I was going for. The lads were cheering, and back slapping me, and I felt a moment of elation. It was, I realised later in life, probably what our ancestors felt on a hunt. Of course, they needed to do this to survive, but we haven't really lost that instinct, no matter how civilized we become. As I have grown older and seen more and more of people, I have long since come to realise that we are chimps with gadgets. If you really want to understand the most basic of human instincts, look at our cousins. They are what they are, with no clutter of ethics or morals, and once we look under these traits, which we need to have to be human, we are just like them, whether we like it or not.

Done a bit of parasailing too, and took a trip out to a pretty decent restaurant to celebrate our last night. These activities had been organised by a mate of Ron's, who joined us at this meal and drinking. He'd brought along an Aussie girl who he'd met hitching out there. She'd sweet talked him into letting her stay at the camp in his tent, which he seemed pretty pleased with. That was, until me and her got talking and laughing in the bar and she came and stayed in mine. I was pretty glad we were pulling out the next day, I wouldn't want an accident with those bloody hippos now.

Actually, she contacted me when I was back, about a month later. I must have given her my Mums phone number, as I knew I'd be staying there when I got back just until I got new digs. I was quite pleased when she said she was at Gatwick, and thought it would be nice to meet up. Except, it became apparent that's not why she rang. She wanted someone to pick her up and put her up. I guess she had her own way of seeing the world too.

Then that was it. The long drive to Mombasa. We hit the road the next day, into Zambia, drove, camped, slept. The day after that was my birthday. It didn't matter. There had been really bad rains, and we spent most of the day getting stuck in the muddy road every half hour or so

We managed five miles in the whole day. Interestingly, I've actually had worse birthdays.

We made good time after that, using the better main roads now we weren't adventure bound. It was depressingly dull, but I caught up on a couple of good books, including On The Road, the Kerouac classic. Wonder how he'd have got on in Africa? We passed through Zambia, Malawi, Tanzania then Mombasa. It took us just over a week. The beach was empty this time, hardly any trucks. We were flying from Nairobi in two days' time, so we just chilled out and did very little. Me, Baz and fuckwit took one last trip to the Green Bar. I got hit on by a pretty young African girl, who was probably a hooker, but I bought her a couple of drinks, and she sat on my knee running her fingers through my hair, which I'd started to leave short rather than shaved, and my plaits were now indeed really just awful dreads which I had to cut out when I got back.

She went to the toilet at one point, and Baz asked if I was enjoying the head tickling thing.

"I am. Why?"

"Really good tickle? Covers lots of your head?"

"Well, yes. What are you getting at?"

He pointed out that she had six fingers on one hand. I looked when she got back. She did as well. She had an extra one growing out of her little finger that wiggled. Oddly, the goth girl I'd met in New York with Ferret also had six fingers on one hand, though in a straight line. I hadn't noticed till Ferret pointed it out. I appear, it seems, to be not very good at spotting extra fingers on my dates. It didn't matter, to be honest. In fact, if anything, I got a really great head tickle out of it.

We had lost most of our numbers now. Baz was also leaving, but Fuckwit, as well as a married couple who'd joined us on the second half, Bruce and Jan, plus one of the student lads called Rob, who really was the most annoying prat I have probably ever met on the road, (so much in fact I had to be pulled off walloping him back at one of the camps), were heading to Cairo. In fact, this Rob had originally set off with his mate to hitchhike to Egypt, but gave up after a few days, and had bought a lift on another truck. He was one of the few people I ever felt it was a good riddance when they left these kind of travellers groupings. On the night before he left, he'd managed to annoy just about everyone, including a quite stocky, and deliberately camp gay guy who's joined us over a few days at camp, who had his own opinion about him.

"Now that one, he's a contemptuous little bitch. I'd be watching my back about that one, but not in a fun way."

I completely agreed.

My heart sank when the idiot turned up at Nairobi airport, still as self-important and pompous as he had been at the camps, which was odd for a bloke who knew nothing about anything at all, and had, much to my amusement, wet his pants on at least three occasions that I knew of when he tried to drink more than two beers. It was typical that he'd bitched about everyone that was left, yet paid his way back to find us when his own pathfinding skills apparently failed him. Nevertheless, here we all were, and we were off to Cairo.

X

I know how a 1940s midwife would feel if she cycled through a desert.

Arriving in Cairo was quite the shocker. Sure, over the last few months we'd passed through cities, but Cairo was more on a par with Bangkok or Delhi when it came to the noise and bustle. I think it was the sound of the perpetual honking horns that got me at first, hitting me with the reality that I was in a completely different kind of Africa. Not so long ago, I had admired a round rainbow at Victoria falls from a microlight. I'd been amazed at the images of the great sand dunes in the Namib desert. I'd been by a lake when the insects swarmed for miles in each direction, and had wrapped my tee-shirt round my mouth as the only way to not breathe them in. Here, I found myself standing on a roadside, looking for a bar called Ali Baba's that the hotel had recommended, with the sound of never ending traffic as a background.

As a moderate Muslim nation, there were bars and clubs to be found in Egypt, but they were not especially a major part of the culture. So after booking in, we headed off to find the bar we kept hearing about with not much luck. As "tourists" we were also constantly hit on by touts and scam artists every few steps. Some of course, were honest tradesmen.

"Hey Mister, you need your shoes shining?"

" I'm wearing sandals."

"I can still clean them. Make them last longer. Your friend has shoes…."

"Actually, we are looking for a place called Ali Baba's, if you know it?

"Yes. Yes sir, that is me. You have found me"

"You're Ali Baba?"

"Yes sir. Ali Baba, the best shoe shine in Egypt."

" I see."

We eventually found the bar, and we could feel the prices going up as we walked in. Never the less, we had a couple of drinks and made plans, while the seemingly huge amount of staff kept coming over, offering us everything on the drinks list every 5 minutes, quoting numbers unrelated to the price next to the list. This really was Ali Baba and the 40 thieving bastards. Tried to take a Felucca trip on the Nile, a Felucca being a kind of small wooden sailing boat, but with no wind it didn't go anywhere. We had quite an argument with the owner about getting our money back, who feigned anger and surprise that we hadn't enjoyed sitting on a non-moving boat looking at other non-moving boats for an hour.

The hotel we were in had a nice rooftop bar and a mixed Traditional and European menu so I hoped I might satisfy this desire for egg and chips. I was out of luck. They didn't do that. We ate in a couple of cafes over the next day to various degrees of satisfaction. From one, where I had hummus and Fava beans which was fantastic, to another back street one we went into that didn't ask us what we wanted, but immediately started bringing out the only dishes they apparently did. Mainly a kind of stew. They did ask, enthusiastically if we wanted meat in it, which with hindsight I foolishly agreed to. Out came this stew with what looked like unidentifiable organs of various colours and shapes floating around. The guys seemed so happy that we were eating there, off the beaten tourist path, that I didn't want to let them know that my usual try anything attitude to food failed me, and instead picked out the more medical looking lumps when no one was looking and put them in my pocket. I disposed of them later on the street near a skinny stray dog, which niffed them and walked off.

There was a man in the lobby - there is always a man in the lobby –
who introduced himself as Doctor Sahid, a dentist. As a side line, he
produced for us student ID which was actually pretty good and would get
us 50% of all places. I was sceptical, but took the chance and it indeed
worked. There were a number of smaller museums, for example, the
papyrus museum (Which against what I first thought I in fact really
enjoyed) and of course the Cairo Museum, or the Museum of Egyptian
Antiquities. Not normally a museum kind of person, this place was
amazing. We were lucky it was at a time to see the Tutankhamun
exhibition too. I was hoping to see his resting place in the Valley of the
Kings, but I guess it would be a bit empty with him and all his stuff being
here.

You could, and I pretty much did, spend a whole day in this place. It
puts the ancient history of Egypt into perspective. We hear of the
pyramids, at about 2,500 or more BC, and we hear of Cleopatra. And yet
it is hard to imagine that this illustrious figure actually lived closer to us
and the age of the moon landings than she did to the builders of the
mighty Sphynx. That's the sort of length of history. There were of course
mummies, statues, amazing artifacts, including things like hair brushes
that were so old yet so familiar to us today. We washed the experience
down with some cold beers in the hotel later, and experimented with a
large Hookah pipe they provided and claimed to be completely legal, and
hit the sack. Tomorrow was the day we would do our last adventure
together as a group.

It could only be one thing of course, and so it was that we headed out to
the pyramids, on the edge of Giza. It is in fact a whole complex out there,
and a couple of us started out with a camel ride around some tombs,
before heading to the three mighty behemoths that we feel we know so
well. Sitting on the back of the camels was possibly the only time we
weren't bombarded with trinket sellers. Even getting off the camels, we
were offered camel rides by other touts.

But it was great to wander around these ancient places. Oddly, I did not
get that awesome vibe quite as strongly as I have at places like Ayers
Rock, or the Church of the Nativity, but this was probably due to the
extraordinary amount of guided tours all shouting to outdo each other
Plus I hadn't expected as much scaffold around the sphinx. However, the
mind is a fantastic tool, and after arriving home I was able, over the

years, to mentally 'photoshop' all the background chaos out, and remember them with the majesty that they deserve.

One thing I couldn't 'shop' out was going into the only pyramid that I could at that time, the pyramid of Khafre. This I was looking forward to, and had been quite excited about feeling the ancientness. In my mind, I saw myself walking through the darkened interior, tuning into the ghostly impressions of the past, and feeling the history swathing me like a gentle silk cocoon. In fact, I went in at the same time as a group of Italian tourists who had hired possibly the loudest tour guide in Cairo. This Giant of a man bellowed out in Italian what I presume to be a history of the fairly narrow corridor we walked along till reaching an antechamber somewhere within. Rather than a burial chamber I found myself in an echo chamber. There was in fact nothing to see in this cavity at all. So I touched the walls to try to pick up some historical vibes, but instead was treated to the guide shouting loudly about lord knows what, and ending in,

"Viva L'Italia!"

"Viva l'Italia!"

"Viva L'Italia!"

He was getting increasingly louder, causing the Italians to all join in happily and loudly. This happiness no doubt contributed to their generosity in gratuity as the guide led them back down the one straight corridor to the entrance, and stood accepting tips. I didn't tip him of course, which got me a sour look. Maybe he thought with my pasty Irish skin and sunburned face I was one of the Italians. Still, I'd been inside a pyramid, and I guess it was the best soaking up of the silent atmosphere in an ancient wonder of the world that I never had.

And so it was that we had our last few drinks together that night, and all caught the same train the next morning. The others had all decided on Aswan, whereas I had opted to just hit Luxor for two reasons. One, my money was really low, and though there were lots to see in the beautiful country, I could really only pick one, so I decided to see the Valley of the Kings. The other reason was that apart from that idiot pant wetter Rob, the rest of the group left were great, but I really needed some time to explore on my own. At the start of the Expedition I had learned that there were overland trucks across South America, China and virtually everywhere else I intended to go to, which struck me as great. But by the end I knew I couldn't spend that amount of time amongst one group of people 24/7 again. I was not alone on this, it's a hard thing to do and you have to be a realist. Maybe a month, maybe even two at a push, but not a day longer. It's a shame, because on the plus side, they are a great way to see strange places that are hard to reach, even if you knew about them in the first place.

So I got off at Luxor, leaving the others to continue their journey. I didn't see Rob as I got off, as we had had a couple of beers on the train due to it being a fairly long journey, and he'd fallen asleep and wet himself again. I believe he was in the toilet when I got off getting changed. I would be lying if I didn't say that that gave me a certain feeling of satisfaction, as did shaking hands with the others, knowing our adventures together were over, and we would never see or hear from each other again.

Actually, that wasn't quite true. I had made a comment about Ingrid when she left, saying that I wouldn't be surprised if she wrote to everybody on the truck. She seemed the type to do that. One of the first words we all learned over there was Jambo, the Swahili word for Hallo, and I also speculated that all of Ingrid's letters would begin with that word. We'd all written out addresses down on a bit of paper Emma had photocopied, with me using my mothers, and sure as hell about a month after I got back, my Mum told me a letter had arrived for me. It was from Ingrid, and written and decorated in colourful felt tips was the word "JAMBO" in huge letters. It made me smile. She had been a character. In fact, at the falls she took a parachute jump and had broken a leg. It turned out that all the falling asleep she kept doing was down to Narcolepsy. She basically jumped out of a plane and fell asleep. Bloody Kudos to her.

Luxor was nicer than Cairo, I felt. It had a more relaxed pace. I found a hotel virtually up the street from the train station, took a shower, and caught up on some sleep. The next day I visited both the Karnal temple and the Luxor Temple, both of which were great to see. Though not as bad for touts as Cairo, I was still permanently approached about a tour to the Valley. I had decided though, for reasons that I really can't fathom, that the spirit of James Starley was still in me, and I would like to travel the mere 26 Km by bicycle. So I found a shop that rented bikes.

"Hi. Do you have any mountain bikes for hire for tomorrow?"

"Yes, sir. Indeed."

"It's just I can't see any. These all look a bit like spare parts stuck together."

"They are all out at the moment. But we will have one tomorrow." Ok, that made sense, I guessed.

"So I want to set off early to beat the sun. Can you guarantee a mountain bike at 06:00am tomorrow morning?"

"Yes sir. No problem. You pay a deposit now. We will see you tomorrow."

I went back to the hotel that evening, relaxed with a couple of beers on the roof, slept well and headed off to the shop in the morning.

"You have my bike?"

"Yes sir. Here you are."

It was not a mountain bike. Not by any description. It was, in fact, a rickety looking old fashioned ladies bike with no crossbar and a basket on the front that looked like a vicar would ride it around a quaint English village. And there, emblazoned down the frame, was the freshly painted word 'MOUNTAIN'.

Sometimes, during your shenanigans, you just have to give in to the sense of the ridiculous and bite the bullet. After negotiating a small discount, I took the bike, which came with a lock and a puncture repair outfit in the basket, and headed off. I had a small bottle of water I had picked up in the hotel which I added to the basket and off I headed. I had to head down the East bank of the Nile till I came to a ferry where I'd been advised just to get on the local one rather than the tourist one, for a considerable saving, which by now was pretty important.

The scenery, mainly white sanded desert with the odd interesting looking building, was sparse, but rugged and a change from the greenery of all but the Namib desert (which was more colourful) of the last few months, and was enjoyable to see and feel. However, the sun came beating down quicker than I expected, and a massive amount of sitting on the back of a truck had clearly depleted my fitness levels somewhat. The bottle of water, now hot, was drunk in no time. All the way along, as I huffed and puffed, luxury air conditioned coaches would pass me and smiling, sweat free tourists would wave admiringly out of the window. I ceased to wave back after a while as I felt I was going to die of the heat, and waving seemed an unnecessary use of energy. I passed some Arab children now and then who would also wave, but their smiling seemed more like bemused laughter.

However, albeit soaked from head to foot, I eventually arrived at the Valley. There was a shop, and I bought a large bottle of water and a carton of orange juice, and pretty much sat and drank them in no time at all. Then bought some more water.

There was also a little kiosk where you could buy a pass that let you enter any three of the tombs. Surprisingly, it wasn't as swamped with visitors as the amount of coaches would have suggested, but then it covered a fair bit of desert. It's unbelievable to think, but they still believe there may be more tombs to be discovered out here. Egypt is indeed quite the enigma.

Firstly, I hit the tomb of Tutankhamun, which was effectively empty, most of his stuff being back in Cairo, but the ornate coffin of which we are all so familiar was in there. It was a fairly simple burial room, but the walls were deliciously painted, and yes, you could feel the age of the place. Quite rightly, no photography was allowed in any of the tombs to preserve the paints and the reliefs. The preservation of these places is hard, even the sweat of so many tourists is enough to give the air in the tombs a humidity that is harmful to the antiquity.

There are , to date, 63 tombs spread across the valley. Good old King tut had been the last one discovered, by Howard Carter, in 1922. The tombs are numbered in the order that they were discovered, and when I was there KV62 was the last number. There is now, I am told, a KV63, but as with many of the others ,they are not sure who this would have belonged to. Obviously, grave robbing , friction, condensation and in later years tourism took their toll on these ancient resting places, but measures to preserve, including rotation of tombs that are open, are in place.

I also visited KV57, or the tomb of Horemheb, which had at some point had flood damage. There is some evidence of other burials also in this tomb. It had been full of debris on its finding in 1908, some of it from a beautifully decorated wall that had not fooled the grave robbers, who had smashed it down meaning that the treasures behind had been looted.

Lastly, I visited KV11, the tomb of Ramses III. This was the most beautiful of the three I saw. Even though known outside of Egypt since James Bruce entered it in 1768, (Though first mentioned by the English traveller Richard Pococke in the 1730s) it has amazingly retained its awe and splendour. Effectively a long corridor, some 188 metres in length, the decoration was incredible. I spent a fair bit of time in here, actually on my own, enjoying the walls and lapping up the atmosphere. It is, in the main, decorated with scenes from the Book of Gates and the Book of the Earth.

I would have liked to see more tombs, but time got the better of me. I had a train booked at midnight back to Cairo, so the valley would be keeping many of its public secrets from me. Enthralled, satisfied and still absorbing my many new found facts, I bought plenty of water, got on my Starley machine, and headed back. I was happy to find that the journey out had been a gradual gradient upwards, so the journey back was indeed more enjoyable, and as I was passed by the air conditioned coaches I waved happily at the tourists, feeling fit, educated and safe in the knowledge that screw the water, I was having a bottle of the local beer as soon as I got back.

And indeed, I did just that. I sat outside the hotel, chatted to some Swedish Backpackers, enjoyed my metaphorical small sherry and a snifter of port, which came in the form of a bunch of beer bottles called, wrongly, Stella, then wandered down to the station 10 minutes till my train was due, boarded and headed off. More backpackers, this time German and Dutch, made for a pleasant journey back, before one last night in the same hotel in Cairo, a taxi to the airport in the morning, then the final flight back home.

Of course, I knew by now that I would be getting off that plane twice. In one life, I would be stepping off it, going for a piss, boarding a coach to Coventry and probably trying to see if there was a pub still open. But in that other parallel life, that crazy, beautiful life on the other side of the looking glass in my mind where I am always on the road and where time runs completely differently, I would be stepping off that plane and straight into my next adventure. That's how the traveller's mind works. We know that the next shenanigans are always just a ticket away.

XI

Because of the situation in Algeria changing the original expedition, I was back earlier than I had originally planned. However, I still had the best part of a month before I was due back at work. But even more than my last adventure, I found that as soon as I got back I was restless. I once again stopped at my mother's house, and figured that I would go into the post office and see if I could restart work earlier.

That's what I thought. However, the very night I got back, I did indeed head straight to the Courtyard pub with my bag and statue, and a drum, to find that as it was a Monday night...or it might have been a Tuesday or Wednesday, who knew....that there was only one guy I knew in there. Probably a good thing, as all I had left to my name was the grand total of 10 English Pounds and about $30us that would need changing. I told my friend about how I still had time left, and he grinned.

"Actually," he said, " I might have a bit of an idea for you......."

And there it was. I would have a couple of weeks at my Mums, which I am sure would be a relief to her, and then the next shenanigans would begin. I turned up there later, had a great night's sleep, and woke up sometime around lunchtime. I came downstairs, and without me having said anything, my mum had a huge plate of Egg and Chips waiting for me. There was also sausage, bacon and fried bread. It was swimming in grease, and a loaf of bread and bottle of HP Sauce sat on the table next to it. It was the best meal I think I have ever eaten.

"So anyway", she told me as I ate and pondered my next adventure. "Your brother Stewart has been away on his travels too, him and his wife. "

"Really? Where have they been?"

"Oh, they've been up to Blackpool."

"Blackpool?"

"Aye. They got me a gift too."

I'd already given my mum her carvings of people, and the little carvings of a family of Elephants, plus a miniature Egyptian vase I had got for her in Luxor. She'd put them in her ornament cabinet, alongside other things I'd brought her from France and Germany, a bronze of the Statue of victory from Russia, a paperweight from Israel and various interesting things from Asia. But there at the front, in pride of place, was a snow globe.

Not just any Snow globe either. This one had a gold painted plastic model of the Blackpool tower in it. My Mum looked at it fondly.

"I don't suppose they make things like that over there, do they?"

Printed in Great Britain
by Amazon